Moral Struggle and the Prophets

WALKING WITH GOD:
THE SERMON SERIES OF HOWARD THURMAN

1. *Moral Struggle and the Prophets*

MORAL STRUGGLE AND THE PROPHETS

Howard Thurman

Edited by
Peter Eisenstadt and Walter Earl Fluker

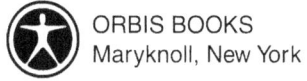

ORBIS BOOKS
Maryknoll, New York

Maryknoll, New York 10545

Founded in 1970, Orbis Books endeavors to publish works that enlighten the mind, nourish the spirit, and challenge the conscience. The publishing arm of the Maryknoll Fathers and Brothers, Orbis seeks to explore the global dimensions of the Christian faith and mission, to invite dialogue with diverse cultures and religious traditions, and to serve the cause of reconciliation and peace. The books published reflect the views of their authors and do not represent the official position of the Maryknoll Society. To learn more about Maryknoll and Orbis Books, please visit our website at www.orbisbooks.com

---

Texts by Howard Thurman copyright © 2020 by Anton H. Wong for the Thurman Family.
Introduction and commentary copyright © 2020 by Peter Eisenstadt and Walter Earl Fluker
Published by Orbis Books, Box 302, Maryknoll, NY 10545-0302.
All rights reserved.
No part of this publication may be reproduced or transmitted in any form or by any means, electronic or mechanical, including photocopying, recording, or any information storage or retrieval system, without prior permission in writing from the publisher. Queries regarding rights and permissions should be addressed to: Orbis Books, P.O. Box 302, Maryknoll, NY 10545-0302.
Manufactured in the United States of America

Library of Congress Cataloging-in-Publication Data

Names: Thurman, Howard, 1899-1981, author. | Eisenstadt, Peter R., 1954- editor. | Fluker, Walter E., 1951- editor.
Title: Moral struggle and the prophets / Peter Eisenstadt and Walter Earl Fluker, editors.
Other titles: Sermons. Selections
Description: Maryknoll, NY : Orbis Books, 2020. | Series: Walking with God: the Howard Thurman sermon series ; volume 1 | Includes bibliographical references and index. | Summary: "The first in a series that collects the "Sermon Series" by renowned African American theologian Howard Thurman, this volume on "Man and the Moral Struggle" and "The Message of the Prophets.""—Provided by publisher.
Identifiers: LCCN 2020012657 (print) | LCCN 2020012658 (ebook) | ISBN 9781626983991 (print) | ISBN 9781608338634 (ebook)
Subjects: LCSH: Christian ethics—Sermons. | Temptation—Sermons. | Bible—Criticism, interpretation, etc. | Bible. Prophets—Sermons.
Classification: LCC BJ1191 .T48 2020 (print) | LCC BJ1191 (ebook) | DDC 241—dc23
LC record available at https://lccn.loc.gov/2020012657
LC ebook record available at https://lccn.loc.gov/2020012658

Contents

Introduction	vii
Acknowledgments and Editorial Note	xvii
Part One: Man and the Moral Struggle	1
Introduction November 21, 1954, Marsh Chapel, Boston University	3
Albert Schweitzer: Spiritual Genius July 17, 1949, Fellowship Church	11
The Prophet of Deutero-Isaiah September 25, 1949, Fellowship Church, San Francisco	19
Jesus October 2, 1949, Fellowship Church	30
Paul October 9, 1949, Fellowship Church	41
Prometheus October 30, 1949, Fellowship Church	52
Job October 16, 1949, Fellowship Church	59
The Undying Fire [H. G. Wells] December 12, 1954, Marsh Chapel	66
Saint Joan [George Bernard Shaw] November 27, 1949, Fellowship Church	74

The Power of Darkness [Leo Tolstoy]
November 12, 1949, Fellowship Church, San Francisco — 84

The Great Hunger [Johann Bojer]
December 18, 1949, Fellowship Church — 93

Faust [Johann Wolfgang von Goethe]
February 13, 1955, Marsh Chapel, Boston University — 102

Brand [Henrik Ibsen]
March 13, 1955, Marsh Chapel, Boston University — 109

Moby-Dick [Herman Melville]
April 17, 1955, Boston, Massachusetts — 115

The Skin of Our Teeth [Thornton Wilder]
February 27, 1949, Fellowship Church — 121

PART TWO: THE MESSAGE OF THE PROPHETS — 129

The Message of Amos, May 25, 1952 — 131

The Message of Hosea, June 1, 1952 — 139

The Message of Isaiah I, June 15, 1952 — 149

The Message of Isaiah II, June 22, 1952 — 156

The Message of Jeremiah I, July 20, 1952 — 163

The Message of Jeremiah II, July 27, 1952 — 170

The Message of Ezekiel, August 11, 1952 — 175

The Message of Micah, August 17, 1952 — 188

The Religion of the Prophets, September 7, 1952 — 198

Zephaniah: Exposition, *Interpreter's Bible*, 1956 — 207

Index of Names — 217

Introduction

I

IN 1926 HOWARD THURMAN, fresh out of Rochester Theological Seminary, started his ministerial career at Mt. Zion Baptist Church, a black Baptist church in Oberlin, Ohio. As a new minister conversant with the latest scholarship, he was, by his own admission, somewhat overly confident. "Initially, the temptation was to try to educate and re-educate my congregation in the light of my own learning." This, he soon found out, sometimes "offended their sensibilities." So he began to find other ways to preach, looking for an approach that both respected the perspective of his congregants and combined his need to instruct with the knowledge that others now looked to him for "support, strength, and for guidance."[1]

He found that "the most creative method was a sermon series," a group of sermons organized around a common theme. His first sermon series was on the topic "knowledge-understanding casteth out fear."[2] These sermons, on medical quackery and fakery, retained a didactic edge, and some of the members of his congregation were upset that Thurman had called out some of their favorite patent medicines. But it also represented some of his lifelong concerns: the relation between the physical body and one's sense of identity, and the pursuit of truth, sometimes difficult and hard-won truths, as the best method of combatting fear. Probably with this sermon series in mind, he wrote in 1927 that he had "a growing conviction that we are fed and clothed by a vast system built upon deceit and adulteration." If this included lies about worthless medical nostrums, his indictment was far broader. He hoped to help inspire "a grand swell of

---

1. Howard Thurman, *With Head and Heart: The Autobiography of Howard Thurman* [hereafter WHAH] (New York: Harcourt Brace Jovanovich, 1979), 65–67.
2. Ibid., 65–67.

spiritual energy" that would lead to a "genuine uprooting" of "existing systems."³ Throughout his long career, the sermon series would remain Thurman's favorite method of preaching, and he delivered sermon series on a vast variety of topics, from the 1920s through the 1970s, always encouraging individuals to find, within their own resources, their own "grand swell of spiritual energy."

Howard Thurman was born in Florida in November 1899. He was raised in Daytona, Florida, primarily by his mother and grandmother, in a poor family with few resources. He came of age as the legal segregation of Jim Crow was tightening its hold on black Southerners, trying to strip them of their dignity and ambitions. Thurman, from an early age, in his own quiet way, refused its grasp. As his lifelong friend Benjamin Mays remarked, he was "free." "He generated in the minds of young Negroes the idea of freedom. When they saw Howard Thurman, most of them, for the first time, saw a free man. When they heard or read Howard Thurman, for the first time they experienced a free man and this freedom was contagious."⁴ By dint of his native intelligence, determination, and ability to circumvent a system that was established to thwart black Floridians like himself, he managed to obtain a high school education, though he had to leave Daytona to do so, attending high school in Jacksonville and St. Augustine. He graduated as valedictorian and was awarded a scholarship to Morehouse College in Atlanta, and became one of a tiny percentage—much less than one percent—of black Southerners able to attend a four-year college. At Morehouse he once again thrived and once again was valedictorian, becoming, as his classmates wrote, "the personification of the Morehouse ideal."⁵

Thurman grew up an introspective loner, an instinctive mystic from an early age, who connected to the divine primarily through nature, through trees, through the disruptive majesty of hurricanes, and through

---

3. To Mordecai Wyatt Johnson, 20 September 1927, in Walter Earl Fluker, ed., *The Papers of Howard Washington Thurman* [hereafter PHWT] (Columbia: University of South Carolina Press, 2009), 1:117–18.

4. Ricardo A. Millet, ed., *Simmering on the Calm Presence and Profound Wisdom of Howard Thurman (A Special Edition of Debate and Understanding—A Journal for the Study of Minority Americans' Economic, Political, Social, and Religious Development* (Spring 1982), 86–88.

5. Morehouse College Yearbook, in PHWT 1:25–29.

the merging of sand, sea, and sky on Daytona Beach. His relation to organized Christianity was complicated, but he soon became a diligent churchgoer at his local black Baptist church; and by the time he was a teenager, he knew he wanted to pursue a religious vocation. After graduating from Morehouse, despite offers to go elsewhere (such as studying economics at the University of Chicago), he opted to go to Rochester Theological Seminary in upstate New York, where Thurman was trained in the tenets of a modernist Christianity that rejected fundamentalism and was deeply committed to the principles of the social gospel.[6] After a stint teaching at Oberlin, in 1928 he accepted a position as a professor of religion at Morehouse and its sister school, Spelman College. In 1929 he spent a semester studying at Haverford College with the renowned scholar of mysticism, Rufus Jones, which gave an intellectual structure to his already pronounced mystical inclination. He had married Katie Kelley in 1926; and from their short union, they had a daughter, Olive, two years later. But Katie's health was not good, and she died of tuberculosis in 1930. In 1932 he married Sue Bailey. They also had a daughter, Anne Spencer, the following year, and Thurman and Sue Bailey Thurman formed a creative partnership that would endure until Howard's passing.

By the early 1930s Howard Thurman was one of the most prominent young ministers in America, much sought after to speak before both white and black audiences. In 1932 he reconnected with his former mentor, Mordecai Wyatt Johnson, now president of Howard University, who brought Thurman to the Howard campus as professor of religion and university chaplain (within a few years the title was enhanced to dean of chapel). In 1935–36, he was chair of a four-person "Negro Delegation" that went on a "Pilgrimage of Friendship" from the American Student Christian Federation to British India. (Sue Bailey Thurman was one of the four delegates.) The tour was a great success, and Thurman tried to present a new image of black Christianity to the Indian public, one that rejected missionary outreach and instead tried to connect to Indians through their shared heritage as people of color challenging white hegemony. The highlight of the journey was a meeting with Mahatma Gandhi, the first

---

6. See PHWT 1:liii–lxii; also Gary Dorrien, *Breaking White Supremacy: Martin Luther King, Jr. and the Black Social Gospel* (New Haven: Yale University Press, 2018), 24–95.

encounter between the world-famous leader of the Indian independence movement and African Americans.

Thurman had been a pacifist since his undergraduate days at Morehouse. His meeting with Gandhi inspired him to further develop his own version of radical nonviolence, which he discussed in sermons and lectures and with his Howard University students. Although he was never a front-line activist—he preferred to offer advice and spiritual counsel from behind the scenes—he inspired many future leaders of the civil rights movement, among them James Farmer, Pauli Murray, and Martin Luther King Jr. He also was an influential proponent of the spirituality of personal exploration and helped shape a new liberal American religiosity, increasingly untethered from the traditional Christianity of creeds and denominations.

In 1944 Thurman left his comfortable position at Howard to become co-pastor of the Church for the Fellowship of All Peoples in San Francisco, one of the first churches in the United States organized on an interracial and interdenominational basis. After 1946 he was the church's chief minister, and this position brought him new national attention. In the fall of 1953 he left Fellowship Church to become professor of spiritual disciplines and resources at the Boston University School of Theology and dean of Marsh Chapel, the first African American to hold such a position at a mainstream, white university. (He was actually Boston University's first tenured African American professor.) His years at Boston University were challenging—he developed innovative courses on spiritual disciplines and resources—and also somewhat frustrating, as he failed to realize his ambition to create a version of Fellowship Church on the Boston University campus. He left his teaching position at Boston University in 1962 to embark on several years of what he called his "wider ministry," which included a semester teaching at Ibadan University in Nigeria, his only extended stay in Africa. He formally retired from Boston University in 1965.

After his retirement Howard and Sue returned to San Francisco. This did not lead to any slackening of his pace as a guest preacher, lecturer, and teacher, which he continued until almost his final days. He took an active role in leading the Howard Thurman Educational Trust, assisting students at historically black colleges and universities, holding seminars with black seminarians, and publicizing and disseminating his body of work. He continued to write, publishing in 1971 the culminating statement of his religious and social philosophy, *The Search for Common Ground*.

He was proud of the achievements of the civil rights movement, dismayed at what he perceived as the turn to racial separation in the Black Power movement, and shocked at the assassination of Martin Luther King Jr. Nonetheless, he continued to find "common ground" with many of the leaders of the new turn to black consciousness, among them Jesse Jackson, Lerone Bennett Jr., Derrick Bell, and Vincent Harding. Although his achievements never received the recognition they deserved, by the mid-1970s he was beginning to receive more attention, with well-publicized interviews on national television networks and the emergence of a coterie of scholars dedicated to studying and analyzing his contributions to religion and American social thought. Thurman published his autobiography, *With Head and Heart*, in 1979. After a long illness, he died in April 1981.

II

Howard Thurman always thought that his most effective medium was the spoken, rather than the written, word. His style was distinctive; slow, with thoughtful pauses and gatherings of thought, offering a glimpse of his carefully examined inner life with a hope that his audience would take the opportunity to explore their own interiority. Although he wrote articles fairly frequently, it would not be until 1944 that he would publish his first book. Twenty more followed, though he remained primarily known as a preacher, not a writer. Because he almost always preached extemporaneously, few manuscripts of his early sermons survive, and there are few early examples of his sermon series. The oldest extant sermon series of Thurman's are five sermons, "The Message of the Spirituals," that he preached at Spelman College in Atlanta in the fall of 1928, the first surviving fruits of what would be a lifelong concern with the religious meanings of the Negro spiritual.[7]

In 1937 six sermons he delivered in Ontario, largely delivered from prepared texts on "The Significance of Jesus," are an important state-

---

7. "The Message of the Spirituals," in PHWT 1:126–39.

ment of his ideas about radical nonviolence.[8] A sermon series on a similar theme, "A Vision of God and Human Nature," also delivered in Canada, survives from 1939.[9] These sermon series survive because someone at the sponsoring institution transcribed Thurman's words. "Mysticism and Social Change," more a lecture series than a sermon series, and probably delivered from a prepared text, also survives from that year.[10] What all of these efforts at sermon series share is that their circulation was extremely limited, and they were never reprinted by Thurman.

The new technology of magnetic tape recording, developed in Germany during the war, became available commercially in the United States in the late 1940s. Thurman was an early adopter. No longer would his sermons vanish into the ether or require the efforts of a trained stenographer to capture his words as he spoke them. By 1948 he was recording many of his sermons at Fellowship Church. When he agreed to come to Boston in 1953 one of his conditions was the availability of a good tape-recording system. Some of the transcribed sermons were circulated by Thurman. In 1956 he published a volume of sermons, *The Growing Edge*, consisting of "transcriptions from the tape recorder and carefully edited."[11] Thurman amassed a library of over eight hundred recorded sermons. In the 1970s the Howard Thurman Education Trust made an effort to transcribe many, but by no means all, of Thurman's sermons, and some of them were made available on cassette tapes.

The editors of Thurman's papers, *The Papers of Howard Washington Thurman*, were faced with a dilemma and an embarrassment of riches, particularly for the period after 1948. (The editors of the current volume were also editors of the documentary edition; Walter Earl Fluker was the senior editor and Peter Eisenstadt was the associate editor.) There was far too much good material to include in the five volumes of the Thurman Papers, and the reluctant decision was reached to omit the sermon series and arrange for publication at a later date.

From the late 1940s through the late 1970s Thurman recorded over twenty sermon series, comprising almost three hundred sermons. Once

---

8. "The Significance of Jesus," in PHWT 2:44–92.
9. "A Vision of God and Human Nature," in PHWT 2:222–35.
10. "Mysticism and Social Change," in PHWT 2:190–222.
11. HT, *The Growing Edge* (New York: Harper & Brothers, 1956), ix.

again, the editors have been obliged to be selective, and are publishing, in four volumes, the best of Howard Thurman's sermon series. In choosing the sermon series for this volume we have tried to demonstrate the breadth of Thurman's interests. We have also tried to select sermon series that cover topics not treated in depth elsewhere in his published writings.

Thurman's sermon series cover a wide variety of subjects. Some are fairly specific, such as "The Message of the Prophets," published in this volume, comprising ten sermons on specific Hebrew prophets. Some have broader rubrics, such as "The Quest for Maturity" and "Seeking and Finding," both to be published in a future volume. The number of sermons in a sermon series ranges from three to thirteen. Thurman generally delivered his sermon series on consecutive Sundays, or as near to this as his busy schedule permitted. Although the editors are publishing some material from Thurman's retirement years after 1965, the bulk of the published sermons are from his years at Fellowship Church and Boston University. Thurman sometimes repeated sermon series to his different audiences in San Francisco and Boston. He often reprised the same topic in entirely different sermon series. (In the series we are publishing in these volumes, there are four different sermons on Second Isaiah.) Since he spoke extemporaneously, all of these versions have significant differences. In these cases of a duplicated topic, the editors have chosen what they feel to be the most illustrative among the alternative versions. Although the editors have tried to publish complete sermon series, in some instances they made a decision to omit a sermon from a series. In some cases, the editors are publishing related material not formally included in a sermon series.

Although Thurman was not a religious thinker who underwent great shifts in his basic views, he certainly was influenced by the context of his times, which, for the sermon series, meant basically 1949 to 1962, years of the Cold War, domestic anticommunism, and the most optimistic years of the civil rights movement. Thurman tended to avoid direct political or racial commentary in his sermons, and this was particularly so when, as at Fellowship Church and Boston University, he was aware that he was speaking to a racially mixed audience and did not wish to divide them along racial lines. (When speaking to black audiences, particularly in the years after 1965, he was sometimes a bit franker.) Nonetheless, the underlying political motivations of many of these sermons are not hidden and would have been clear to his audience. Finally, these are sermons of a congregational minister, speaking to his regular congregation. Like all successful ministers and lecturers, Thurman had favorite sermons that he preached, with some variation, numerous times. When preaching to his own congregation, he needed new material, and the sermon series are a reflection of this. If the sermons convey his need to instruct and inspire, there is also a friendly, almost bantering familiarity with his audience, a desire to include his congregation as equals in his thoughts and ideas.

In this, the first of four volumes, the editors are printing two sermon series, "Man and the Moral Struggle" and "The Message of the Prophets." For Thurman, there is a moral struggle when "the end that a man seeks involves him in reaching for that which is outside of or which transcends his personal private ends." When this involved a search for ends "that are transcendent and boundless, it involves me in the kind of struggle in which there is at stake the ultimate destiny of my life." The sermons in "Man and the Moral Struggle" are sketches of individuals involved in this sort of life-transforming moral struggle. Some of these are sketches of religious figures, such as Jesus and Paul, while others are of literary characters, such as Captain Ahab in *Moby-Dick*, or Goethe's Faust. Thurman delivered two sermon series on "Man and the Moral Struggle," one at Fellowship Church in 1949, the latter at Boston University in 1954–1955. The current version is a composite of both series. In cases of duplication of topics the editors have chosen the version that best fits the purposes of this volume. We have added another sermon on a literary topic, from the same time period, on Thornton Wilder's *The Skin of Our Teeth*.

Although it is a separate sermon series, "The Message of the Prophets" exemplifies what Thurman meant by "moral struggle": personal and social transformation through the seeking of transcendent ends. Although the theology of Thurman and that of the prophets was quite different, the Hebrew prophets were always of central importance to Thurman's view of religion. Thurman felt their social witness, their closeness to God, and their insistence that holiness is not only a personal quality, but that entire peoples and nations can, and must, be holy, and that it is the job of prophets to call a nation to holiness, whatever the reception they might receive or, if their message is unwelcome, the maltreatment they must endure. The editors have supplemented "The Message of the Prophets" with a published commentary on Zephaniah that, for reasons of space, they were unable to include in *The Papers of Howard Washington Thurman*.

In 1980, toward the end of Thurman's life, he told an interviewer that he was "convinced of the unity of life, and that in living my life I am making a single statement even though I live it in terms of particular moments, incidents. So that if today I had a motion picture reel that had recorded the story of my life from my birth up to this present moment, and if I unwound it backward, I would see that every single moment, every single step was an unfolding of the same basic, fundamental idiom."[12] These sermons are a collection of "motion picture reels" of other lives—some familiar, some quite obscure, some existing solely in works of literature—that Thurman wished others to watch with him.

In the end it is our hope that those who read these sermons will, like Thurman, see *Walking with God* as an apt metaphor for the ways in which spirituality and social transformation are conjoined, so that the walk with God is at the same time a walk in the world of nature, people, and systems that create contexts for engagement and renewal, and that their respective pilgrimages are not confined to a narrow and myopic vision of the church or to Christianity for that matter. Thurman believed that the transformative power that is discovered in one's inner life must of necessity be worked out in the political and social dimensions, as well as in a search for "a friendly world under friendly skies."[13]

---

12. "Interview on Religion and Aging" [May 1980], in PHWT 5:307.
13. Howard Thurman, *A Strange Freedom: The Best of Howard Thurman on Religious Experience and Public Life* (Boston: Beacon Press, 1998), 308.

Acknowledgments and Editorial Note

The editors thank former managing editor of the Howard Thurman Papers Project, Silvia P. Glick; Hazel Monae Johnson; and Nora Graciela De Arco for their assistance, and Robert Ellsberg of Orbis Books for his support of this project. A special thanks to Professors Shively Smith and Benjamin White for their reviews of the documents to ensure the best scholarly attention to the sermons on Jesus, Paul, and Ezekiel.

Most of the texts in this volume are taken from transcriptions of audiotapes; the transcriptions were made under the auspices of the Howard Thurman Education Trust in the 1970s. When possible, we have checked the accuracy of the transcriptions against the original audio tapes. In a few instances, we directly transcribed the text from the original tape source. The editors have silently corrected obvious mistakes and resolvable confusions in the transcriptions. The original audio sources differ in their comprehensiveness; some include initial meditations and opening illustrative quotations; others do not. Whenever possible, the editors have included the full sermon.

Throughout his career Thurman used masculine language to refer to persons or people in general, and the editors have not changed his wording.

The editorial procedures used in preparing this volume closely follow the editorial statement in Walter Earl Fluker, ed., *The Papers of Howard Washington Thurman: The Wider Ministry*, vol. 5 (Columbia: University of South Carolina Press, 2019), lvii–lxi.

Abbreviations

HT   Howard Thurman
PHWT   Walter Earl Fluker, ed., *The Papers of Howard Washington Thurman,* volumes 1–5 (Columbia: University of South Carolina Press, 2009–19).
Moffatt   Bible translation of James Moffatt. New Testament, 1913; Old Testament, 1924.
WHAH   Howard Thurman, *With Head and Heart: The Autobiography of Howard Thurman* (New York: Harcourt Brace Jovanovich, 1979).

PART ONE

Man and the Moral Struggle

Introduction

November 21, 1954
Marsh Chapel, Boston University

Central to Thurman's view of religion was the notion of "moral struggle," the spiritual resources to call upon when an individual is faced with the responsibility to make a decision on which path to take when faced with a crucial moral fork in the road. In the sermon series "Man and the Moral Struggle," all of his subjects are figures challenged by what Thurman calls "frustration," the consequence of individuals finding their transcendent goals thwarted as a result of forces outside of their control and internal inhibitions that restrict the private will. This becomes a moral struggle for the realization of goals that seem, at first, to lie beyond reach.

When Thurman was teaching at Morehouse and Spelman colleges, probably in the 1929–30 academic year, he organized Religious Emphasis Week[1] around the theme of "Man and the Moral Struggle."[2] He delivered sermons on Job, Jesus, and Paul and invited a controversial speaker to campus, the labor leader A. Philip Randolph.[3] The week was capped by a stu-

---

1. Religious Emphasis Week was a common practice on many college campuses in the first half of the twentieth century, particularly in denominationally affiliated institutions. As at many other colleges at the time, chapel attendance was mandatory at Morehouse except for seniors, and this obligation was resented by the underclassmen. As a consequence, Thurman tried to make the services "so interesting that the men would want to attend for their own sakes, their own enrichment" (WHAH 81–82).

2. Ibid. Although Thurman states that the Morehouse sermon series on "Man and the Moral Struggle" was from "his second year on the Morehouse faculty," or 1929–30, there is other evidence that places the *Macbeth* performance in December 1931; see PHWT 1:cii.

3. A. Philip Randolph (1889–1979) was a socialist, a labor leader, and founder of the first black union admitted to membership in the AFL, the Brotherhood of Sleeping Car Porters. He is best remembered for successfully pressuring President Roosevelt in July 1941 to issue Executive Order 8802, banning discrimination in the defense industry, and for organizing the March on Washington in August 1963. For Thurman's friendship with Randolph, see WHAH 82, 85, and PHWT 2:16–18.

dent production of Shakespeare's Macbeth.⁴ Appropriately, "Man and the Moral Struggle" included sermons on religion, with literature and a little politics. Thurman liked the idea and the combination, and would at least twice more organize sermon series around the title "Man and the Moral Struggle," one at Fellowship Church in 1949, and another with the same title in Marsh Chapel in 1954–55.

Thurman was an assiduous reader of fiction but rarely discussed his literary tastes, and the sermon series provides his perspectives and reviews on a number of plays and novels, some quite well-known, others rather obscure. All of the subjects face life-altering decisions. There is no assurance that their struggle will succeed, and some, such as Prometheus or Captain Ahab, seem to be monumental failures. Not all of the moral struggles are, on their surface, of equal weight. Thurman, for example, offers a moving account of his unease at having to kill a family of mice. But for Thurman, gaps between ends and means represents what he called in a 1948 sermon the "tragic sense of life," the "gulf between what I say and what I am able to achieve, the gulf that is never quite filled in," as a result of which we act out our "hoping, yearning, aspiring" over a "churning abyss" into which we are likely to fall.⁵

In the first sermon presented here, taken from the 1954–55 series, he illustrates the moral struggle through the biblical story of the Syrian commander, Naaman, in 2 Kings 5. "Where do you draw the line?" asks Thurman, or when do I with genuine integrity and full commitment to the ethical ideal say, "Here is the stand I take in the light of my commitment to ends which for me are the ends that are ultimate, the ends of God; then whatever it costs, even my life, I give it."

The sermon series published here is a composite of the two extant "Man and the Moral Struggle" series. For subjects that were duplicated in both sermon series, the editors have chosen the version they feel best suited to the goals of the current publication.⁶

Thurman was urged, probably by the Morehouse board of trustees, long reliant on the financial largess of the Rockefeller family and other northern capitalists, to cancel Randolph's appearance, but he resisted the pressure.

4. *Macbeth* was Thurman's favorite play of Shakespeare (conversation with Edward Kaplan, November 2019).

5. "The Tragic Sense of Life" (November 28, 1948), in PHWT 3:293–97.

6. Both the 1949 and 1954–55 sermon series have sermons on Paul, Job, Second-

Nestled underneath a sheaf of old papers,
Carefully protected from prying eyes and softly treading cats,
I found five moist-eyed mice.
A surging impulse of destruction gushed into every muscle,
And all the thirst of a thousand aeons of the Will to Kill
Paralyzed my new-born dream that life was sacred.
And yet, I paused!
Deliberation, the armored foe of action, caused me pause!
Who am I that I should crush in one fell swoop
The throbbing pulse of life caught in these tiny forms?
Are they not life?
To let them live would be
To run the risk of pestilence, disease and death.
How to destroy and yet not feel
The curse of power—
And not atone in all the subtle ways?—
    There—a slight increase in carelessness,
    Here—a bit more callous,
    Again—less mindful of another's plight.
    Where no persistent duty claims me.
Does a mouse enjoy life?
Is there no secret which he holds that I dare not miss?
But I had power to withhold death or to yield!
To the nestling mice was I not Omnipotent?
Can Omnipotence know aught else but its own sure strength?
Standing on the pinnacle of that awful moment
I saw the heights and depth of all brutality;
The bloody clue to the crimson stain in all man's dreadful
Past flashed before me.
To Power, stark and Omnipotent in its narrow
Sphere of time and circumstance,
What are ethics, morality, tenderness, religion?
Weakness, sentimentality, betrayal!

Isaiah, Prometheus, and Goethe's Faust. The editors have omitted a sermon on King Lear (February 27, 1955).

It was all clear.
To grant man power and hazard the trust
That he would make life safe for aught but that which keeps it
Fat and strong:
This was God's great gamble
When into man He blew the breath of life![7]

We begin this morning our thinking along lines upon which we shall be engaged for some time: man and the moral struggle. There is an unoccupied area of vitality that broods over the life of man, and the moral struggle is one of the creative means by which man moves into this area. Man may be said to be frustrated when the end that he seeks cannot be realized, whether it is a simple end or a complex and involved end. In the face of frustration, a resolution is found either by altering the ends, revising the ends, fixing the ends, changing the ends, so as to fit into the scope of the realizable, if I may put it that way, or by attacking the environment, elements which make it impossible for the end to be realized. Now there is a third thing. If the end that a man seeks involves him in reaching for that which is outside of or which transcends his personal private ends, needs, desires, then as the man struggles for the realization of these ends that are out beyond, what he struggles for now involves the whole destiny of his life; and struggle of that character for our thinking during these mornings is moral struggle. Now my temptation is to repeat that, but I won't. I have a feeling of vacuity.

When the ends that I seek whether they be within the context of my personal life and needs and desires or beyond always fail me, then I begin examining the ends. Maybe something is wrong with it. Perhaps I do not quite understand it. Or I begin attacking my environment which

---

7. This prose-poem, under the title "Rejoiceth Not in Iniquity," appeared in Thurman's first published book, *The Greatest of These* (Mills College, CA: Eucalyptus Press, 1944), 15–16. Elsewhere, he relates another version of this episode. The Thurmans were moving and discovered the mouse family, and though he "did not feel that he had the right to take their lives," he felt he had a responsibility not to leave them for the new tenants. As he raised his broom to swat them, one of the doomed mice "raised himself on his haunches . . . with a squeal of defiance, affirming the core of his mouse integrity in the face of descending destruction" (*Jesus and the Disinherited* [New York: Abingdon-Cokesbury, 1949], 81–82).

seems always to keep the thing from coming off. When that involves me in ends that are transcendent and boundless, it involves me in the kind of struggle in which there is at stake the ultimate destiny of my life.

Now [the] setting as found in our scripture lesson has to do with the man Naaman who had leprosy,[8] and he heard through his servant that there was a way by which he could be healed, if he could make contact with that way. And you know the story. I need not take the time to go through it except to say that Naaman was instructed to dip a certain number of times in the Jordan River, and his reaction was immediate. "Why that's stupid. If this prophet would ask something very important to do, something tremendous, then it would make sense, something to match the intensity of my disease." It is like the lady who prayed to God that she might learn how to surrender her life to him and she kept praying, but she always held back just a little because she was afraid that if she surrendered to God, God would require something of her that was so tremendous she couldn't do it and then she would have double embarrassment. Finally, she surrendered her life to God, and the thing that God asked her to do was to clean out her bureau drawers.[9]

So that was the way Naaman felt. If you had asked me to do something tremendous! All he had to do was dip in the water a certain number of times. But he did it finally because the leprosy made him do it. And then when he was healed, he tried to give the prophet something, and he made him a promise. Something new moved on the horizon. He began now to see that there had been emptiness in his life. He had been worshiping a God that was a no-God as he had thought of him, and now that I have found the God of Israel, I am still the right-hand man of the king. So get the figure now. He says to Jehovah, "When I walk into the temple of the other gods and his majesty is leaning on my arm as he has always been doing, and when he stops before the altar and genuflects, I must genuflect also. Will you understand it?"

---

8. See the story of Naaman, commander of the Syrian (Aramean) army (2 Kgs 5:1–27). For another treatment by Thurman, see "The House of Rimmon," in "The Power of the Spirit and the Power of the World" (November 1950), in PHWT 4:27–28.

9. Jane Steger, *Leaves from a Secret Journal: A Record of Intimate Experiences* (Boston: Little Brown, 1926), 72–73. For Thurman on Steger, see "Men Who Walked with God: Jane Steger," June 21, 1953, reprinted in the volume on Mysticism, next in this series.

Now, let's work at that just a few minutes. We are dealing here with an illustration of the moral struggle, with the question of compromise. Compromise. What was the alternative before Naaman just to mention that again? Either to say to the king, "I can't do this anymore," give up his job and lose his head, or to say to his God, "Do you know, I am in a tight place, and I hope you will understand."

Do you remember the story of the other wise man?[10] He was seeking Jesus, the Christ child, and he had these precious stones which he wanted to offer to him; and one by one he lost them, meeting some sort of need. And finally he came to a courtyard, and he went into the courtyard, and into a cottage. A woman was crouching in the corner, protecting her little male child under two. In the distance were the marching feet of Herod's squads going into all these places trying to find male children and killing them and presently the captain came to the courtyard, and the other wise man met him at the door. The captain said, "Is there a male child in this house?" The wise man said, "No, but here is a ruby," to the captain who has sense enough to go to the next house.

Now what am I getting at? This: that the individual as he seeks the realization of his goals, his desires, if he decides that his ends, his goals, are ultimate ends, ultimate goals, one with the mind of God, then the degree to which he surrenders to the quest, and the fulfillment of those goals, to that degree does he yield every secondary consideration, even if it means the yielding of his life. If, however, he decides that the goals are not ultimate goals, but are goals that can be juggled, manipulated, then he may try so to adjust the goal that his sense of frustration may be released, or he may decide if he cannot adjust or juggle the goal, so to operate upon the context in which he is living and working as to change the end, to make the climate more congenial for the fulfillment of the goal.

Now you see that in another interesting way, in the concept, for instance, of the reverence for life which seems to be inherently a part of the Christian ethic but interesting enough, you see, the ethical concept of reverence for life, once it is embraced, involves the individual in what

---

10. Henry Van Dyke, *The Story of the Other Wise Man* (New York: Harper & Brothers, 1895). Van Dyke (1852–1933) was a Presbyterian minister and a prolific and popular author, primarily on religious subjects.

Albert Schweitzer, I think, calls a boundless ethic rather than a limited ethic.[11]

The story of the mice, for instance. Or take the bacon that you had for breakfast this morning. At one time it was a hog enjoying life, grunting his thanksgiving to God. And then without any suggestion, without any permission granted, he found himself involved in death, and he had to give up his life for us; and he enjoyed [life], but if I did not make that demand of him, I would not have had bacon.

Where do I draw the line? Where do I draw the line? I have reverence for life if it is expressed in human beings. Is that it? But I draw the line at reverence for life if it is expressed in a cobra, or a rattlesnake, or a mouse. Where do I draw the line? If I draw the line at the rattlesnake, and if I can ever decide, as I look at a man, that his behavior is identical with the behavior of the rattlesnake, may I not destroy the man with the same ease of mind and conscience?

Where do I draw the line? But if I do not draw the line anywhere, which is to yield to all empiricist insistence of an absolute ethic, then ultimately my final compromise is the yielding of my own life. That is the way the martyr thinks, isn't it? That is the way he thinks. So if I want to keep myself intact, if I want to be involved only in a limited way with the moral struggle, I define my goals so that they will not involve me in a commitment of life that may demand that I sacrifice my life. But when I start juggling with these goals, I am never sure when I am being honest. You see? I may not retaliate, for instance, taking that as an ethical dimension of this concept of reverence for life. I may not retaliate when violence is visited upon me because of this ethical concept, or I may not retaliate because I am afraid. I may get this all confused. It is not a question then of compromise or no compromise for the human spirit. It is a question, where? At what point do I draw the line?

Let me illustrate it in one other way. You do not believe in war because you believe in peace. And you will not support the war system. Where do you stop? There was a young man who worked with me for several years in San Francisco. He decided that he could not register for the draft. He was twenty-six on August 31st. The last day that one could register was

---

11. For Schweitzer, see "Albert Schweitzer, Spiritual Genius" (July 17, 1949), in this volume; "Albert Schweitzer," PHWT 4:309–14 (January 1962).

August 30th. And he felt if he registered even as a conscientious objector, he would do violence—but he still paid his income tax.[12] He still paid his income tax. Where do you draw the line? The question is concerned with all of my endeavor, with the completest commitment when and if I say, "Here is the stand I take in the light of my commitment to ends which for me are the ends that are ultimate the ends of God; then whatever it costs, even my life, I give it."

When I walk with my king in the House of Rimmon[13] and I genuflect my knee as he does, O Jehovah, wilt thou understand?

Enter our hearts and minds, illumine with Thy spirit and Thy mind and Thy heart, O God, to the end that we may not be left to stumble in our darkness. Dismiss us with Thy spirit and grant unto us Thy peace.

---

12. For Robert Meyners, an assistant minister at Fellowship Church, and his decision to register as a conscientious objector when a peacetime draft was reintroduced in September 1948, see PHWT 3:254 n. 2, 280–81.

13. Ben-Hadad II, the king of Aram-Damascus, in the time of Joram, king of Israel. See 2 Kings 5:18 for the Rimmon reference. Rimmon was a god worshiped in ancient Damascus (Syria).

Albert Schweitzer, Spiritual Genius

July 17, 1949
Fellowship Church

Although Thurman was planning to deliver his series on "Man and the Moral Struggle" in the fall of 1949, he delivered this sermon a few months earlier, to coincide with the publicity surrounding Albert Schweitzer's only trip to the United States.[1] Thurman was a great admirer of Albert Schweitzer; and, as he states in this sermon, he had "read much of Schweitzer."[2] Schweitzer's commitment to a "boundless ethic" of the reverence for life in all of its forms was an influence on Thurman's own views of the unity of all life.[3] He was an admirer of the ethic that drove Schweitzer toward his compassionate and redemptive activities in Africa and elsewhere that he believed teach us much about our own possibilities of commitment to vital causes. Yet Thurman also has an ambivalence toward Schweitzer, detecting an underlying trope

---

1. Schweitzer was in the United States from June 28 to July 27, 1949, speaking in Aspen, Colorado, Chicago, New York City, and Boston.

2. Albert Schweitzer (1875–1965) was born and raised in Alsace, which after the 1870 Franco-Prussian War was incorporated into Germany. (It returned to French control after World War I.) He began studying at the Kaiser Wilhelm University in Strasbourg in 1893, and studying medicine at the University of Strasbourg in 1905, receiving his degree in 1913. The same year he moved to Lambaréné, in French Equatorial Africa [now Gabon] to establish his clinic and hospital, which remained his home for the remainder of his life. The first English-language edition of some of Schweitzer's works are *The Quest of the Historical Jesus: A Critical Study of Its Progress From Reimarus to Wrede* (London: A & C Black, 1910); *J. S. Bach*, 2 vols. (London: Macmillan, 1911); *Paul and His Interpreters* (London, A & C Black, 1912).

3. For Schweitzer the "reverence for life" was a "boundless ethic" including all living things and was an influence on Thurman's thinking; see Charles R. Joy, ed., *The Animal World of Albert Schweitzer: Jungle Insights into Reverence for Life* (Boston: Beacon Press, 1950), 174. See HT, "Community and the Unity of Life" [March 1964], and HT, *The Search for Common Ground* (New York: Harper & Row, 1971), 56–74.

of paternalism in Schweitzer's view of Africa and Africans.[4] *Nonetheless, for Thurman, Schweitzer was a "spiritual genius," and his life is exemplary. If we all placed ourselves under the sort of "necessity" that animated Albert Schweitzer, "who knows but the pressure for atonement would be so great in us that resources that we had never tapped would begin to stir in us and overflow in the richest expression of creative living?"*

THIS REALLY BELONGS in the series of sermons which we shall be doing during the month of August and September on "Man and the Moral Struggle," but it seemed very important to pull him out of that sequence and think a little with you about him this morning. The first and simple observation that I would make about him represents in a rather dramatic manner the result of great and detailed planning of his days. That's a very simple observation and an uninspired one, but it's impressive to me because the tendency that is present in us all, to which in varying degrees we succumb, is to live our lives without a sense of plan, without a sense of order, without a sense of direction. We apply a sense of order, a sense of direction, a sense of plan to our business—out there are other things that seem to be tangible and objective—other aspects of our experience in which it is comparatively easy to have a sense of judgment when plans do not go through; but in the most crucial thing, the most important thing, the living of our own lives, we do it at random.

I shall read just a little to illustrate the Albert Schweitzer timetable: at age twenty-one, he decided that he would devote nine years of his life to science and music, after which he would give all of his life to human service as a man to his fellowmen. That's at age twenty-one. At twenty-three he passed his first theological examination. At twenty-four he published his work on Immanuel Kant, took his doctorate in philosophy, and was appointed the preacher at St. Nicholas Church in Strasbourg. At twenty-five he was awarded his licentiate in theology and a full professorship. At twenty-six he was principal at St. Thomas's Theological College at the University of Strasbourg. At thirty appeared his *Life of Bach* in French, and he began his seven years study of medicine. At thirty-one appeared *The Quest*

---

4. Albert Schweitzer, PHWT 4:309–14 (January 1962).

of the Historical Jesus. Also he published his strategic and debatative book *Organ Building and Organ Playing*. At thirty-three there appeared the German edition of his *Life of Bach*, an entirely new work with three hundred additional pages. It had appeared some time previously, in French, you recognize; and now an entirely new work appears in German. At thirty-six he published his *Paul and His Interpreters* and passed his medical examination. At thirty-seven he resigned as a teacher and a preacher and became an intern to finish his medical preparation; and he married. At thirty-eight he became a doctor of medicine and published as his dissertation *The Psychiatric Study of Jesus*. And at the same age, he brought out with Widor[5] a six-volume edition of all of the works of Johann Sebastian Bach.[6] At forty he made his monumental and spiritual disclosure relative to his conception of reverence for life, and the rest of his story was written on the banks of the Ogowe River in Africa. Now when I read that, the temptation is to become completely discouraged. But that is not necessary.

It is impossible, or course, to fill in the picture of the life of so amazing a man, so creative, so powerful, so dynamic, so resourceful. You have been reading in all of the current magazines, and in *Vogue* there is an article about Albert Schweitzer that ends up, really, in discussing Mrs. Schweitzer[7] in relation to Albert Schweitzer, but they have to get it worked around so as to justify its appearing in *Vogue* and increase the sale. *Time Magazine* has a long definitive piece on Schweitzer, all the newspapers and so forth and so on.

What I have to say about Schweitzer this morning is very simple and very direct. Here is a man, a European, the heir of many generations of culture and discipline and refinement and religious insight, and also a man who by his social heritage was a part and parcel of the mood of our civilization that has sent the Western culture into all of the different parts of the world as an agent of exploitation and power. He inherited the good and the bad from his culture and his civilization, and yet he decides to go to Africa.

---

5. Charles-Marie Widor (1844–1937), French organist and composer.

6. C.-M. Widor, *Johann Sebastian Bach: Complete Organ Works*, 8 vols. (New York: G. Schirmer, 1912–1914).

7. Helene Bresslau Schweitzer (1879–1957) met her future husband in 1898, and they soon entered into a relationship; in 1912, they married and resolved to move to Africa. She trained as a nurse to assist her husband's work.

As a youngster he was walking through a park in Strasbourg, and he saw a statue of a European, and kneeling at his feet was a native African boy. There was a look of anguish and pleading and yearning in the face of the African. And Albert Schweitzer felt as he looked at that—Albert Schweitzer, the sensitive youth—felt that somehow in the African-European necessity he had to do something about it. His rationalization for the decision is very far-reaching and significant, I think. He said, "I went to Africa as a missionary to put at the disposal of the African the skills which I acquired, the powers of my mind and my spirit and my sense of urgency because I wanted as a white man in Europe to atone to the African for the blood and the tragedy and the suffering that the white man in Europe had perpetrated on that continent."

I have read much of Schweitzer, and I am frank to confess to you that when I first encountered him, I encountered him with all of the limitations of my own background and culture and religious experience and sensitiveness. I felt, as I read *On the Edge of the Primeval Forest*,[8] for instance, that during a long period of Schweitzer's life in Africa, he was battling with certain spiritual and psychological problems of which he himself was not aware. He had to come from under the burden of a sense of racial superiority and cultural superiority and religious superiority and meet the African as one human spirit encountering another human spirit, and all through the pages of the first edition of the *On the Edge of the Primeval Forest* there seems to me evidence of this inner struggle that the great doctor was passing through.[9]

Finally the moment of tremendous emancipation came when one day an African came into the compound, bent at right angles, suffering from a case of acute hernia. His teeth were chattering, and he was in a great and living agony. An operation was indicated, and Dr. Schweitzer says that he performed the operation; and after the operation was over he sat by the bed of this man, as the man worked his way out of the influence of the anesthetic and as he became conscious, the first thing he remembered was that there was no more pain. No more pain. And he reached out

---

8. Albert Schweitzer, *On the Edge of the Primeval Forest: Experiences and Observations of a Doctor in Equatorial Africa* (London: A & C Black, 1922).

9. Thurman explores his ambivalence in greater detail in "Albert Schweitzer," PHWT 4:309–14 (January 1962).

to touch the doctor's hand, and the doctor, as he grasped the hand of this African, felt—said he—that the difference of religion, difference of culture, differences of background, differences of race, all melted away. And on the edge of the primeval forest he met as a man another man. Albert Schweitzer became free.

Now this other thing that interests me about Dr. Schweitzer is that because of his revolutionary and radical ideas, particularly as touching the significance of the life and the person and the teachings of Jesus, he was regarded in many circles as a heretic, as a religious iconoclast. But he presented himself to the missionary society to go out, after giving Bach concerts for the money to finance it all, he had to go out through a sanction, you see, for one of the ways by which colonial governments are held is that no person is permitted to go out to deal with the minds and the spirits of the colonials unless the official colonial government says "yes." And that is common sense if imperialism is going to remain in power. It has to do that, and all missionary activities in any of these possessed places are cleared officially by the body in the country and the government that has the destiny of the people in their hands. So you can't go free-wheeling among these people lest you do things that will be deadly for the guaranteeing and the perpetuation of the established order. But as I say after you get the sanction of the society—and he wanted to have it, too, I don't want to exaggerate that—there was one thing wrong. He was a good doctor, apparently, well-disciplined, well-trained, but he had ideas, religious ideas that were bad for Europeans; so what on earth would happen if his ideas were turned loose among simple people in Africa, went the logic? So they said, "all right you may go, but you can't preach." We put a ban on your lips. So he served his first section of his experiences in Africa under a ban. He was not to talk religion. He was not to explain anything, and that's a wonderful thing, you see. Suppose we had a ban like that, and indeed, if the tremendous spiritual revolution in the midst of which the world is placed at this moment, would indicate that the time will come when that will be true; but what would happen if you couldn't talk about what you believe? You couldn't teach anybody. The only thing that would be left for you to do would be to demonstrate. Tremendous thing, isn't it? So that people would have to catch it by contagion as they catch the measles. The righteousness, then, you see, would be under a great urgency to perforate all of the many-sided manifestations of one's daily life.

I spent an afternoon with one of Dr. Schweitzer's secretaries about five years ago, and apropos of that aspect of Dr. Schweitzer's experiences, he told me this interesting story.[10] He said that one day the doctor, after a delivery, the woman asked the doctor if he would name her child, since her tribespeople were far away, and give him his fetish—that is the banner—the private banner under which he would be going to live his life if he were going to be healthy. One of the problems that Dr. Schweitzer had to face in this country was the problem of drinking—rum had been brought there at another time. So Dr. Schweitzer, who was not permitted to do any preaching about anything, said, "His name shall be so and so and so, and his fetish is that he must never taste rum."[11]

You see? Now, I think that it was a very good thing for Dr. Schweitzer and the world that he was under that ban for that first time, for it meant that energy that would have been spent in preaching as such, doing the overt things in connection with the ministry which he always regards as paramount in importance, could now be spent in thinking and writing; and indeed it was a part of the whole plan of his life that every day, even on the banks of this river in Africa, every day he did a certain amount of reading, a certain time for reflection and study and writing. And in addition, when his metallic-bound organ came out, he spent a certain number of hours in the evening playing his organ.

Now there is a third thing. And this to me is the most significant thing about Dr. Schweitzer. And this reveals the character of his spiritual genius. The interpretation he gives—or shall I say the interpretation that was given to him—of the concept of "reverence for life." For this concept is at once one of the central, ethical problems of man. For there can be no ethics if the individual does not affirm life. Even the notion of ethics is

---

10. The exact date of the meeting with Schweitzer's secretary and the name of the secretary are unknown, but it probably was in 1944; see "From Albert Schweitzer, 1944" (a short postcard in French). The two men had further contact; see "From Albert Schweitzer, 23 September 1956," in which Schweitzer compliments Thurman for his work at Boston University (correspondence in the Howard Thurman Papers, Howard Gotlieb Archives, Boston University).

11. Thurman had told a version of this story before in "The Missionary Spirit and World Peace" (April 1934), in PHWT 1:250.

one that is derived directly from life-affirming rather than life-negating. One of the reasons that men say that the mystic can never be ethical is because the mystic is engaged in a spiritual experience that denies life—that it is life-negating; it is withdrawing from the pulsing, creative process of existence. It is retreat. It is burrowing oneself more deeply into one's own center, while ethics insists always that men will move out in constant affirmation of life and the living process.

Now, Albert Schweitzer, who by temperament was a man, as a youngster even, who affirmed life, who had sensitiveness towards life—a sensitiveness so dramatic that he was almost morbid about it. We recall one of the instances that appeared in *Time Magazine*, how he wrestled with a boy who was larger than he, but he threw him, and the boy said, "It is small wonder that you threw me because you have good soup to eat every day and I don't have that kind of food because I don't have your security"; and for days after, Schweitzer the youngster couldn't enjoy his food. Sensitive. Or how he would drop a little of his grapefruit juice on the floor in order that the ants may have a little quiet time together. Sensitive. Now the feeling that he expressed even in the use of chemicals, or what have you, to destroy microbes; the battle with disease germs, all of these living expressions of life he had to destroy: so that on a naturalistic level, without regard to the religious sensitiveness, Albert Schweitzer was in a very difficult psychological position as he tried to work out a creative orientation for his own life and make his life useful without having in that endeavor to destroy other lives and other forms of life. It is natural then that he would turn to India and to Brahmanic mystics and to Buddhism and all of that particular kind of oriental climate to see what was the meaning of the concept there.[12] Then he would also look into Chinese culture and into Greek culture and into the culture of which he was a part and into the relevant aspects of the religion of Jesus and the meaning of the religious experience of Paul. Always trying to see if there can be a satisfactory ethical answer to the problem. "Reverence for life," which has at its center, compassion.

Now the concept of "reverence for life" is not new. Even though it came to Albert Schweitzer one afternoon in his boat, as a gift from God under the aegis of a flash of blinding inspiration, it was not new. For the

---

12. For Thurman's (not entirely favorable) review of Schweitzer's *Indian Thought and Its Development*, see PHWT 2:19–20 (December 1936).

concept of reverence for life as a metaphysical concept is a part of certain of the great Oriental religions, and indeed it is true that Buddhism makes its appearance in the history of religion rather in the culture of India because there was something in the Indian spirit that protested against the impersonal aspects of metaphysical concept of "reverence for life" as found in Hinduism. Buddhism arises as an ethical answer to that metaphysical generalization, and Buddhism says that there must be placed at the center of the metaphysical concept of reverence for life the notion and the experience of compassion, which notion and which experience are ethical in character because essentially it is life-affirming.

Now, Albert Schweitzer, the Christian, draws on that resource and brings to bear upon the considered religious and ethical judgment of the past, his genius and his insight. And what does he get? He says, "Reverence for life" means that in the affirming of my life I must always under every circumstance be sensitive in the bearing that the affirming of my life has upon the jeopardizing of your life or of the life of something that is not a human life. "I can't live," say Albert Schweitzer, "without some participation and destruction of life. I have no choice, but I shall reduce my destruction of life even on behalf of the affirmation of my own life, to a minimum. To an honest, authentic minimum. And wherever I must participate in the destruction of life, for ends of compassion which seem to transcend the urgency merely to sustain life under any conditions, I shall do so with a sense of sin. And all of my days then, my life is a living atonement for the life of animals, of grass, and flowers, of disease germs, of human beings that I have destroyed in order to fulfill what seems to me the high destiny for the ethical man."

It is small wonder that by any standard he seems to be working himself to death, but he doesn't die. It is no wonder that with this kind of urgency placed upon all of the total powers of his personality, he seems to burst out in a manifold expression of the richest variety of creative ability. What would happen to us, limited as we are, without the great gross or required talents of an Albert Schweitzer—what would happen to us if we placed our lives under that kind of necessity? Who knows but the pressure for atonement would be so great in us that resources that we had never tapped would begin to stir in us and overflow in the richest expression of creative living? And great, high and holy, but redemptive activity.

The Prophet Deutero-Isaiah

September 25, 1949
Fellowship Church, San Francisco

The author of one of Thurman's favorite religious texts, and a favorite sermon topic,[1] is the unknown prophet who occupies most of the second half of the Book of Isaiah, chapters 40 to 55.[2] This sermon was the first delivered in the 1949 Man and the Moral Struggle series and serves as its introduction. Its theme, and that of the entire Man and the Moral Struggle series is that "frustration is the mood of spirit that obtains in an individual when the ends that he seeks are not fulfilled," and "frustration takes on the character of moral struggle when the ends that I seek extend beyond the frontier of my little life."

The frustration felt and lived by the author of Second Isaiah, who likely lived in Babylonia after the destruction of the First Temple in Jerusalem in 586 BCE, was the condition of exile. For Thurman, a prophet must

---

1. Other treatments of Deutero-Isaiah by Thurman include the following sermons: "The Meaning of Loyalty V: Deutero-Isaiah I," June 3, 1951; "The Meaning of Loyalty VI: Deutero-Isaiah," June 10, 1951; "The Message of Deutero-Isaiah," June 29, 1952; "Man and the Moral Struggle, II: Deutero-Isaiah," November 29, 1954; and "The Creative Encounter—Isaiah [on Second Isaiah]," December 14, 1958.

2. The division of the Book of Isaiah into First and Second (or Deutero-) Isaiah has been widely accepted in critical studies of the Hebrew Bible since the nineteenth century. Recent scholarship is less certain than Thurman was that all of the second part of Isaiah was written by a single hand, and some scholars have posited a further distinction between Deutero-Isaiah (chaps. 40–55) and Trito-Isaiah (chaps. 56–66), and there are other theories of complex and divided authorship. As early as 1926, while serving as pastor of Mt. Zion Baptist Church in Oberlin, Thurman made a special study of the treatment of the "suffering servant" passage in Isaiah (52:13–53:12) with the esteemed professor of Old Testament at Oberlin College, Kemper Fullerton (1865–1941). Thurman remarked that this was a "great creative adventure" and that since the seminar he had "never since lost sight of the far-flung mystery and redemption of the sacrament of pain (WHAH 70). In this sermon, he draws heavily on this early research capturing the theme of redemptive suffering.

rearrange, reinterpret, and manipulate the very events of his times in order to maintain a sense of transcendence in the far-reaching purposes of God. This is the moral struggle of Deutero-Isaiah, who is caught in the clutches of the history of Israel and the movement of imperial powers over which the people of God have no control.

The essence of the moral struggle, Thurman tells us, is precisely in our wrestling with the events and experiences, great or small, over which we have no command—and yet devoting ourselves to understanding the transcendent within them. This struggle for the transcendent within us comes at a price; it involves suffering for a higher end or the realization of God's will in history. Thurman suggests that three great ideas emerge from his reading of Deutero-Isaiah: (1) the special destiny of the people of Israel "not only as the strategic political capital, but [as] the center of the animation for the redemption of the world"[3]; (2) the universality of God's outreach to humanity is not confined to a political or geographic location but to a binding moral relationship to YHWH, an "ethical monotheism"[4]; and (3) that the Jews, through their history of oppression and suffering, will become the moral and spiritual teachers of humanity. The "suffering servant" motif of Second Isaiah speaks to the universality of this mission, which is to all who dream of a just and loving world. Moreover, this quest for "a vast creative manifestation of the spirit of God [can] throttle the political movement with moral and ethical insight" only in humility of spirit and of mind.[5]

---

3. Or as Thurman said elsewhere, "to be a Jew was equivalent to having an automatic spiritual relationship with Jehovah. . . . In other words he had to redefine what it meant to be a Jew. And now he arrives at a conclusion that a person is a Jew who is related spiritually, in attitude of mind, in attitude of spirit to Jehovah and not merely because he was born in a certain family, or he belonged chronologically, to a certain tribe etc. Now, the logic of that meant, that if it be true that the thing that determines whether or not a man is a Jew is not his birth, not his roots, but his moral and spiritual awareness and character, then any man who has that awareness becomes, in the language of the prophet, a Jew" ("The Message of Deutero-Isaiah," 8).

4. Ibid, 10.

5. See "The Meaning of Loyalty V," 6–7, on the moral and spiritual mission of Israel.

MAN AND THE MORAL STRUGGLE: it is not as formidable as it sounds. We are picking up one of the insights about which we talked in the series on prayer which closed last Sunday. You may recall a phrase "the unoccupied frontier of vitality," descriptive of that area in human experience disclosed by the thing that happens when, under tremendously overwhelming pressure growing out of needs for oneself or for another, the individual human spirit discovers a dimension of desperation that is not an ordinary part of its working arrangement.[6]

The proposition on which we shall be working for several weeks is this: frustration is the mood of spirit that obtains in an individual when the ends that he seeks are not fulfilled because of the operation of forces over which he has no control, or because of a limitation which seems at the moment to be resident in his personality. It expresses itself in simple ways—when I want to go out of the door and the door is locked and I don't know where the key is, all the way up to the profound stalemate that arises when my desire for the highest and the best is unfulfilled.

Frustration takes on the character of moral struggle when the ends that I seek extend beyond the frontier of my little life. Frustration itself is always tied up with the personal and the private outreach; but when the end that I seek is pushed out until it involves more than my private destiny, and that end–which is then a transcendent one—cannot be fulfilled, I move into a qualitative struggle that from my point of view takes on the character of moral struggle. Because now it is not a conflict between my little private will and something that blocks my little private will, but it is projected now in terms that are as wide and as comprehensive as life itself.

Each one of us is involved in that kind of a struggle, so please do not think that it is some kind of academic exercise done to stimulate your minds, and leaving your spirits unconvicted. That can happen, but it certainly is not my purpose. Sooner or later each of you will find that

---

6. The phrase "unoccupied frontier of vitality" is one that Thurman associated with the moral struggle. It appears in the introductory sermon to the 1954–55 Man and the Moral Struggle series (November 21, 1954), published in the current volume, where Thurman claims that "there is an unoccupied area of vitality that broods over the life of man, and the moral struggle is one of the creative means by which man moves into this area."

the thing you most want in life is defined in terms that are as broad and as wide and as deep as life itself. And in your effort to get fulfillment, you find that you are involved in a struggle that is no longer private and personal but that encircles all of the pulsing desires and weaknesses and strengths of the entire human race.

Take a simple instance. I want to love people; I want to love somebody. I want somebody to love me; I want to feel that I count; I want to respond and I want to be responded to—I reach out for that kind of fulfillment, and very soon I find myself involved in all kinds of struggles of other human beings. I find myself face to face with a human being who would love me, using it in the broadest possible sense of the word, but who somehow finds that it is almost impossible because of circumstances that worked on his mind when he was most innocent, when he was growing up. Even with all of the will in the world to respond to me in pure and wonderful and creative affection, he finds that he cannot implement that will because there is in him a paralysis that came even before he knew what was happening to him. Therefore, in order to make it possible for him to release his spirit to me in warmth and fellowship and redemption, some major something must happen in the society that created him. Thus, you see, I have embarked myself upon a struggle that is as wide as the human family, and the ends I seek are stymied.

Ends may be stymied because they are too selfish and too narrow; so perhaps I redefine my ends, because I refuse to admit that an aim which seems to me to be high and holy and fully desirable cannot find fulfillment in this kind of universe. If I am forced to admit that, then my confidence in the integrity of the whole moral fabric of life is undermined, so the fault must be in the character of my desire—so I work to change it.

Or the fault may lie in forces operating on me, holding up my fulfillment; forces over which I have no control; forces that are not responsive to me, however good and high and holy my end may be. Then I say, "Perhaps it will not be fulfilled now." If the forces close in upon me with too much terror and madness, I will say, "No, it cannot be fulfilled now. It must be fulfilled outside of time and space." So I become one who lives with his end in a dimension outside of the reach of the hopes and fears of ordinary human beings. We have these nice technical words for it: predestinarianism, apocalyptic, eschatology. What all these wonderful words really mean is that this is the sort of world that is closing in on me, taking all the oxygen out of the air so I can't breathe. So I must learn how to get my air from another dimension, and I say, "That's all right, I can be destroyed now, but there will come a time when I won't be: I'll get my way."

Now the way in which these forces drive you to disclose the very grounds of your integrity, the way these forces strip you of all your pretenses and literally push you into this area of vitality, this frontier of vitality, is the essence of the moral struggle.

I want to begin this morning by applying this principle to one figure; next Sunday to another, the next Sunday to another. I want to begin with the unknown prophet of the exile, Deutero-Isaiah, Second Isaiah. You understand the principle under which we are working; now you can see it operate. Watch it carefully as the story of Deutero-Isaiah unfolds, and if you keep looking you will see yourself.

Nebuchadnezzar[7] had taken the Jewish community into captivity. Jerusalem had fallen, and Nebuchadnezzar had carried all of the prestige-bearing people of Jerusalem into captivity in Babylon. Ezekiel was the prophet of the exiles, and in his mind there began to emerge a very great and interesting idea: the idea that God can't quite be limited; can't quite be limited to the soil of Israel.[8] We take it for granted now that God is universal, but—oh my, the long lead-footed centuries of staggering agony through which the whole race passed before an idea like that began to break into the minds of men. God was a god that belonged to a place, to a soil, to a people; so if you are taken into captivity away from your soil, your God can't follow you, because when you move into another soil another god takes over. When people were agonizing about being taken captive away from the holy soil of Israel, it was not only because they were losing their homes and all that sort of thing, but because they were now getting out of reach of Jehovah, and they would be under the domination and control of a god who did not know them, whose worship they did not understand, into whose spirit they could not enter because deep within

---

7. Nebuchadnezzar II (reigned c. 605–562 BCE) was king of the Babylonian Empire, remembered for his conquest of Judah and the destruction of the First Temple in Jerusalem in 586 BCE.

8. For Thurman on Ezekiel, see "The Message of Ezekiel" (November 8, 1952), published in the current volume.

them there was an alien feeling growing out of their allegiance to their god. For these people who were exiles in Babylonia the spiritual problem was very great, and their prophet Ezekiel began talking with them about the idea that Jehovah really is here. He was pushing out the frontier of their minds so that they began to feel that Jehovah could be worshiped in Babylon. That is very revolutionary, but we won't tarry with it at the moment.

Nebuchadnezzar was a hard man; he put the king into chains for thirty-seven years.[9] He was a smart man also; he didn't forbid everything. He allowed room enough for movement and growth of a certain kind, so that if the people had anything and they belonged to him then he would have more. But the unknown prophet of the exile was not among these people down in Babylon; he stayed in Judah. He was a peasant prophet; he wasn't a city man.[10] In every community into which he went in Asia Minor he observed the units of Jews carrying on their lives, functioning as part of the common life of the community by which they were surrounded. They were scattered, because Jerusalem, the central worship place, had fallen.

An idea began to take shape in the prophet's mind:

—What should I do with my life? I have gifts; I have abilities; I have strange stirrings sometimes in the long nightwatches when I'm on the hills in meditation. What is it? Ah, it is that all of these knots of Jews scattered over Asia Minor are part of Israel, to whom the sense of the true and authentic character of God has been revealed out of the evolution and development of their long and sometimes tragic history. These Jewish people, who understand from insight the moral character of God, are now serving an apprenticeship all over Asia Minor, getting acquainted with different cultures and different people. If they can come back to

---

9. Jeconiah was king of Judah briefly in 598 BCE until he was overthrown and captured during Nebuchadnezzar's first invasion of Judah; he was held in captivity until Nebuchadnezzar's death in 562 BCE.

10. This is speculation on Thurman's part. Nothing is known specifically about where the author he identifies as Deutero-Isaiah lived, but most scholars argue, from the focus on exile, that the prophet lived in Babylon, not Jerusalem. Thurman's identification of the author as coming from a poor peasant background has much in common with his views on the social background of Jesus and prophets such as Amos and Hosea.

Jerusalem as a center and pool all of their accumulated knowledge, they can, with this knowledge and this religious sense, become the redeemers of all the peoples of the earth!

Beautiful, isn't it? Now that became his desire, the end that he was seeking. Meanwhile, things began happening in Babylon. Nebuchadnezzar died, and the new king corrected certain policies of Nebuchadnezzar.[11] He tried to make friends out of people who were enemies, so he released the Jewish king who had been in prison for thirty-seven years, on the theory that when enemies arose and began to close in on the empire, if even conquered peoples had a loyalty that sprang from within for the kingdom, then they would fight on behalf of the empire against the invading enemy. Good policy. The Jewish community breathed a sigh of relief because at last they were going to get official status, and that is different from just status. Some men in the kingdom had other ideas. They said, "Nebuchadnezzar built his empire on force. It was the might of his arms that caused the other kings to cringe before him, and if you don't keep force always before the subject peoples, they will rise up and destroy you." So they hatched a plot and killed the king, and the status quo was resumed.

But when the Jewish king had been released, the unknown prophet of the exiles had said:

—Ah, God is a god of history; God is in history, and the first act by which God confirms my private dream about the destiny of Israel is to move the heart of Nebuchadnezzar's successor to release the king.

He began prophesying about it; and then, when the king was killed, where was he?

—Is God in history now? I don't know. Let's see.

There is a long series of verses in which he talks, revealing the beginning of his frustration. Then something else happened. A little man whose name was Cyrus began stirring way over somewhere.[12] Nobody paid any attention to him, but this little man had a lot of courage and a lot of other things, and he began conquering. Before anyone realized it,

---

11. Amel-Marduk, whose reign was probably from 562 to 560 BCE.

12. Cyrus (c. 600–c. 529 BCE) established the Achaemenid, or First Persian, Empire, conquering Media, Lydia—where Croesus was king from c. 560 to 546 BCE—and the Babylonian Empire, establishing his reign over most of the Middle East.

Croesus (who has come down to us in our childhood stories as the richest man in the world—everything he touched turned to gold) heard that this little upstart was going to attack him. Since he was the most powerful man in the world he paid no attention to it, and one morning when he got up there wasn't anywhere for him to go. Cyrus had simply circled him and the great Croesus fell.

At that the unknown prophet said:

—Cyrus is the angel of God.[13] Even though he doesn't know it, God is using Cyrus as his instrument to bring in the world the climate which will make it possible for this dream that has possessed me to find fulfillment. Cyrus will make it possible for all the Jewish captives to come back to Jerusalem.

But Cyrus didn't order anyone to go back. He set up very narrow limits on which temples could be built, and he did many things that were disagreeable and disappointing.

But the prophets said:

—Of course you couldn't expect any more of Cyrus. He didn't know that he was God's arm, so he did as much as he could without any awareness. But God is at work in the hearts of the captives. Now that the barrier is removed, they will go to Jerusalem and block out the city, and they will take the preliminary steps toward the transformation of the moral order of the world.

Then what happened? The Jews who had settled in the different communities had no particular interest in returning to Jerusalem, and only a handful came back. The prophet said:

—What is this? Lord, where art thou? I can understand what happened to Cyrus, but does this mean that I am wrong? That I have misunderstood the fact that thou hast revealed thyself in moral quality to Israel?

He became bitter and disillusioned, and retired. Then he came back, because something else began to dawn upon him.

—I had assumed that all the people of Israel were aware of the revelation of the Spirit of God in their lives, but that isn't true. There are people in Israel who aren't sensitive to the moral spirit.

---

13. Isaiah 45.

You see what happened? He had been sure that just to be a member of the House of Israel meant, ipso facto, you are aware of the presence, the moral presence of God. When the unfolding of the vicissitudes of fortune revealed to him that that wasn't true, he asked:

-Is it true that there is no revelation of God in Israel? Or must I revise my idea in some other way?

So he said:

—Oh, this is it. There are those in Israel who have heard God's voice, who have responded to his spirit, and there are those who have not. God will work his will through those of Israel who have responded, but of course that is not enough, if God is the God of all the people.

Now he took the great transcendent step that has been the source of inspiration and guidance for all morally and ethically sensitive spirits, since he prophesied:

—Wherever God finds the righteous, responsive soul, there God will reveal himself, whether the man be a Jew or a Gentile, for God's approach to man's spirit is a moral approach.

—God does not care whether I am a Gentile or a Jew, or, in our language, a Baptist or a Presbyterian, or an Episcopalian, or a Quaker. Wherever the spirit affirms the declaration to yield the life to the moral and spiritual imperative of God, there, with that remnant, will the dream find fulfillment.

So the function of Israel had again to be redefined. And with that revision he came upon the final truth of his life: he had been thinking in terms of an external thing; he had thought that God could only work through people who have political, economic, and social power coupled with their righteousness, and now he arrived at the staggering conclusion that the role of Israel was to redeem, yes, but to redeem through agony, through suffering. They were to be the martyr nation, the self-effacing nation; they were to be the suffering servant. That is why this prophet is called the prophet who states the position of the suffering servant. This is what he says about it:[14]

> Behold, my servant shall prosper,
> He shall be honored and greatly exalted . . .

---

14. Isaiah 52:13–53:12.

> For as much as many were appalled at him
> For his face was marred more than any other . . .

(He would be exalted because his face was marred more than any other.)

> So shall the mighty ones be startled at him.
> Kings shall be silent before him,
> For what hath not been told them.
> They shall see what they hath not heard.
> They shall understand
> Who hath believed our report they shall say
> And whom has the Lord's arm revealed.

Now listen to the beautiful majesty of this.

> "For eagle Israel." (This remnant he is talking about now. We have used it in another way in the development of the Christian religion, but that is not on the point.)[15]
>
> For he grew up as a slender shoot before us, as a root out of the arid ground
> He had no form or charm that we should notice him, no beauty that we should admire him
> He was despised and forsaken of men, a man of sorrows and acquainted with pain
> As one from whom men hid their faces he was despised and we esteemed him not.
> Yet it was our woes that he bore, and our sorrows that he carried.
> While we accounted him punished, smitten of God, and afflicted
> But he was wounded for our transgressions, bruised for our iniquities,
> On him fell the chastisement that made us whole, and with his stripes were we healed.

---

15. The phrase "eagle Israel" is not in Isaiah, and perhaps refers to personifications of Israel's relation to God as that of a soaring eagle, as in Isaiah 40:31 or Exodus 19:4: "I bore you on wings of eagles and I brought you to me." This is followed by a selection of passages from Isaiah 53:1–53:10.

> All we like sheep had gone astray, we had turned each to his own way
> And the Lord laid on him (on Israel, this remnant, not all of Israel) the penalty, charged upon him the guilt of us all
> And his life then shall make an atonement for sin.
> He will see his seed, and he will prolong his days."

From a simple desire, growing out of an ordinary but highly sensitized national interest (a patriotism), this man went through frustration after frustration; and every frustration caused him to redefine the spiritual character of his intent, and to reinterpret the march of impersonal social forces that were hammering away at his desires, until at last, stripped to the literal substance of himself, having no defense of philosophy, no defense of dogma, no defense of theology, no defense of race or culture or civilization—stripped to the literal substance of himself—he said:

—Ah, he who would redeem must be one who gladly takes upon himself the aches, the tragedies, and the wickedness of human beings. In that travail he will discover the meaning and the mystery of life and God, and find there a solution to his frustration and a fulfillment of his moral struggle.

And we, each one of us who has ever walked through the valley of the shadow, understand what this means.[16]

---

16. Thurman here is not concerned with some traditional Christian interpretations of this narrative that see this as a precursor of the life of Jesus. Rather he is concerned here with the ways, the mental maneuvers, that the individual seizes upon to actualize what seems to him or her the transcendent moral imperative, which in this case is resident within the imagination of the prophet. By implication, Thurman argues, the prophet's moral struggle mirrors our own need to come to a sense of resolution with the transcendent, which visits us in our need to fulfill the deep sense of our destiny and place in the world. Thus, Thurman's treatment of "the suffering servant" is a psychological examination that carries the weight of the mythic and historical struggle of the individual who is seeking a synthesis from disparate frames of meaning and the nagging moral demand of commitment to the higher calling of self and society.

Jesus

October 2, 1949
Fellowship Church

In this sermon Thurman offers his familiar perspective on Jesus, seeing him as a "religious subject, not an object of religious devotion."[1] (He tells the congregation at Fellowship Church that he had said this "many times from the pulpit, and perhaps it is almost redundant now.")[2]

Thurman places the beginning of Jesus's ministry not at his birth but rather at his baptism by John, which was the divine imprimatur of his commitment by God.[3]

---

1. HT, *Jesus and the Disinherited* (New York: Abingdon-Cokesbury, 1949), 15. For an earlier version of this argument, see "The Significance of Jesus IV: Prayer Life of Jesus," in PHWT 2:68–74.

2. A careful reading of Thurman's treatment of Jesus in this sermon and elsewhere reveals that he often treats the stories as "facts" of the life of Jesus—indeed sometimes as reports of Jesus's own consciousness and experiences—though all of the gospels were written decades after Jesus's lifetime and represent stories about Jesus's life written in hindsight and retrospection, rather than in the moment. Yet, what complicates this is the fact Thurman constantly demonstrates knowledge of the historical-critical issues related to individual biblical texts. He is engaged in a sophisticated hermeneutical dance between history, his commitments to the moral religious life, and the contents of Scripture.

3. Thurman's views on Jesus have affinities with the christological doctrine known as adoptionism, which holds that Jesus was adopted as the Son of God at the time of his baptism. (Other versions hold that Jesus was adopted at his resurrection or ascension.) Adoptionism is antitrinitarian, and Thurman, as early as 1924, rejected the dogma of the virgin birth ("Virgin Birth," in PHWT 1:32–36). Thurman, however, nuances his perspective by noting that Jesus was an "experiencer of religion." For Thurman, it's not just that God commissioned Jesus but that Jesus himself was involved in the commissioning process. Thurman is asserting that Jesus not only participated in the "religious ends" of his work but that he opted into it as much as one would say he was adopted by God to do it. For the fullest previous discussions of Jesus by Thurman, see "The Significance of Jesus" (September 1937), PHWT 2:44–92. See also HT, *Temptations of Jesus* (New York: Harper & Row, 1962).

Thurman claims that one can best understand Jesus's moral struggle by living out the distilled white-heat intimacy of the moment of commitment, at his baptism, which inspired his commitment to the lofty, transcendent ideal of the Kingdom of God. Jesus, according to Thurman, felt entrusted with this transcendent goal; and in order to realize it, he had to decide between his response to the day-to-day challenges of Jewish resistance under Roman domination, as well as his own inner temptation to defy the consequences of his actions rooted in material necessities, religious heritage, and natural law.

Jesus, Thurman argues, "decided that he would worship God, that he wouldn't be God." Jesus's decision to pursue his vision of the Kingdom of God led him to Jerusalem, the epicenter of his moral struggle and his death. Thurman thinks that it was Jesus's faith in God, expressed in his despairing cry "My God, my God! Why have you forsaken me?" that was the focus of the moral struggle for him and for all who dare pursue such transcendent ends that pull them beyond their private ends of comfort and security. This is, says Thurman, "the ultimate paradox of the moral struggle, and I love Jesus for this shaft of light which his moral struggle throws across the pathway of all who stand at that point in the darkness."

THE PROPOSITION upon which we are working, simply stated, is this: that frustration is the common lot of the experience of man; that frustration arises when the end that a man seeks cannot find fulfillment because of the operation of factors or forces over which he as an individual is not able to exercise any immediate control. These forces may not be resident in his environment, but it is altogether possible that they may be resident in him; sometimes with his full consciousness, sometimes without his being aware of it. The solution to his frustration can only be found when he either alters the ends that he seeks so as to make those ends congenial to his environment or to the factors that limit those ends, or when he is able to operate upon his environment so that the things in his environment which frustrate his end no longer exist and the end can be fulfilled.

Now moral struggle is of the same anatomical character, with a difference at one crucial point. When the end that a man seeks extends so far beyond his private concern, his private will, his private desires, that it becomes one with ends that are transcendent (with which he is identified, to be sure)—when this transcendent end with which the individual is identified cannot fulfill itself because of limiting factors in the environment (factors which may be entirely temporal; that is, factors that are present because there has not been enough time, or factors that are due to the stubborn or recalcitrant nature of men's minds and spirits, or factors that may be due to what, for lack of a better term, are invisible, demonic forces in life)—the moral struggle takes place because there is always the assumption that the high end that is transcendent can be fulfilled. The process by which the individual works over himself or over his environment in an effort to implement this transcendent end is the measure of his moral struggle.

Last Sunday we applied to Deutero-Isaiah, Second Isaiah, and I forgot to say that Deutero-Isaiah is found beginning with chapter 40 in the Book of Isaiah, and going twenty-six chapters. This morning I want to do a much more difficult and, perhaps, pointed application, because I want to apply this thesis to the life of Jesus Christ. To what I am going to say, I hope you will listen—and listen with your minds and your spirit, and not with your prejudgments. For in our thinking about Jesus in this connection I am regarding Jesus as religious subject rather than religious object.[4] I have said that many times from the pulpit, and perhaps it is almost redundant now. By religious subject I mean one who himself was the experiencer of religion; one who sought religious ends, who was involved in the religious and moral predicament of man—rather than one who is the object of religious devotion and thereby finding himself outside of the realities of the moral struggle.

Jesus at the baptism had a clarification. John was preaching a gospel of repentance for the kingdom of God is at hand. Many, many people came to hear and be baptized, and among those people was Jesus of Galilee. Why did he come? Is it enough to say that he came in order that he might fulfill some law operating outside himself of which he was but the instrument? Or perhaps it is better to regard his coming as the movement of one who sought that which was involved in the announcement

---

4. HT, *Jesus and the Disinherited*, 15, published in the same year as this sermon.

of John the Baptist. He came as a son of Israel, involved in the struggles of Israel. And after baptism he had a primary religious experience of great illumination, for it seemed as if the heavens opened and the spirit of God descended upon him (like a dove, one of the gospels puts it), and he heard the voice of God saying to him, "Thou art my son, my beloved, in whom I am well pleased," or as one of the old manuscripts puts it, "This day have I begotten thee."[5]

He felt the most wonderful thing that a human being can ever feel in life. And what is that? That the thing you are doing, your dream, your hope, your life, has the ultimate approval of God. There is nothing like it. You know how you felt when you were a little child when you did something and your father and your mother just beamed. This pleased them right down to the bricks, as we say. They gave to you their approval, their imprimatur, their stamp. And you forget all about the fact that you had ripped the nail off your big toe, or that your best friend wasn't speaking to you because you didn't give him part of your all-day sucker. You just forget all about that because your life, your little life, had the parental nod. Now that is the thing that happened at the baptism.

He went from the baptism to the temptation.[6] At the temptation there was only one problem:

—How must I live? What must be the most adequate, the most complete expression of my life so that my life will be the living "for instance" of God? Shall I give all of my energies to taking care of the physical needs of people? Everywhere I look, people are hungry. Everywhere I look, they are under some kind of hammer. Outside of Israel they are oppressed; inside of Israel they are oppressed. How can I be a sensitive, responsive person to the mind and to the spirit and to the will of God? How can I be true to the genius of Israel and fulfill the insights of the prophets, which is the potential destiny of every thoughtful son of Israel? How can I do that?—in the presence of the poor, of so much destitution. Is that it? There is nothing more important.

---

5. Matthew 3:17.
6. See Luke 4:1–13; Matthew 4:1–11; Mark 1:12–13. For Thurman's first discussion of this, see "The Significance of Jesus II: The Temptations of Jesus," in PHWT 2:54–60. See also *The Temptations of Jesus*.

—But if I do that, then what happens to the other things that I feel and see? Can I work out some kind of synthesis? Can I give myself over to the meaning of these needs and at the same time have enough surplus energy left to devote my mind and my spirit to the things that cannot be measured in terms of food, of clothes, of money? How important is bread anyway? And what would happen to me if I started out saying this sort of thing about bread, about meat, about raiment? Would not Israel feel that I have betrayed it? Would I not then fall right into the hands of the Roman exploiters who want to get their hands on all of the economic security that Israel has? And if I do not point up the significance of raiment and clothes and the rest of it, then can I really be a loyal son of Israel? And yet the prophet did say that the spirit of God is upon me for he has anointed me to preach the gospel to the poor, to open the eyes of the blind, to unstop the ears of the deaf. Is that it? I can't do it all. If I spent all of my time feeding hungry people, if I spent all of my time getting clothes for the naked, when I get through working, the number remaining naked and the number remaining hungry would still be infinite. Would that be a solution to my struggle? Man should not live by bread alone! Is that it? Bread alone? But he has to have bread, but for every word that proceedeth out of the mouth of God, do I really betray my—I don't know.

—And then if I am really close to God as my private religious experiences have indicated—if in me at last all that God has been saying, and the prophets, all that has been meant by the peculiar relationship of Israel to God, if it is true that all of these things are rushing upon me, and in some sense I seem to be the fulfillment of the law of Israel (and mark you the fulfillment of the law of Israel, not the beginning of a new religion, not the making of something new, but the fulfillment of the law, of the unfolding of the mind and the heart of God to Israel), the climactic moment of the divine declaration in the heart of these people—then I can throw my weight around. I can actually go up to the pinnacle of the temple and jump down and not get hurt because I belong to a people; I am nurtured in a womb that has been brooded over by the direct intervention of the mind and heart and the ethic of God. And, therefore, I can do that; I can go up there and jump down, and I won't get hurt because God has spoken to Israel, and the light that has broken in Israel is a light that can light all the Gentiles who are also God's children. But, if I go up there and jump down, it may be that I will break my leg. Maybe I will.

And then there was something going on in him that said,

—Oh, no you won't. You won't break your leg, because for him who has the order of God in himself there is nothing binding of an orderly character in the universe. That's it.

—So if I have the order within, then I can ignore the order without. Very simple; we do that, don't we? Or do we? Because you have it in you, then you don't need to be bound by anything outside. Don't you say that about your own values? "I know what's right! I know what's wrong!"

One side of him said,

—Well, this is not an orderly world; no, it isn't. Not an orderly world so far as people who have God in them.

And have not men always felt that way? That they can transcend natural law any time they wish—if the pressure becomes great enough? The history of all peoples is that now and then men just ignore natural law. They heal where there seems to be no possibility of healing; they do the impossible all the time; they live on the verge of the possibility of the miraculous, and here and there the relentless momentum of their past experiences infused with the dynamics of their desire pushes them into the realm of the miraculous.

—Well, can I stand it myself? If I go up there and jump and nothing happens to me, but I just land on my feet. Can I stand that kind of thing myself? Not stand it physically, but can I stand to stay on the same planet with the rest of the human beings if I can do that? Is it arrogance on my part to think that I rate, that I merit that? If so, what becomes of what God is doing through me, what becomes of the purpose of God which I glimpsed with very tremendous clarity at the baptism? What becomes of that if in one radical expression I throw myself out of bounds so that I can no longer feel myself as being an agent of the divine purpose and the divine mind, but become my own agent? I shall become the divine mind. I shall be God, and have my own purposes and my own ends which I may throw into the face of my early commitment.

Well, he decided that he would worship God, that he wouldn't be God. He worshiped God, and he moved out across Palestine preaching and teaching and doing all manner of wonderful things. With the full burst of enthusiasm of this new sense now, the sense of triumph, of buoyancy, he was sure that when he started talking to men about God and about the kingdom of God—not about his kingdom, not about Jesus's kingdom, but the kingdom of God; not about the will of Jesus, but the will of God—that men would respond—just as Deutero-Isaiah thought that once Cyrus gave the decree and it was possible for them to go back and build they would come running from all over Babylon, but they didn't do it. And they didn't respond to Jesus.

Even in his hometown they said:

—Isn't that Joseph's son? On what meat does he feed that he has grown so bold that he can tell us something about the meaning of life? Let's get rid of him.[7]

Even his family said:

—Don't be too hard on him, because he is a little off—not crazy, but a little off—so that you can't take him seriously.[8]

And then they began to close in on him, close in on him, and what is happening to his spirit at the time?

—Is this the vision? Is this the thing that gripped me, that made me know that I must make of my life the expression of the will of God, on the assumption that the will of God would be so radiant in me that its impact on the minds and the spirits of other people would elicit in them a response of the same character and quality? What has happened to it? Maybe I missed it. Maybe I was wrong. Perhaps—No.

So he disappeared; he traveled incognito all across a certain area and finally got way up to Tyre and Sidon and there, with his disciples, tried to get himself reorganized, get this thing reestablished—and then what happened? There came bursting in on their retreat a woman of another race, with a great urgency.[9] You remember the story, don't you? She said,

—My child! (And who was going to stand between a mother and her child?)—My child. If you really will do it, you can help her.

And what did Jesus say?

---

7. Luke 4:22; John 6:42; Matthew 13:55; and Mark 6:3.
8. Mark 3:20–21.
9. The reference here is to Jesus's encounter with the Syrophoenician woman and her daughter, from whom he cast out evil spirits. See Mark 7:27–28; Matthew 15:26–27.

—It is not right. (Listen to him; listen to him with your minds and your spirits.) It is not right that the food for the children should be given to dogs.

That is what he told her. He was wrestling with the inner moral problem of the ethical and spiritual fulfillment of the mind and life of God in Israel and in himself as a part of Israel, and Israel had buffeted him in a way that he thought was not in accordance with the purposes of God or of the ethical and spiritual insights that were a part of the very warp and woof of Israel. Somehow they had not responded, and:

—I've got to get myself straightened out. I can't turn my back upon the commitment which I experienced when in that moment of illumination at the baptism I was sure that my life and my dream of fulfillment had the approval of God.

Once he was reestablished in his original faith and insights, he and his band of disciples moved back down through the area of Palestine until they came to the road which led to Caesarea Philippi. As they were walking along, Jesus said to his disciples:

—What are men saying about me? What is the general rumor that is being spread among them concerning me? I mean, when they are not talking for general consumption, but when they are sharing their innermost thoughts with each other concerning me. What do they say?

And the disciples said:

—Some say one thing and some say another. There are some who say that you are Elijah, that you are Elijah having returned from the dead.

Interrupting the statement of the disciples almost with a flash of blinding insight, Jesus said:

—What do you say? What do you really think about me?

One bold and audacious, but inspired disciple said: "Thou art the Christ, the Anointed One." Suddenly Jesus replied:

—Don't say that. Don't say that!

Then quickly on the heels of that he uttered those fateful words: "Flesh and blood did not reveal that to you."[10] And why did he say that? Because what the disciple had confessed concerning him was one with the early commitment which was his at the baptism. He was the Anointed One

---

10. Matthew 16:13–20; Mark 8:27–30.

of God, the one who, as a result of his religious experience, had glimpsed in some full-orbed manner the living mind of the living God and was so imbued with the glory of that vision that he dared to believe that in the details of his living this revelation could find a fulfillment.

A little later we find him coming with his disciples outside of the city of Jericho. They are walking along when suddenly Jesus bolts ahead of his disciples, and with a look of astounding resolution on his face, a look so pregnant with emotion that when his disciples beheld his countenance they were frightened, he turned to go down the road which led to Jerusalem.[11] They had approached a fork in the road; one fork led back up to Palestine, to Nazareth, to his hometown; the other to Jerusalem. It was the decision to go to Jerusalem that had generated the emotional upheaval. And what did it mean to go to Jerusalem? It meant that he would be at the very citadel of those who regarded him as one whose insights into his fate, whose utterances with reference to the meaning in the life of Israel were so profoundly disturbing that their position would be forever untenable if his insights were valid and were permitted wide circulation. This meant that the issues would be brought to a head. And what were the issues?

Let us point out once again that if Jesus had been regarded by the custodians of the religious life of Israel, or even if he had regarded himself, as one who was projecting a new religion, then there would have been no reason for opposition or resentment. There were many religions by which they were surrounded that were not a part of the religious experience of Israel, and if Jesus had separated himself from Israel and started a new faith, then the most that they could have said about him was that he was an apostate Jew, a renegade, who was completely disclaimed by them, who was separated completely from Israel and could be regarded as one who did not even live. But because Jesus insisted on remaining within the community, because he insisted that he was speaking on behalf of the God of Israel, because he regarded himself as the fulfillment of the law of Israel, he was a threat to all of the security of those who regarded themselves as the custodians and the trustees of the mind of God and of the law of God.[12]

---

11. Luke 19:41–48.
12. Matthew 5:17–20.

He went to Jerusalem. It was during high holy days. The experiences through which he passed there I need not relate, but it is enough to point out that a showdown between him and the priests and the scribes was inevitable. If they had permitted him to do what he was doing and remain within the fellowship of Israel as he insisted upon remaining, then much of what they stood for would be vitiated and the grounds of their authority would be undermined.

So sensitive was Jesus to the possibility of judgment and possible death that every day at the going down of the sun he and his little group of disciples went outside of the city of Jerusalem to spend the night. It seems clear to me that they were in hiding overnight because he did not wish to be the victim of assassination. If he had been the victim of assassination he would have died like a dog in the street or in an alley. The whole feeling on my part is brought out in the fact that when the betrayal came, the proposition which Judas gave to them was: "For this amount of money I will take you to his hiding place at night." It was clear that if he were arrested openly in the daytime the arrest would have precipitated the kind of crisis with which they were not prepared to cope. When Judas said, "I will take you to his hiding place," the obviously implied question would be: "Well, how shall we know him in the dark?" "I will kiss him."[13] The whole point, it seems to me, of the kissing of Jesus is clear in the light of the tension of the situation and in the light of the fact that with eleven or twelve men resting in the dark it would be very easy to select the wrong man.

When he is arrested and sentenced, he is crucified on a tree outside the city wall. This means the climactic fulfillment of one aspect of his life, and as he is stretched out on the cross, dying, over and over the thought must have come into his mind:

—This can't be! Is this the answer to the dream which I have? Is this the way God's law is to be fulfilled in me? I have followed the path which stretched before me with relentless logic and abiding enthusiasm, conscious always that I was doing the will of God and that I was deeply at one with the divine purpose. And where is God now? I have kept my end of

---

13. Matthew 26:14–50; 27:3–10.

the bargain. I have followed my dream. I have done the will of God, and now even God has deserted me.

Out of the depth of that tremendous agony Jesus cries, "My God, my God, why hast Thou forsaken me?"[14]—the most audacious utterance in the entire literature of religion, for here is one who declares that he is surer of God than God is of him, and it is significant that the Gospel of Mark, the oldest of the Gospels, pulls the curtain down on this part of the career of Jesus with these fateful words. Does it mean that Jesus is dying in despair, or may it not mean that in the moment of the cry "My God, my God, why hast Thou forsaken me?" he is surest of God and of God's presence? For over and over again in the religious experience of men, they have discovered that they are closest to God when in their moments of agony, in their moments of desolation, they seem to be farthest away from him.

"My God, my God, why hast Thou forsaken me?" are words which ring through the centuries, for they say that the key to the unfolding of the mind of God is often to be found in the great inner struggle, the great moral struggle, in which men find themselves stripped to the literal substance of themselves, with no pretensions left, with no props left, just the naked spirit laid bare to the mind of God; and in that primary exposure of radical desolation they become conscious that God is articulate in them. It is the ultimate paradox of the moral struggle, and I love Jesus for this shaft of light which his moral struggle throws across the pathway of all who stand at that point in the darkness.

---

14. Matthew 27:46; Mark 15:34, quoting Psalm 22:2.

Paul

October 9, 1949
Fellowship Church

Thurman's best known treatment of Paul is in Jesus and the Disinherited. *It is not complimentary. Thurman compares Paul unfavorably to Jesus, in part because of Paul's statements that seem to be justifications of slavery.[1] But this is at best a partial view of Thurman's perspectives on Paul.[2] Thurman had an immense appreciation for the "moral struggle" of Paul and the spiritual creativity involved in his efforts to resolve the tensions between his heritage of Jewish monotheism and the demands of his new belief in Jesus Christ. In addition, Thurman felt that Paul had to contend with his transformation from a persecutor of the followers of Jesus to a worshiper of Jesus, as well as the fact that he was not one of the original disciples. In this sermon, Thurman identifies three major elements that shaped Paul's moral struggle: the martyrdom of Stephen; Paul's vision on the Damascus Road; and Israel's sense of election as the chosen people of God.*

One of Thurman's rare discussions of Christology, this sermon also reveals some of his own perspectives on questions of salvation and the significance of Jesus and Paul in shaping continuing schools of thought in Christian history and practice. Thurman sees Paul as a follower and one of the creators of what he elsewhere calls "the religion about Jesus." But, Thurman argues, Paul, unlike many of his successors, despite being "wrapped up in the infinite clutches of a tremendous moral and spiritual problem," does not quite see Jesus as divine because he was rooted in an "ethical and spiritual monotheism" that insisted "that there shall be no other God before me, even though I name that God the Son of God." Instead, for Thurman, Paul's reasoning is along these lines: Jesus Christ is the Law; and, therefore, since he

---

1. HT, *Jesus and the Disinherited*, 30–35.
2. For Thurman's other writings on Paul, see "Man and the Moral Struggle: Paul," delivered at Marsh Chapel on January 9, 1955, and "Jesus and the Disinherited: Jesus and Paul," April 1969.

"expresses and reveals God's life with more fullness and power than anyone ever before," Jesus Christ is the Son of God. But Paul thought that while "Jesus is the Son of God," he is the "Son of God as the For-Instance of the divine mind and will and purpose—but he is not God. But he is in God; God is in him—and if I can get him in me, then God will be in me and I will be in God."[3]

I WANT TO PAUSE for a moment to read a few lines from one of the Pauline letters:[4]

> For when we were unspiritual, the sinful cravings excited by the Law were active in our members and made us fruitful to Death; but now we are done with the Law, we have died to what once held us, so that we can serve in a new way, not under the written code as of old but in the Spirit.
>
> What follows, then? That "the Law is equivalent to sin"? Never! Why, had it not been for the Law, I would never have known what sin meant! Thus I would never have known what it is to covet, unless the Law had said, You must not covet. The command gave an impulse to sin, and sin resulted for me in all manner of covetous desire—for sin, apart from law, is lifeless. I lived at one time without law myself, but when the command came home to me,

---

3. Although Thurman was familiar with the Pauline scholarship of his day, his view of Paul was built on premises that, by the standards of contemporary Pauline scholarship, are outdated. Thurman's view of Paul relies heavily on Acts rather than the genuine Pauline epistles. Acts and the Third Gospel, traditionally ascribed to Luke, was written twenty to fifty years after Paul. The account of Paul in Acts is secondhand and reflects later developments in the history of Christianity and Judaism, such as the destruction of the Temple in 70 CE. See Michael F. Bird, *Introducing Paul: The Man, His Mission, and His Message* (Downers Grove, IL: InterVarsity Press, 2009); Thomas R. Schreiner, Luke Timothy Johnson, Douglas Atchison Campbell, and Mark D. Nanos, *Four Views on the Apostle Paul* (Counterpoints Bible & Theology; Grand Rapids, MI: Zondervan, 2012); A. Katherine Grieb, *The Story of Romans: A Narrative Defense of God's Righteousness* (Louisville, KY: Westminster/John Knox, 2002); Bruce W. Longenecker and Todd D. Still, *Thinking through Paul: A Survey of His Life, Letters, and Theology* (Grand Rapids: Zondervan, 2014). For current thinking on Romans and Thurman's reliance on older scholarship, see n. 13 below.

4. Romans 7:7–25, Moffatt.

sin sprang to life and I died.... Then did what was meant for my good prove fatal to me? Never! It was sin: sin resulted in death for me by making use of this good thing. The Law is spiritual; we know that. But then I am a creature of the flesh, in the thralldom of sin. I cannot understand my own actions; I do not act as I want to act; on the contrary, I do what I detest. Now, when I act against my wishes, that means I agree that the Law is right. That being so, it is not I who do the deed but sin that dwells within me. For in me (that is, in my flesh) no good dwells, I know; the wish is there, but not the power of doing what is right, but wrong is all I can manage; I cordially agree with God's law, so far as my inner self is concerned, but then I find quite another law in my members which conflicts with the law of my mind and makes me a prisoner to sin's law that resides in my members. (Thus, left to myself, I serve the law of God with my mind, but with my flesh I serve the law of sin.) Miserable wretch that I am! Who will rescue me from this body of death? God will! Thanks be to him through Jesus Christ our Lord! (says Paul).

Without seeming to repeat the general proposition too often, we are working on a series having to do with man and the moral struggle. Our fundamental concept is that every human being is involved in a moral struggle at one point or another. Every human being is involved also in frustration, and frustration and moral struggle are one and the same up to a crucial and decisive point, and that is: when the end that a man seeks is finite, personal, and he is unable to fulfill that end because of factors that operate upon him in his environment or factors that are within his own spirit, then he is frustrated. Either he has to work on his environment or he has to work on the end, or he can juggle the end, or operate on the environment so that the end will be more convenient to the environment or the environment more convenient to the end.

Now moral struggle takes place when the end that a man seeks extends beyond his private concern, and becomes involved in processes that stretch out beyond the span of his particular life or his particular problem, and the degree to which he identifies himself with that transcendent end and the degree to which that transcendent end cannot find fulfillment within the time span of his life, to that degree does the moral struggle become for him acute and intensified

We applied the principle first to Deutero-Isaiah, and then to Jesus of Nazareth, and today we want to apply the principle to the apostle Paul.

There are three basic elements in the inherited conception of God to which Paul was heir, and also Jesus. There was the fundamental trunk line—roots, idea: that God is Righteous Will in the universe. Righteous Will! God is therefore a person in the mind and in the thought of Israel, which mind and thought were shared equally by Jesus and by the apostle Paul. In the second place, not only is God Righteous Will (a person whose will is righteous), but this Righteous Will acts, and it acts in time; it acts in history, and it manifests itself by a series of mighty acts. The first and most crucial one was the act by which the world was created and man was set on his way. Then all the various ways by which God operated upon history, in history and upon history, were summarized by them as expressions of God's mighty acts.

Now in order that these mighty acts may have the kind of significance that is important and intelligible, there must be some group of human beings who are uniquely responsive to this God who is Righteous Will, who is operating in history and upon history by the series of mighty acts. Therefore, the notion of a unique and special people, Israel, becomes the inevitable logic of the assumption made about God; and one of the ways by which these mighty acts of God are dramatized in human history can be best disclosed by understanding how God has worked with Israel: going into captivity, being delivered from captivity, and so forth, are expressions of the way by which God worked in history, revealing himself in his concern and his brooding over the life of Israel, the chosen, the gifted people.[5]

Then there was a third fact: the presence of a literature that expressed also the will and the mind of God, and described the operation of God in

---

5. Thurman's description of Israel as a "special people" underscores how important the Letter to the Romans, particularly chaps. 9–11, is to his discussion in this sermon. Indeed in Romans 9:21 Paul uses the metaphor of the potter and the clay to transform objects of "special use" to "ordinary use." This text echoes the potter and the clay imagery that appears in Isaiah 45:9–11 (cf. Isa 64:8); and, as Thurman stated in the opening, he has been using the Isaiah text as well in this discussion about the moral struggle.

history upon the life of this people that he was shaping and molding, that they might be the living For-Instance of his will and his mind. That was the thing that Paul inherited.

We find him, a Jew proud of the fact that he was a Jew, who lived in Tarsus,[6] which was a metropolitan city—a Gentile city, largely. Paul was a city man; Jesus was rural. Jesus was a small-town individual; Paul was a city man. He was trained as a rabbi. We don't know whether he ever saw Jesus or not—the traditions are confused.[7] There are many things in his letter that would indicate that perhaps he had had very primary contact with the earthly Jesus, but there is no specific statement for confirmation of that.[8]

The first time that he appears in our records he is standing to watch the clothes of the men who were stoning Stephen.[9] A sensitive, trained rabbi who understood the inner workings of the spiritual process which is Israel is brought face to face with a radical expression of a manifestation of the genius of Israel, which manifestation was completely outside the scope both of his psychology and his religious experience. Here is a man, a Jew, Stephen, who is being stoned to death in a fit of fury. He is the expression of this terrific thing that had turned up in Judaism. He is still a Jew, still a practicing Jew; mind you, don't forget that; but he is now participating as was Jesus in a heresy within the framework of Judaism, not a new something. But Stephen says, as he is dying, "Behold, the heavens

---

6. It is Luke who claims Paul was from Tarsus, not Paul himself. See Acts 9:11; 11:25; 21:39; 22:3.

7. Most contemporary scholarship does not think Paul saw Jesus in the flesh. There is no evidence from the source documents that Paul did. In fact, Paul himself claims he did not encounter Jesus in the flesh, but as a revelation of the resurrected Jesus Christ (1 Cor 15:3–9; Gal 1:11–19).

8. If Acts is accurate, Paul was born in Tarsus, in Asia Minor (now in Turkey), probably in about the same year as Jesus. Little is known about the first half of his life, other than that he was a Greek-speaking Jew, a Pharisee, and a persecutor of the followers of Jesus. His received his call to follow Jesus around 36 CE and spent the remainder of his life as Apostle to the Gentiles. He died in Rome in 62 or 64 CE. Current scholarship is very skeptical of claims that Paul had contact with Jesus before the latter's crucifixion.

9. Reference is to the martyrdom of Stephen, Acts 7:54–60: "Then they dragged him out of the city and began to stone him; and the witnesses laid their coats at the feet of a young man named Saul" (v. 58).

have opened, and I see Jesus Christ on the right hand of the Father"—this one who had been killed outside of the city wall of Jerusalem. Stephen says now he isn't dead; he is on the right hand of God; he is next to God.[10]

—Now either he is right—Stephen is right in what he is saying (says Paul) or Stephen is wrong. If Stephen be right, then the whole basis of my orientation is groundless. But further, the thing that I am seeking with my life seems now to be possible because all the time I have wanted salvation, a salvation that would rescue me from the burden of my sinfulness, a salvation that would make it possible for me to participate in Life spelled with a capital "L." I have worked over the Law. I have studied the Law.[11] I have become obedient to the Law. And yet the Law promises that this consummation, which will be for me salvation, will take place at some remote time in the history of the universe; but what I need is something that will rescue me now. I obeyed all the minutiae of the Law. I have kept everything in order that somehow there may be visited into my spirit some fleeting overtone of that ultimate consummation, and I can live the present life with a sense of hope and redemption. That's what I want! All around me the religious insist that they have it, these mystery cults—and I know that it is in Israel, but I have not been able to find it because the thing that I want, the thing that I must have, I can't wait until the consummation of the age when the Messiah comes on the clouds and redeems all the sons of Israel.[12] I can't wait for that. I want to behold now.[13]

---

10. Reference is to Acts 7:59–60: "While they were stoning Stephen, he prayed, 'Lord Jesus, receive my spirit.' Then he knelt down and cried out in a loud voice, 'Lord, do not hold this sin against them.' When he had said this, he died." Most scholars put Stephen's martyrdom in 34 or 35 CE, several years after the crucifixion of Jesus.

11. Thurman is referring to Paul's rabbinical training with Gamaliel the Elder, a leader in the Jewish Sanhedrin in the first century CE, who is mentioned in Acts 5:34–39 and 22:3. Some recent scholarship questions the historicity of Paul's studies with Gamaliel.

12. "For the grace of God that brings salvation has appeared to all men, teaching us that, denying ungodliness and worldly lusts, we should live soberly, righteously, and godly in the present age, *looking for the blessed hope and glorious appearing of our great God and Savior, Jesus Christ,* who gave Himself for us, that He might redeem us from every lawless deed and purify for Himself His own special people, zealous for good works" (Titus 2:11–14).

13. In an influential article, Krister Stendahl has argued that Paul's dialogue in Romans 7, quoted in the beginning of the sermon and the basis of Thurman's argument here, is not about his personal doubts about Judaism as it was practiced in his time,

So he sees Stephen die, and the problem is at once brought into focus in his mind, for he goes on with his persecutions,[14] and he intensifies his persecutions, and I can imagine—and you will find, letting your imagination play with it a little—that as he hounded these Christians he would examine their statements, and every now and then he would run into one and would say:

—Now look here. What is this thing? Why is it that you are able to die with composure; why is it that you have no sense of retaliation, no arrogance of spirit? What has happened?

And every time they spoke to him he argued, and yet he watched them, watched them.

—I wonder, is Stephen right? If he is right, if he is right! If he is right! I must know it.

Oh, that old cry of hope. So it went in his mind. Then on his way for a fresh investigation, according to the records and Acts, and according to his personal testimony,[15] something happened to him. He had a vision; he saw God, he saw Jesus, and Jesus was living. And he recapitulated the dream, the vision, of Stephen. And then he went away to try to think the thing through. He says that he went away into the desert and stayed three years.[16]

—I must think the thing through. What does it mean? How can I—what can I do with it? I've had the same thing, and I'm still confused. I'm still at sea. I still believe that the Law is right, and I still think we should keep the ceremonial perhaps, but oh, I now experience a new dimension of life, and that is what I have been looking for, and that is what I have found, and now how can I take my mind—how can I take all of the knowledge that I have of Israel—and accommodate that body of living stuff which is "I" to the tremendous impact of this new experience?

---

but his need to find a continued rationale for his halachic observance when all people can be saved from sin by sharing in the death and resurrection of Jesus; see Krister Stendahl, "The Apostle Paul and the Introspective Conscience of the West," in Krister Stendahl, *Paul among Jews and Gentiles and Other Essays* (Philadelphia: Fortress Press, 1976), 78–96.

14. Acts 8:1–3 and Galatians 1:13.

15. Thurman is again relying on Acts to explain Paul's behavior and psychology rather than the more reliable source of the authentic Pauline epistles.

16. Galatians 1:15–18.

He decided that Jesus Christ is God's special representative, that what the Law had been trying to coach man into understanding, Jesus had For-Instanced. And the most important and crucial thing in Paul's thought at this point is the fact that the significance of the life of Jesus, based upon the peculiar religious experience of Paul, is rooted in the resurrection.[17] Jesus Christ becomes the Anointed; Jesus Christ becomes the Savior; Jesus Christ becomes the one who is active always on behalf of God and on behalf of men, making of himself the nexus, the connecting link, between the two, so that the man who affirms a confidence in that connecting link could ride over and be once again restored to the mind and to the life and to the beauty and richness of God. So, he goes out to preach that. And as he preaches it he is brought face to face with two very crucial problems. One of them is the fact that he is saying to the Jewish community that this Jesus is the Lord, is the Messiah for whom we have been looking; and they answer when they face him with the fact that it is also written in our book which you recognize that "Cursed be the one who dies on a tree."[18] He died on a tree, so how can the Messiah be cursed of God? It is a contradiction in terms; it has no meaning.

—Ah (said Paul), the meaning is best expressed in the resurrection, for in the resurrection there is the reversal of the judgment of the cross. But, the Messiah, what dared you for the cross?

And the more they pushed him—you see, the more they resisted—the more Paul worked over the significance of the doctrine of the resurrection. It is just as if you started out with a very simple remark about something and then somebody said, "Oh, no," and then you answered, and then that person just came back with more pressure. Before you get through you are making, you are seeing things in your position that you didn't see at the start. And that is true of Paul. Very simple, too.

The second thing that he faced was:

—What can I—how can I substitute, how can I make up for the fact that I was not one of the disciples? I am sure God has forgiven me for this

---

17. The significance of resurrection for Paul in Romans, especially the resurrection of Jesus, is that the event confirms Jesus's sonship. The claim to "believe in the resurrection of Jesus as the Christ" is the faith claim sitting at the center of Christian confession and identity, according to Paul (Rom 6:5–11).

18. Galatians 3:13; see also Deuteronomy 21:23.

persecution that I have done. I was acting wholly within the compass of my understanding at the time; but I can't forgive myself, and one of the ways by which that lack of forgiveness is constantly burned into me as if by acid is the fact that every time I look at one of the other disciples who knows Jesus, it seems as if he is looking at me with his tongue in his cheek, "You can preach, Paul; you are brilliant; you have all this dazzling wisdom and the imagination of a poet with all of the sensitiveness of the mystic—you have all that, Paul. But you weren't there!"

So, he would have to run to cover, get himself reorganized again, and then start back. Little by little, there appeared in him—and I don't want to be misunderstood—what I would call a compensation for this lack of earthly continuity with Jesus, and that compensation expressed itself in one or two ways. One very human way: the Nazarene community, after the death of Jesus, were members, as I pointed out before, of the synagogue; they practiced the Jewish Law, circumcision, and the rest of it. Then one day Paul said—he didn't know he was saying it this way, I suppose, but he said:

—This is my opportunity now, for probably Peter and some of the others who were there are insisting that before you become a Christian you must become a Jew!

So Paul made an issue of it—and watch! He insisted that the Law is in the heart; the Law is the unfolding of the mind of God, and particularly the ethical responsibility of man in Life and God's ethical relationship to man—that is what the Law is. It is not washing hands; it is not going through tiddlywinks—and I imagine Paul put his tongue in his cheek as he put Peter and the others in their place. And now we come to what is his greatest moral struggle:

—If Jesus Christ is Law, if Jesus Christ expresses and reveals God's life with more fullness and power than anyone ever before, then Jesus Christ is God! No. No, not quite God. (Paul is rooted and grounded in monotheism—there could be only one God.) Jesus Christ is my Savior, my Redeemer. It is he who makes it possible for my life to be restored, and for my own sense of significance to be vindicated and validated. For all practical purposes, he is God! But if he is God, then I am a dualist; and if I am a dualist, then I must renounce the very genius of the ethic and the religion of Israel in which I was nourished. So he comes up with an interesting concept: Jesus is not God. Jesus is the Son of God, but Son of God officially, Son of God as the For-Instance of the divine mind and will and purpose—but he is not God. But he is in God. God is in him—and if I can get him in me, then God will be in me and I will be in God. So for me to live in Christ, I will know him in the power of his resurrection—for if somehow Christ is in me, that makes sense, that he lived on earth just as I am; he participated in human flesh; he believed what I believe. Except one thing separated us: he relaxed any responsiveness to sin.

Paul makes Jesus a man, but not quite. He makes him God, but not quite. He always comes out at the same point:

—He answers my moral struggle because the Life that I have been taught, spelled with a capital "L," the Life that I have been taught would come to pass at the consummation of the age when the redeemer with a sign would come back on the clouds and redeem Israel and all the people who were responsive to his will and his Law. That Life I am experiencing now, and it is a Life that transcends death. If I can be as full of Christ as Christ was full of God, then Christ will become for me the answer to all of my needs just as God became for Christ the answer to all his needs.

On that basis he solved his moral problem and decided that the relationship between man and God is an ethical relationship, and he who has faith in God as, in Paul's words, "as it is revealed as He is revealed in Jesus Christ," will participate now in the Life without which there can be no meaning and no fulfillment. And so Paul, wrapped up in the infinite clutches of a tremendous moral and spiritual problem, worked his way through to a concept which has identified him for all time, not with God, but with Jesus Christ. For all practical purposes, Jesus Christ and God, in the thought of Paul, are one, but he is never able, quite, to say that.[19] It remained for the theologians who built upon his thought to make the statement, because the theologians were not rooted in spiritual and ethical monotheism as was Paul. Perhaps the degree to which we are rooted in an ethical and spiritual monotheism we shall always accept it, and in the degree to which we are not rooted in an ethical and spiritual monotheism we may be inclined not to make that distinction, but instead to express a

---

19. However, in Romans, Paul names all three figures—God, Jesus Christ, and Holy Spirit—and assigns them different roles, albeit related. See Romans 15:16 and also Romans 5:5; 9:1 (cf. 1 Cor 6:19; 2 Cor 13:13).

rationalization of concept, which has for us only the meaning that comes from a rejection of the ethical insistence that God places upon man, chief of which is that there shall be no other God before me, even though I name that God the Son of God. And that is the challenge. What are you going to do about it?

Prometheus

October 30, 1949
Fellowship Church

In each of his two sermon series on Man and the Moral Struggle Thurman spoke on the myth of Prometheus.¹ In both sermons, he contrasted the two most famous versions of the story, the ancient Greek tragedy, traditionally ascribed to Aeschylus, Prometheus Bound,² *and Percy Bysshe Shelley's* Prometheus Unbound.³

In Aeschylus, Prometheus, who gave the secret of fire to humanity, is bound to a rock by Zeus and daily tortured for refusing to divulge his secret of fire. Thurman stated that "in Aeschylus, the thing that kept Prometheus alive was the bitterness, the hatred that he had of Zeus for this obvious and dramatic miscarriage of justice and decency. He was being unjustly punished, not because he was innocent, but because he did that which to him was the fullest expression of his dignity and his meaning as a god, namely, to be a benefactor to man."

In Prometheus Unbound *by Shelley, Prometheus is freed after realizing that the problem with hate "is to say about the wicked thing that it is permanent. It is to say that the contradictions in life are final." The lesson is that one must "do the right as you see it, taking into account the consequences for taking the position." Thurman argues that Shelley's point is "that men do worship gods, yes, and they obey the gods they worship; but the gods they worship are unworthy gods," and "men become like the gods they worship." But the search for better gods can end in tragedy. He closes the sermon*

---

1. For the alternative version, see "Man and the Moral Struggle: Prometheus" (January 23, 1955).

2. The authorship of *Prometheus Bound* is traditionally assigned to the Greek tragedian Aeschylus (c. 525–455 BCE), but there is considerable debate about his authorship of the play.

3. *Prometheus Unbound* (1820) is by the English poet Percy Bysshe Shelley (1792–1822).

not by quoting Shelley's uplifting conclusion but another poet's "hymn to the conquered," which was dedicated to those "who fell in the battle of life," the "hymn of the low and humble," those "who strove and failed," dying "with the wreck of their lives all around them," with "all but their faith overthrown."[4]

Today we are dealing with an aspect of the life of the race, which aspect belongs to human experience in almost all of its dimensions.

The problem is the same. The ends that I seek do not find fulfillment, even though I am willing to adjust my thinking about the ends that I seek and make those ends conform to that which is within reach; but even in the fulfillment there appears a subtle sense of guilt because I have lowered my standards. Of the ends that I seek to become involved in, ends that affect the life and the destiny of the race, then these ends become in themselves transcendent—they reach beyond my little world of hopes and fears and even my little world of dreams. This is true with reference to my ends whether they have to do with ambitions, with legitimate hopes and dreams, or whether they have to do with the problems of human endurance under odds that are unyielding, whether they have to do with the meaning of life in general or whether they have to do with my life in particular as I live it within the shadow of my tragedies.

The problem with which Aeschylus and perhaps, if there is time, Shelley deal in *Prometheus* is the problem about which I have been talking. The myth is very simple; doubtless you all recall it. The setting is in heaven. Prometheus, who is a god, steals fire—and by fire is meant in the myth the magic of understanding and knowledge, that which fans the dreams, that lifts the spirit, that makes for the reduction of the impersonal aspects of nature to manageable units of understanding and control and power, in order that dreams may be fulfilled and civilizations may be possible—fire means all of that. Prometheus takes it and gives it to man who is under the curse of Zeus. Because he gives fire to man—this ability, this push, this growing edge—he is banished from heaven; not only

---

4. "Io Victus," in William Wetmore Story, *Poems Vol II: Monologues and Lyrics* (Boston: Houghton Mifflin, 1886), 177–79. William Wetmore Story (1819–1895) was an American sculptor, writer, and poet, who spent most of his adult life in Italy.

banished, but sentenced. The sentence is that he shall be chained to the rocks on the side of the Caucasus Mountains so that he can't bend his knee—riveted there. That is the myth. Aeschylus takes that myth and reworks it, dealing with certain important problems of human destiny.

In Aeschylus the scene opens with Prometheus being chained to the rocks. The god whose job it is to chain him—to rivet the chains, to make them fast—is rather glad to have a job like that because it gives him a chance to feel good for himself. It is interesting. Then Prometheus is very bitter; he feels that he is being punished by Zeus because Zeus is omnipotent, but temporarily so, and also because he has no sense of responsibility for his creation. The gods urge Prometheus to submit, to bow before this omnipotent will, and Prometheus says:

—I defy this will! I did the thing that was right with reference to man, and if Zeus is against that, then I am against Zeus! I must bear what is ordained for me with patience, realizing that necessity doth front my universe with an invincible gesture. Bring on your tormentors! I can take it. I know that his days are numbered.

In the myth Prometheus is blessed with forethought—sometimes he is called Fore-thought, and that means he can look a little ahead, a great distance ahead, and knows the secret. The secret is that omnipotent power as expressed in Zeus cannot possibly survive because the clue to the understanding of Life, the clue to the secret of Life, is not to be found in the impersonal operation of blind power.

So when the rumor (even among the gods the rumors move) gets to Zeus that Prometheus knows something that Zeus, being omnipotent but not omniscient, does not know, that creates a problem for him. Prometheus is omniscient at that point but not omnipotent. Zeus says:

—I'll bargain with you. I can give you freedom if you will give me your secret.

What would a man give in exchange for his secret? Is it for sale? Prometheus would not sell it, because the price that had to be paid was one that would make Prometheus repent of what he had done! Therefore Zeus called out all the furies, and things begin happening surely enough! In the last scene, the lightning and the earthquake and the elements conspire to bring down their bitter judgment upon Prometheus, and you see him being thrown from the side of the mountain into the depths of Tartarus,[5] the dwelling-place of doomed souls.

—If (says Zeus) you will not yield, I will destroy you.

That is all in Aeschylus. The rest of the play is lost; we do not know how he resolved the problem.[6] Five thousand years later,[7] Shelley picks up the theme. The scene opens in Shelley just as it does in Aeschylus: the bare, stark Caucasus Mountains, and here is this man, this god, Prometheus.

In Aeschylus, the thing that kept Prometheus alive was the bitterness, the hatred that he had of Zeus for this obvious and dramatic miscarriage of justice and decency. He was being [unjustly] punished, not because he was innocent, but because he did that which to him was the fullest expression of his dignity and his meaning as a god, namely, to be a benefactor to man.

But in Shelley, Prometheus, who now is back from Tartarus and is again upon the side of the cliff, says:

—I hate no more. Down in the lower regions I have laid bare my soul to all of the agonies and the bitterness that come from my profound and deeply moving sense of injury, until at last all of my will for revenge has been exhausted. Out of that exhaustion, out of being spent by antagonism, in that darkness there has grown up in me something else, that is, that hate can never release me from this. Hate, if I keep it, I must pass on with all the good things that I have given to man. There is only one answer, and that is: the thing which will dethrone love is love, love.

The man who said that, the man who put those words upon the lips of Prometheus, was a man who in his own life time was condemned and hounded, ejected and rejected again and again in the name of Christian love. Brooding over the tumults of his own experience, he finally distilled all of the ceremony and bitterness out of it; and he came upon an irreducible residue which to him marked the ultimate meaning of the dignity and the destiny of man. So he worked it out in this drama.

---

5. In Greek mythology, Tartarus is both a god and the underworld, a place of doom and torment.

6. Classical Greek tragedies were performed as three separate plays, like the *Oresteia* of Aeschylus. Only the first play of the Prometheus trilogy has survived.

7. Thurman doubles the time span between Aeschylus and Shelley.

He had someone visit Asia, Prometheus's wife, who had been banished when her husband was chained, to give her comfort:

—Prometheus has held his ground! Prometheus has not been broken. Prometheus has become mellow, enriched, deepened, but not broken, and I want to comfort you with the tiding that he has been true to his dream.

—And what has been happening on the earth when men have been learning? They have learned art, crafts; they have learned various things about knowledge, about the stars and about the earth. They have learned how to subdue nature—but they have not learned how to get along with each other.

—One man came among them who talked about gentleness and kindness and decency and the kind of fellowship that should exist between men who had been given this tremendous gift of fire, this illustration of the mind, and the only thing they could [do] to him was to nail him on a tree outside a city wall, so he is dead now.

—Is it as bad as that?

—Well, almost; but here and there, hovering in the minds of unknown men, there is the making of a new kind of dream. That dream is that behind Chance,[8] behind all of the shifting scenes of nature, behind the creation of the world, behind fate, behind all of the impersonal operations of the world of nature or the impersonal operations of the social order, behind all of that, there is an eternal love.

He reaches the conclusion that when man has learned to say that, then the redeemer breaks his chains and he is free to love and to live. When Prometheus becomes released, in Shelley's interpretation, something tremendous takes place all throughout the length and breadth of nature. The hills rejoice; the rivers have a new rhythm; all of life takes on a new glory because at last that which is the dream of God is walking the hills of the earth.

It is very interesting that Shelley attacks the problem of man's brutality, man's stupidity, man's error, and the problem of the suffering of the benefactors of the race, by projecting a notion—and I want to call your attention to it—that the world is not finished yet; that men do worship gods, yes, and they obey the gods they worship; but the gods they worship

---

8. In Greek mythology, Chance is identified as the goddess Tyche.

are unworthy gods. If, somehow, they could lift their sights of religious worship and devotion until their sights apprehended ultimate goodness and ultimate beauty, then perhaps their lives would increasingly conform to the impact of that kind of religious devotion.

—But the tragedy of human life (says Shelley) is that men become like the gods they worship. There are not atheists. Men become like the gods they worship. If they are bad men, it means that they are worshiping bad gods. The curious thing about the worship of your god is that you work over it and work over it and work over it until you make your god the God of the universe, and automatically you shut out all others who do not worship that God.

—Now, says this man, life isn't made—you are not made—the world isn't made. We are all involved at varying stages of fulfillment.

He does not say that evil has no existence; he does not say that sin is not sin. But he does insist that the destiny of the world is good, and that contradictions of life are not ultimate contradictions.

The love which is behind the universe, the eternal love that is pressing, pressing all of the time; pressing upon frustrations, pressing upon disorders, combing out this difficulty, reshaping this, refashioning that, letting civilization rise and fall, always digging among the ashes of a dead culture to find one live coal and breathing upon that live coal—breathing upon it until it begins to glow, to light the way in the darkness—if that is the thing you believe and demonstrate and live and exemplify, then don't be surprised if the powers that are blind to that destroy you. Don't take it personally; don't think, "Oh, I'm a martyr," that because I am this or that or the other, I am this or I am that, or I am the other, that this is being done to me, to me. No, not that.

You are involved in the unfolding of the dream of God, and the degree to which in your little spot you are able to anticipate that dream, then, if those who are working on the other side reject you, you must make their rejection your strength. If you do that, you'll die, you'll die. Of course, you are going to die anyway. You may hurry it up a little. Your heart may ache—it is going to ache anyway, so it is nice to have it ache for something significant. It really doesn't make any difference as far as what happens to you, for you aren't made yet. You are on your way; but if in one little way, if in just one tiny way, you are able to be, which has no graduations in it, just one little bit with reference to one simple human relationship, with reference to one simple deed, you just are, then that is an indication of what all of life will be, and you go down to your end with a shout. If that is your faith, then nothing can destroy you.

> I sing the hymn of the conquered who fell in the Battle of Life—
> The hymn of the wounded and fallen, the beaten who died overwhelmed in the strife
> Not the jubilant joy of the victors, for whom the resounding acclaim
> Of nations was lifted in chorus, whose brows wore the chaplet of fame
> But the hymn of the low and the humble, the weary, the broken in heart
> Who strove and who failed acting bravely a silent and desperate part,
> Whose youth bore no flowers on its branches, whose hopes burned in ashes away,
> From whose hands slipped the prize they had grasped at, who stood at the dying of day,
> With the wreck of their lives all about them, unheeded, unpitied, alone
> With Death swooping soon o'er their failures, and all but their faith overthrown.

That's it! For the contradictions of life, however terrible, are not ultimate. How wonderful that God created Aeschylus, and how passing our understanding is the creation of a poet like Shelley.

Job

October 16, 1949
Fellowship Church

There are few characters in the Bible or literature that better exemplify moral struggle than Job. In the late 1940s and early 1950s Thurman gave several sermons on Job.[1] For Thurman, Job is a story of how individuals respond to personal calamities and catastrophes, and wrestle with the question of divine justice. "If there were no reward, if there were no punishment," as Thurman paraphrases Job's questions, "would I still be interested in the life of integrity and the life of decency?" None of Job's questions have easy answers.

Job discovers that transcendent goals are often whittled down to innocence and guilt, reward and punishment, honor and shame. Yet, Thurman suggests that even within the exigencies of existence, there is something in human experience that will not relinquish the moral quest; and even though the human mind cannot fathom the ways of God, the spiritual strivings to reach the transcendent that is within still emerges as our destiny. In various places,[2] as in this sermon, Thurman identifies integrity (a sense of wholeness) as the goal toward which human endeavor must be directed.

A consistent theme in Thurman's corpus is that innocence is given without knowledge or experience; integrity, however, is achieved only through

---

1. In addition to this 1949 sermon, Thurman spoke on Job in "The Meaning of Loyalty IV: Job's Dilemma"(May 27, 1951); and "Man and the Moral Struggle: Job" (May 17, 1954).

2. For Thurman on integrity, see *Meditations of the Heart* (New York: Harper & Brothers, 1961), 41; "Results Are Not Crucial," in *The Inward Journey* (New York: Harper & Row, 1961), 65; "The Creative Encounter-Integrity," sermon delivered at Marsh Chapel, Boston University, November 9, 1958; "Leadership," in *Torch and Trefoil* 35 (February 1960): 4, reprinted in *A Strange Freedom*, ed. Walter Earl Fluker and Catherine Tumber (Boston: Beacon Press, 1998), 61; "The Responsibility of the Professional Person to Society," *Nursing Outlook* 5 (June 1957): 334–35, reprinted in Fluker and Tumber, *A Strange Freedom*, 229; "Knowledge . . . Shall Vanish Away," in *The Inward Journey*, 95–96.

struggle for knowledge, freedom, and responsibility. Job comes face to face with God as a result of his integrity—his willingness to confront the transcendent within himself, even though he may not fully attain it. In the final dilemma of the human spirit, one must ultimately place one's trust in ultimate ends beyond our reach.[3]

THIS DISCUSSION deals with the moral struggle as it expressed itself in one of the very amazing and, in some ways, most deeply moving dramas in our literature. No one knows who wrote the Book of Job; no one knows when it was written; no one knows where it was written.[4] It is a drama of the first magnitude because it deals with the essential dignity of man.

It is rather curious, just in passing, that, in a period during which men have weak, or mediocre, or inadequate sense of human dignity, there is no great drama. There is a lot of melodrama; but no great drama that seems somehow to purge, to wash clean. There is something ennobling about drama, but about melodrama there is something that is dingy.

The drama of Job opens in a manner that raises one of the most persistent and unanswerable problems of human existence; that always, behind the scenes in human life, there seem to be operative forces, factors, powers, to which human life is responsive but for which human life is not responsible. In this drama, the sons of God, one of whom is Satan, come together in their regular conclave, and each one reported about his goings-on. (It is interesting that Satan was in good standing in the family.) And God says to Satan,

"Where have you been?"
"Oh," says Satan, "I've been up and down the earth, looking around."

---

3. For more on Job, see "Man and the Moral Struggle: The Undying Fire" (December 12, 1954), printed in the current volume.

4. There is no consensus on when or where the Book of Job was written, though most scholars date it around the sixth century BCE; it was written in Hebrew, possibly by a native speaker of Aramaic.

"Have you considered my servant Job?"
"Yes, I saw him."

And then a plan is developed: that Satan will work Job over—but he can't take his life; he can frighten him almost to death, but he can't take his life. So the drama unfolds on the earth as the result of a design that was projected down to the earth by God and the spirits.

Here is a perennial problem: it is a problem in Greek drama: the gods on Olympus decide to do something that affects human life, and human life begins moving in certain directions as if human life itself had decided to move in those directions. But it was the gods on Olympus that had worked it out; and if, for some reason, human life seems to be getting out of hand, then one of the gods participates in incarnation and comes down and begins pushing things around. He is half man, half god—it is curious, isn't it? In your life and in my life, too, it seems sometimes that behind the scene there is this manipulation of human life; and yet all the time each human life is sure that it is autonomous, that it has made its own decisions. Some say that the stars really control all of this and that if we can understand how the stars impinge upon the destiny of man, then we can always come out without destruction, for we can anticipate. Now we who are modern and sophisticated talk about the great hidden, abysmal things in human life that the psychologists have turned up for us, about the "unconscious," the "x," the "y," the "z." But this is just another way of saying that we are moving on one plane but the thing that controls what we do is somewhere outside our sphere; that we have no freedom; that there is no such thing as an autonomous human being. When we run out of all these invisible things, we talk about the "social heritage," the "social behavior pattern," the "mores," the folkways; all those jugglers of man's destiny that crowd him so that he has no moment that he can call his own and be free. Well, that is the setting of the story of Job.

The drama begins to unfold. Without any warning whatever, Job's wealth is wiped out. Then his children die. And in all his disaster, his wife comforts him by saying, "Well, that is all right. I remember a time when we had no children. I remember a time when we had no wealth. So you can take it."

But then Job's body begins to disintegrate, and at this he seems to become directly involved in the demonic operation of life. It had been an impersonal act of God, the whirlwinds and storms, that killed his children, and Job said, "I can deal with that." When the Sabeans and other people came down and wiped out his flock,[5] he could deal with that because they didn't know really that he was Job, and it might be that the operation of the laws of God were fulfilling ends and purposes that Job himself did not understand, ends and purposes that involved the whole fate of His people rather than anything personal and private. But when Job's body began to disintegrate, then Job said, "I know that whatever else may be operating, this thing at last is getting personal. What shall I do with it? I don't understand this. There is, I know, in me the willingness always to pursue ends and goals (and he is moving into his moral struggle now), to pursue ends and goals which I thought had to do with the good that extends beyond my private welfare and my private fate. But maybe I am really interested in goodness only because I know that this is the kind of universe that guarantees and sustains the man who is upon goodness bent. I didn't think I was interested in helping the widow, and in being gracious, and in showing compassion to the needy, just for personal reasons. But maybe I am! Maybe I am interested in helping the widow because I have a feeling that if I do not help her I will not be blessed. Is that really the basis of my behavior? Left to myself, what would I do? Would I be interested in goodness and decency and right, if I did not deeply believe that goodness and decency and right were somehow always involved in what happens to me personally? I don't know. Maybe that is why I insisted that my children should offer sacrifices to God, not merely for things that they had done that were wrong but extra offerings for the unuttered thoughts of their minds and hearts, which unuttered thoughts might be evil, and, as a result of that evil, wickedness would descend upon them. So, in order to be sure that nothing is left uncovered, I had them offer sacrifices for the unknown. Is that why I did that, not because of my religion, but because of a certain superstition that I have? Am I really afraid to be unkind because of what will happen to me if I am unkind? Or am I really interested in ends that transcend my particular fate?"

---

5. Job 1:15. The Sabeans were a people native to southern Arabia, mentioned in Genesis 10:7 and 25:3.

That was Job's problem. It is my problem; it is your problem. Is my life ordered on the basis of my response to a good that transcends my particular fate and fortune, or is my eye focused upon the logical bearing between reaping and sowing, between reward and punishment? If there were no reward, if there were no punishment, would I still be interested in the life of integrity and the life of decency?

—Well, I don't know (said Job), I don't know, but let me review my life.

So he went over all the details of his life to find out whether there was this balancing. That was perfectly human. I remember when I was about nine or ten, I broke my arm running from a dog, broke two bones in my wrist. My hand was put in a splint, and I comforted myself by trying to find out what in my past had rated that kind of thing. I thought of all that I had done, that I hadn't done, that I hadn't thought of for a long time; and I finally decided that my arm was broken because I had been selling tickets on Sunday, for that seemed to have been the worst thing in my little catalog of sins. That is what Job did.

—Things don't just happen (he told himself). There is a logic, and that logic is moral! Not impersonal, not metaphysical, not biological, not moral! "Nothing walks with aimless feet."[6] We are surrounded all the time by a moral monitor. Reaping, sowing; reward, punishment. Wherever there is punishment, it is a reward for evil done.

—But I haven't been that bad! (Job said) I know that I am innocent. Where, where is the judge? Why doesn't he come forward and talk to me? Behold, I go forward and God is not there; backwards, I cannot perceive him. He knows that I am innocent, and he is hiding from me; for, if I am being punished because of sins that I have not committed knowingly, if this is the kind of universe in which men are brought to judgment for deeds with reference to which they have no sense of moral or spiritual or ethical responsibility, then this is an immoral universe! For what is the meaning of judgment if it does not locate responsibility? But this cannot

---

6. Alfred Lord Tennyson, *In Memoriam* 54, lines 5–9:
That nothing walks with aimless feet;
That not one life shall be destroy'd,
Or cast as rubbish to the void,
When God hath made the pile complete.

be an immoral universe, for I remember how I felt when I heard about the widow and her hungry children; I know what surged through me when I beheld the injustices around me, and how my strength became the strength of ten men as I sought to put to right the diabolical and the wicked. That was a pure, sheer, neat impulse without any of the dross and the limitations that belong to one who is trying to juggle his universe to meet his private ends. I know that.

Then his friends began talking with him. They said, "God is pulling the cover off you. You have been pretending that you were a good man, and we all thought so. We were sure of it, but we didn't know the truth, and now the truth is coming out. Why don't you admit it? Admit your pretensions; admit the fact that you fooled all men but that you can't fool God? Why don't you confess your sin? If you confess your sin, God will forgive you." And do what? "God will restore the status quo."

(Job said) No . . . but you may be right. Why was I born anyway? Life is a nightmare. I didn't ask to be born; I had nothing to do with the process. Here I am. Why has all of this befallen me? I look around and see some other people. Look at you, and you, and you (to each of his three friends). I know you aren't any better than I am, and yet none of these things happens to you, and they happen to me. Maybe you are right. Maybe there are secret sins that are working away at the fiber of my character and the integrity of my mind and spirit—secret sins of which I am dimly aware or scarcely aware. Perhaps that is the logic of what is operating upon me. Oh, I curse the day I was born! Cursed be the moment when they announced that a male child was born! Why did I not die in my mother's womb and be delivered from all of the tragedy, the brutality, the wrath of life that victimizes man, squeezes his life, and yet will not let him die! If I could die, then I would sleep the sleep of the dead. Nothing would trouble me, no thoughts, no frustrations, nothing. Why doesn't God kill me? Then I would be at rest, but I can't die. I'm conscious; I feel pain; I know frustration and disorder, and I can't die. Since I cannot die, then I will take my stand, and my stand is this: I do not know why, I cannot fathom the mystery that has created the terrors of the moment, but I know that I am innocent. I take my stand on my integrity. I know that my Redeemer lives, and even without my flesh I shall see him and when I see him, he will answer.

And then God moves in, and he says to Job, "You are just a man. Why do you think you can understand everything? Do you know what makes the horse strong? You can't even answer that. Do you know what makes the snow fall? Have you visited the nest of the hawk and know what the hawk says to the little hawk? You don't. If you cannot understand the secret of the ordinary ways of nature by which you are surrounded, if you cannot penetrate the mystery that is a part of the garden-variety expression of the life of nature, how can you, Job, how can you understand morality, God, suffering, innocence, guilt?"

Oh God (Job replies), I am a stupid man. I put my hand over my mouth. It was my agony that cried out. My pain was more than I could bear. My frustration was more than I could handle; out of the anguish that stirred in me I became articulate, vindictive, and arrogant. Oh God, I won't do that anymore. I won't. I still don't understand, but I'll wait. I'll wait, and, perhaps, in the quietness there will steal into my heart not the answer but the assurance that I am not alone. That's all I want. It was because I could not face the loneliness of desolation; it was because all of the things that happened to me made me fear that no one anywhere cared for me. But now you have assured me that you care, and I've seen the travail of my own soul, and I'm satisfied. Why the innocent suffer, I don't know, but God does not leave them alone; and if I can be sure of God, God becomes the answer and the solution to my spiritual problems, even though, even though, with reference to my frustration I continue to be agnostic.

This was Job's answer. This was as far as Job could go. We shall see, as the aspects of the moral struggle unfold in the lives of some other people, whether there is an improvement on Job's answer.

THE UNDYING FIRE
[H. G. WELLS]

December 12, 1954
Marsh Chapel

In this sermon in the Man and the Moral Struggle series, as a follow-up to a sermon on Job,[1] Thurman explores a little-known novel by H. G. Wells, The Undying Fire, *which presents a contemporary updating of the Job story. Thurman explains how the Job-like figure in the novel, after suffering a series of reverses and contemplating the evil in the world in the aftermath of World War I, decides that his life, human life, and life in general cannot be reduced to the natural and social forces that drive its worst elements. This is the undying fire, and Thurman states that "every time I overcome the impulse to negate you, every time I relax my fear in your presence and embrace you with tenderness and understanding . . . I shall become a conflagration."*

AS OUR BACKGROUND for our thinking together and the continuation of our series on Man and the Moral Struggle, I am reading the final paragraph of *The Pilgrims of the Lonely Road*:[2]

---

1. "Man and the Moral Struggle: Job" (December 5, 1954).
2. Gaius Glenn Atkins, *Pilgrims of the Lonely Road* (New York: Fleming H. Revell, 1913), 338–39. The excerpt from this volume of essays on religious topics was a favorite passage of Thurman, which he included in sermons on numerous occasions. This part of the sermon, which exists only on audio tape, has a gap in which someone recorded over Thurman's voice. We follow Thurman's versions of Atkins in "Christian, Who Calls Me Christian?" (January 1938) and "Kingdom of God" (June 1938), in PHWT 2:107–8, 171. Thurman's version of the paragraph differs in some places from the original, noted below. Gaius Glenn Atkins (1868–1956) was a Congregationalist minister and a noted preacher and author.

Life does not grow more simple with the passing years, but its deeper needs are unchanging. The secret of peace is not to be found at the end of the road, but in the spirit in which we journey. It is to be sought in the sustaining love of God who is committed[3] to a real participation in all our strife;[4] who does not set us free from the possibility of pain and tears, but who feels the hurt of our wounds, the salt bitterness of our sorrow; who spends Himself, not only with us, but for us, and in the travail of redemptive passion, anticipates the victories of the spirit. And, finally whatever pilgrimage we undertake, must be undertaken, in spite of the interior loneliness of all great spiritual processes.[5] We are never to forget that we are all so tied up in one bundle, that peace and reconciliation in which others are not involved are quite impossible. The note of service must be deepened and in our care for those who lie wounded or broken along the road, we shall forget our own wounds and our own wearinesses. So conceived, so reinforced, life is never impossible, but does indeed become, so these books and leaders teach us, an adventure whose greatness is its own best justification and whose difficulties may become for the faithful and the discerning, but stairs of ascent to radiant and triumphant regions.

H. G. Wells[6] wrote a modern parody on or an interpretation of the drama of Job and the title of H. G. Wells's story is the title of our subject, *The Undying Fire*.[7] We discovered last Sunday—that is, I think we did—that Job was caught in the grip of the moral struggle precipitated by the events of his life, which events caused him to examine the meaning of his life. And when he examined the meaning of his life in the light of the events of his life, he found that there were searching and crucial questions

---

3. In original, "by the very nature of his Godhead."
4. In original, "who does not release us from the battle, but who shares the fight."
5. In original, "in the comradeship of our kind and all well-being must always be our goal."
6. H[erbert] G[eorge] Wells (1866–1946) was a well-known British author of novels, science fiction, and works of history and political commentary.
7. H. G. Wells, *The Undying Fire: A Contemporary Novel* (New York: Macmillan, 1919).

for which he had no answer, but from which he could never be relieved of the necessity for seeking the answer.

He rested his case, finally, upon his own integrity, and he sought to place his integrity over against the God of nature and the great impersonal force that, out of a quality of being and knowing that his little mind could not grasp, was dealing with all living things; and, even though it would not be possible for Job to find this transcendent God and face him with Job's judgment, he, Job, felt that ultimately God could not escape him. "I go forward, and he isn't there; backwards, and I can't receive him, but that's alright. I shall find him either with my flesh or without my flesh. Somewhere in the vastness of the universe, he will have to deal with my integrity." The important and searching question as to why the vicissitudes of life acted as they did with Job is a question that he leaves unanswered; it's a question which you and I finally leave unanswered even though we may be smart and wise. Annoying.

Now H. G. Wells takes this drama and tells it in a contemporary manner and just to sketch the basic ideas, for this is not a book review. The hero is Job Huss.[8] This is very interesting. He is the headmaster of a school in England. A man of very great wisdom and a good and wise teacher. And then calamity begins falling his way. First, his assistant headmaster dies in an accident. Then, a fire burns down one of the dormitories and two of his boys are killed in that fire. Then the headmaster's son, who is a soldier in the British army, is killed behind the German lines. The setting is the First World War. Then his oldest friend commits suicide. And then, the headmaster himself gets tidings from his solicitors telling him that his life's savings have been wiped out due to the curious manipulations of some conscienceless individuals so that his dream of retirement, when he would not have to work, goes up in smoke, as it were. But that isn't all. He gets sick. And he gets sick with cancer. And while he is ill, and he has long hours to think, which hours as a teacher he doesn't have, except with reference to the tasks. And as he thinks about what has happened to him, a very curious thing begins operating in his mind. He says, "Why am I complaining? Why am I thinking that I am different from the way life is?"

---

8. "Job Huss" was an attempt by Wells to invoke both Job's name and place of residence, Job of Uz.

And out of this vast learning, he begins to trace in his mind, the struggle of life on this planet. How always there is this killing, this bloody business at various levels of sentient development. He talks about it in detail with the various species in the whole kingdom; and then finally in his reflection, he comes upon man, and he says man does the same thing. Man has this evil in him. This meanness. This cunning. That even when he takes his mind and is able to devise things that are good for healing and for redemption and for the salvation of the race, he turns his genius to work on those things that make for the destruction of life through wars. And not only that, but man looking at other men involved in this begins to figure ways by which [through] the promotion of organized destruction and violence they themselves may make more money and become more secure, as it were.

And at the climax of that kind of thinking, his friends come to see him. They are trustees in the school. And there are three of them, as in the Book of Job. And these trustees are amazed to discover that this man, to whom they had entrusted their sons, this man who was always the very essence of optimism, of character, of goodness, is now talking like a heretic. And they wonder whether or not they were mistaken in giving him so great a responsibility. And as he listens to their indictment, and as they push him more and more and more against the wall, something else begins to stir in him. It occurs to him that all of life is not like this. There are impulses in me that work against all of this. There have been moments when I have been kind, when I am kind, when I do not accept as ultimate or as permanent aspects of life—these evil, diabolical, negative and wicked expressions of life. I hadn't been conscious of it before, but there has always been in me a struggle going on between these two, and I have never said about the evil deed that it was a good deed. I have never said that the bad thing was a worthy thing. I have never relaxed my interest in trying to overcome the evil—trying to overcome in me, in my boys, in the world—those things that work most against goodness and decency and wholeness and love and beauty. This a part of the universe also. "And I will call it that undying fire in me and in you," he said to his inquisitors.[9]

---

9. Probably Thurman is referring to the passage where Job Huss says, "There burns an undying fire in the hearts of men. By that fire I have. I know the God of

Now if it be that I can cultivate this quality—if it be that I can educate this quality so that more and more it invades the deliberate and self-conscious actions of mine, then it may be that, together, mankind might do this. And it may be that what mankind is doing as it seeks always this overlapping growing edge—on the side of the positive and creative and redemptive—that that really is what the God of the universe is doing as he seeks to bring out of the chaotic stuff a manifestation of existence, some measure of order, some measure of purpose, some measure of wholeness. "So the spirit of God, somehow in my mind," says this teacher, "must be separated from the power of God." Now if I can teach, train this quality in me; then there is a rallying point around which all of the disciplines of life may take on character and meaning. What if I cannot see the end? Maybe a part of the end is in the process itself. That was his second insight.

Now, I need not go on with the rest of the story because it turns out as the Book of Job does. Things happen and he gets better, and we will just leave that alone. The undying fire. The spirit of love, joy, peace, wholeness. The hunger. Is that the human spirit, which is what one of the philosophers in his groups said to him? Why do you patronize it by calling it the spirit of God?—this undying fire? Why don't you call it the spirit of man? Why patronize it by calling it the spirit of God? The teacher says, "I can't call it the spirit of man because the spirit of man is selfish. The spirit of man is narrow. The spirit of man is the generator of anxieties and fears as that spirit broods over the stuff of the man's experience and living. But this is another kind of spirit that seems always to be warring against this spirit that is in man, so I will call it the spirit of God because God is in man, deep within man, working away to overcome this other spirit."[10]

He doesn't attempt to account for this other spirit. The only thing that he does is to emphasize the fact that the spirit of God is not out in the vastness of the universe, sowing the hills with pines, handling the

---

my Salvation. His will is Truth; His will is Service. He urges me to conflict without consolations, without rewards" (*The Undying Fire*, 132).

10. "It is not humanity, it is not the spirit of men. Humanity, the spirit of men, made poison gas and the submarine; the spirit of man is jealous, aggressive and partisan. . . . But this spirit in me, this fire which I call God, was lit. I know not how, but as if it came from outside" (ibid., 196).

cataracts, putting the stars in their courses. Not the transcendent God way out there, but the God within the spirit, the life of man. Now he says that you can be taught how to develop this.

That is very interesting, and if I may digress for a moment to tell you a story. It's fresh in my mind because one of the scientists who developed this other idea about this coming together spirit, which is the symbol of this undying fire in other aspects of nature, is the Russian sociologist Kropotkin,[11] for whom my dog is named. Now it is an experience that I had with my dog last week that illustrates, that ties it right up. Kropotkin was becoming very difficult. He would not respond when he was outside of the house, which threatened his life constantly and jeopardized my emotions. With the result that he was turned over to a man whose business it is to teach dogs how to be what they ought to be on behalf of tranquility and peace. And when we turned the dog over to this man, he said, "I will call you at the end of two weeks and then I will tell you that the dog can remain for the rest of his course which will be four weeks longer, or you must come and get him." He said, "I, through long years of feeling, and thinking and experience, I love all dogs. And this is so deeply embedded in my whole organism that there is an atmosphere that surrounds me into which any dog comes so that whatever may be his name—I don't have to know—but as soon as he comes within my field of awareness, he is surrounded by this love that is accumulation of the discipline of my experience, my atmosphere. But it will take me two weeks, in my experience, to teach a dog how to love me. And if I cannot teach your dog to love me, then I cannot teach him anything else. And it will take me two weeks, and if at the end of two weeks I find that I have taught him how to love me, to be at rest and at ease and without any fear or sense of being bounded or limited in my presence, then on that foundation, I can teach him how to do anything."[12]

---

11. Prince Pyotr Alexeyevich Kropotkin (1842–1924) was a prominent Russian anarchist who lived much of his life in exile, primarily in England, though returning to Russia after 1917. As Thurman indicates here, his social and scientific works, especially *Mutual Aid: A Factor in Evolution* (1902), was an influence on his social and religious thinking.

12. The story of Kropotkin the dog—"beautiful, charming, friendly, but a bit stupid"—did not work out as Thurman hoped. The trainer told Thurman that he could not teach him, and Thurman gave the dog to a friend in San Francisco. Every

That's just a dog. I wonder how we ever fare with ourselves when we look out upon the world at this moment with all of its madness, with all of the fears and anxieties and organized evils by which our days are surrounded and our moments are strangled, and say it's the way life is, it's the way man is. May it not be true that if we put the resources of our minds, of our personalities, of our wealth, of our possessions at the disposal of the tutoring of the spirit so that there will not only be an individual condition of thinking and responding and behaving, but the staggering possibility of there being a collective condition so that the possibility of a decent world, the possibility of living without fear, and in some measure of increasingly profound tranquility, is not the whisper of the prophets in our ears, not the dancing dream of the seeker for utopia, but the rational possibility of the very stuff of our existence if we dare learn how to teach this spirit about which we are talking, to possess our lives.

Every time I overcome the impulse to negate you, every time I relax my fear in your presence and embrace you with tenderness and understanding, I light in another part of my behavior the undying fire until at last, perhaps, I shall become a conflagration, and you and you and you. What a possibility for life! And to sense that possibility and do nothing about it, it were better that we had never been born. This is the hope in this season of hope. What shall we do about it? What? Our Father, Our Father, Our Father.

> *Meditation*
> When we are most ourselves, we are conscious of the struggle within us, between the impulses and desires, leading and prompting us to do the good thing, to say the generous word, to be understanding where understanding is needful. And the wide seaways of contrary impulses deep within us, to say the ungracious word, to close the doors of our compassion against the needy, to devote our minds and our energies and our thoughts to those things that make for our own private security, our own private well-being, day and night, through event after event, the struggle goes on of pace. And yet there are moments when one part of the struggle

---

time Thurman returned to the city, "always he remembered me and I did never forget," WHAH 232–34.

seems to be more favorable than another. There are clear, wonderful moments when we know that, for the rest of our lives, we shall be on the side of the good impulse and the gracious deed, the kindly act, the loving spirit, and from those moments of awareness and wholeness, we wonder why we have been so blind. And then, without notice, without warning, we lose our way, we lose our struggle and we wonder whether or not there is any health in us, anything that is clean and worthy and worthful in us. Therefore, Our Father, in the quietness of this room this day, we yield our struggle to thee. Not merely for good impulse, the kindly deed, the loving spirit, but the meanness, the weaknesses, the selfishness—our whole selves. Holding back nothing, we lay bare to thee, to thy spirit, to thy mind, without apology, without embarrassment, but with confidence. We do this, making no demands, just being ourselves as we are before thy brooding spirit and thy loving heart. This, for us, is enough, O God. With that, we trust tomorrow and all that it may bring of good or ill. O God, Our Father.

SAINT JOAN
[GEORGE BERNARD SHAW]

November 27, 1949
Fellowship Church

Saint Joan, by George Bernard Shaw,[1] *premiered in 1923, three years after the canonization of Joan of Arc by the Roman Catholic Church, and almost five hundred years after she was burned at the stake by the Roman Catholic Church for heresy.*[2] *For Thurman, Shaw's play highlights the ways the individual conscience needs to struggle against the imperatives of the institutional sources of power. No person can escape their "responsibility as a member of society." Those who rebel against the dominant practices of society know that there is no ironclad "guarantee against self-deception,"*[3] *and that*

---

1. George Bernard Shaw, *Saint Joan: A Chronicle Play in Six Scenes and an Epilogue* (New York: Brentano's, 1924). George Bernard Shaw (1856–1950) was a prolific Irish playwright and polemicist, and the most honored English-language dramatist of his era. He was awarded the Nobel Prize for Literature in 1925. For other references by Thurman to works of Shaw, see PHWT 1:171–72; PHWT 2:80, 249, 294; PHWT 5:124.

2. Joan of Arc (c. 1412–May 30, 1431) came from an obscure peasant background to inspire a French army during the Hundred Years' War. After her capture by Burgundian forces allied with the English, she was tried for heresy and burned at the stake. A papal court nullified her conviction in 1456. Long before her 1920 canonization, Joan of Arc had become a figure of legend and a symbol of France.

3. Self-deception is a key theme in Thurman's interpretation of the religious experience. He is acutely aware of the danger of subjectivism and privatization of meaning implied in the emphasis on the development of inner consciousness. He tries to guard against this tendency by accentuating the need for external empirical verification of what one experiences in his inner life. "The real questions at issue here," he contends, "are, how may a man know he is not being deceived? Is there any way by which he may know beyond doubt, and therefore with verification, that what he experiences is authentic and genuine?" Rational coherence between the inner experience of self and the external world, in St. Joan's case religious institutions, is the methodology employed to test for self-deception. He argues, "Whatever seems to deny

"it is the logic of society to guarantee itself by getting rid of heretics." In the end, Thurman counsels, the religious person must, like Joan, recognize that *"that which seems to me at the moment of my greatest honesty to be the truth for me"* is the will of God.

TODAY WE ARE THINKING about Bernard Shaw's *Saint Joan*. The story of *Saint Joan* is familiar to all of us for the most part. It is the story of a French maid who is gifted with a sense of other-worldliness. She hears voices, and she identifies these voices. The voices tell her what to do to save her country. Her country is being overrun by the British, and there is nowhere a single voice that is able to speak with the kind of authority that inspires men to action brave and glorious. Everybody is either frightened or tired; and Joan of Arc is neither frightened nor tired, and it is to her that the voices come. She goes to see the man who has charge of all of the army in her area, someone whose name is Robert, whose last name I do not remember.[4] Of course he tries to dissuade her; he is a little troubled. She is a young woman, and the soldiers who are in the outer court like her. She is different from the women that they know. They even feel that there is something unclean about saying bad words when she is around.

So Robert is impressed with the quality in her; something about her impresses him because she isn't afraid, and she believes that France can be saved. It is refreshing. But she wants to see the king himself, the prime mover; and in Bernard Shaw's play she is taken to the king. The king is weak—a weak child. Yet there is something fascinating about him because he is sure that this king business is something in which he personally should not be involved. We see introduced in this historic drama as a secondary theme the idea that there is almost always a conflict between the demands that are personal and private and the demands that are impersonal and public. Left to himself as a man, or as a youngster, the

---

a fundamental structure of orderliness upon which rationality seems to depend cannot be countenanced" (HT, *The Creative Encounter* [New York: Harper & Brothers, 1954], 57–58).

4. Robert de Baudricourt (c. 1400–1454). He first met Joan of Arc in 1429.

king wanted to dream his dreams and, as Joan says, "suck his candy."[5] But he is a king, and the responsibilities of office are upon him, the impersonal demands; and he cannot give priority to his personal life. So he is constantly in a state of rebellion. That is very interesting, though it is not the point of Bernard Shaw's play, but it is one of the interesting secondary ideas that he works out.

Now the king will not see her unless the archbishop says so, and the archbishop finally concedes that she might come in; so she comes in and something begins to happen. The archbishop recognizes something that is inevitable if this girl keeps going, and what is that? He recognizes that she is introducing into life the kind of authority which conceivably may conflict with the authority of the church. But he can't do anything now because she is going to save France, and she has power. But an institution can wait, you know. It can wait. So the archbishop lets her come in, and the story moves very rapidly. They haven't been able to go against the armies of England; they have to cross a river, and they can't cross because the wind is bad. They have spent all their money getting the priests to pray for the wind to change, but the wind hasn't changed. So they don't have any more money, and they don't have any more friends, and the wind hasn't changed either. While Joan is talking with them about it, they say to her: Go to a church or chapel somewhere and pray for us; that is the best thing you can do. You know about God. If you pray for us, pray that the wind will change; then we can do the rest for we are soldiers. You aren't.

Joan said, —I've done my praying. I am on a mission now and I can't take the time to go into the chapel now. But they insist, and she says, — Well, I might do it. And as she turns to go, one of the messengers rushes up, saying that the wind was changed. Of course that is a miracle, and I guess it is, you know, for no one knows why winds change anyway. The explanation is a description; it is not an explanation. So it is a miracle, so it is all right.

They move on, getting more and more success, and, finally, when they come to the coronation of the king, she insists that they should

---

5. Joan contemptuously tells Charles, the uncrowned king of France, that his "business" has been merely "petting lapdogs and sucking sugar-sticks" (Shaw, *Saint Joan,* 44).

drive the English away until they get to the city where the king is to be crowned; and she is going to do it. She is going to do it, not the archbishop. There again, you see, the logical stepping up of this conflict. Joan, with her voices, speaking on behalf of the voices, will anoint the king. She has done with her voices what the archbishop with all of the cumulative momentum of fifteen hundred years of religious monopoly has not been able to achieve. The archbishop doesn't like it, and you wouldn't like it, so don't sit feeling full of pride about the archbishop. Then when the king is crowned, Joan says:

—We aren't through yet. We must go on. We must drive them out of Paris.

They said: —Don't waste your time now. The king said, —I'm crowned and we have defeated them up to this point. Why don't you go back home and milk the cows? You have saved us.

Then the archbishop says to her:

—You do not speak in the name of the church.

The army says: —We can't really follow a girl.

Joan discovers at this moment, in one of the moving scenes in Shaw's play, that the army, after it has exhausted all of her resourcefulness, is through with her. She has been a means to an end. She discovers that the church was silent as long as she was in the ascendancy with her voices and her spiritual power, but now that the climactic moment has come and it seems as if her stars are on the decline, the church leaves her, as indeed it had all along. Then the archbishop says to her, and let me read this to you:[6]

> You stand alone: absolutely alone, trusting to your own conceit, your own ignorance, your own headstrong presumptions, your own impiety in hiding all of these sins under the cloak of a trust in God. When you pass through these doors into the sunlight, the crowd will cheer you. They will bring you their little children and their invalids to heal: they will kiss your hands and feet and do what they can, poor simple souls, to turn your head and madden you with the self-confidence that is leading you to your destruction. But you will be nonetheless alone: they cannot save

---

6. Shaw, *Saint Joan*, 93–95.

you. We, and we only, can stand between you and the stake at which our enemies have burnt that wretched woman in Paris.

Then Joan says:

> —Yes: I am alone on earth: I have always been alone. My father told my brothers to drown me if I would not stay to mind his sheep while France was bleeding to death: France might perish if only our lambs were safe. I thought France would have friends at the court of the king of France, and I find only wolves fighting for pieces of her poor torn body. I thought God would have friends everywhere because He is a friend of everyone, and in my innocence, I believed that you who now cast me out would be like strong towers to keep harm from me. But I'm wiser now; and nobody is any the worse for being wiser. Do you think that you can frighten me by telling me that I am alone? France is alone; and God is alone; and what is my loneliness before the loneliness of my country and my God? I see now that the loneliness of God is His strength: what would He be if he listened to your jealous little counsels? Well, my loneliness shall be my strength too: it is better to be alone with God: His friendship will not fail me, nor His counsel, nor His love. In His strength I will dare, and dare, and dare until I die. I will go out now to the common people and let the love in their eyes comfort me for the hate in your eyes. You will be glad to see me burnt, but if I go through the fire I shall go through it to their hearts for ever and ever and so, God be with me.

Well, that was a strong potion for the archbishop. The story moves very rapidly, and finally it is decided that she shall be burned at the stake. I wish I had time to read it. Sometime you read it. The scene of the trial is, in my opinion, one of the greatest, if not—well, it isn't the greatest perhaps, but it is one of the greatest scenes in all dramatic literature with which I am familiar at any rate. The decision of the state and the church, and the pawn is this innocent little girl. She is burned at the stake. First they tell her that if she takes it all back, if she says that her voices aren't really voices, if she recants, then she will be forgiven. So she says:

—I'll sign a confession.

They take her hand—she can't write, you see, so they take her hand and draw her name just like that, then after that she has to make her mark in her own strength. So she makes the mark. Then she hears them read this and she says: —Well, all right.

Something in her dies it seems. Her voices are stilled.

When that is done and she expects to be freed, they say:

—Now for all these things you have done, we will now send you to the dungeon; we won't kill you quickly; we will kill you slowly, and you will be shut out from the light forever and ever until you die.

She leaps from her chair, runs over, snatches the confession that she has signed, tears it up, and says:

—I knew my voices were right. You are all children, or manifestations of the devil. Take me to the stake.

Then, of course, they take her to the stake. Outside they make the great funeral pyre, and she is chained. Then they light the wood; and as she is dying in her agony she asks to see the cross, and a man makes a cross out of a wooden stick and holds it up before her glazed eyes until the flames begin to leap around him, and she says;

—Oh, be careful. You might be burned. I can die now.

And she dies, saying in the language of her own Catholic faith,

—Blessed Jesus.

These hard men are stirred. They are stumped, and that is the way the play ends.

But you can depend upon Bernard Shaw to have an epilogue, so he had an epilogue; and in the epilogue the king is now an old man, fifty[7] or sixty or seventy years old, and he dreams. And in his dream—well, he is in bed asleep, then he wakes up and starts reading; and then there is a wind and people come in. Joan comes in, and talks to him. Then one by one all these people who participated in her destruction come in, and a lot of things have happened to them since then. There is one man, a soldier; he did only one kind thing in his life, and for that he is permitted one day from hell every year. That kind thing was to hold the cross in front of this dying girl. All are repentant; all are very sorry. Then Joan says:

---

7. Shaw describes Charles as being fifty-one years old.

—But suppose I came back.

One by one they make their excuses and disappear because if she came back each one is sure that he would act now as he did then, for he was involved in a network of relationships which forced him to act as he did. Bernard Shaw has Joan say: "How long, Oh Lord, will it be before this world can receive thy saints?"[8]

Now that is the story. Now let me take two or three minutes to point up something that just has to be said. This is the lesson of Bernard Shaw's Joan of Arc; we are all involved in moral conflict. Now the difference between the moral struggle as we have been developing it in the seven addresses before now and this one is at one crucial point. In this play, this historic drama, the moral struggle goes on between two vast profound impersonal forces in life, in the world. That is the struggle of the institution as over against the individual who is involved in the institution's predicament. The conflict between church and state is another dimension as expressed in *Saint Joan*. Now it happens, you see, that the girl herself is merely the battleground on which these two impersonal forces struggle. She is merely incidental. The issue is an issue that involves the whole structure of the social order and the destiny of Man, for to what shall I give finally the complete and thoroughgoing assent of my spirit? What shall be for me the source of authority? Shall I depend upon the leanings of my own conscience? Shall I be guided by the truth as God gives me strength to observe the truth and to discern the truth? Or shall I defer, or shall I give the right to determine the truth, to some other than self-reference—even though it may be the state or the church or some other family or social unit? Shall I listen to my voices? Or shall I be told what the voices say to me? That is the problem! Shall I be guided by what happens inside of me when the spirit of God broods over my troubled waters until at last there begins to appear in the midst of my conflict order and meaning and direction? Shall I follow that, even though it goes against everything I have been taught, everything that I have been inspired to say is true, everything that the organized relationships say that men recognize as being valid? That is the problem.

---

8. Joan's words are, "O God that madest this beautiful earth, when will it be ready to receive Thy saints? How long, O Lord, how long?" (Shaw, *Saint Joan*, 163).

During wars we always deal with that. During the First World War, for instance, it was illegal to read the Sermon on the Mount publicly in the United States. Couldn't do it during the First World War.[9] Now suppose you just had to read it. (You could read it in church service.) But suppose you had to. It is a decision that some men make when they decide they will not go to war but will go to jail instead. It is the decision that somebody makes in a very simple way, that he will not wear a hat. Everybody else wears hats. Simple thing, but how far can you depend upon the integrity of your own insight? Is there any guarantee—this is the crux of it; is there any guarantee against self-deception? That is the point. Is there any way I can protect myself from being wrong, being mistaken? Must I always recognize in an other than self-reference, some other group—the validity of the thing that I feel in myself? It was the early problem of the Quakers, for instance, when they were trying to develop some sort of organizational structure based upon a religious and mystical experience and insight. So if I had a concern, I took it to the first-day meeting, then I took it to the quarterly meeting, then I took it to the annual meeting; and then if it were a heavy concern that involved many issues, I might take it to the five-year meeting; and the theory is that from this point and this point and this point I will get an other than self-reference saying, "Yes," to my light.[10] But suppose they say, "No" all the way up to my light, then what do I do? Do I dare say, "Yes," to my light in the presence and in the face of all the "Nos" to my light? And if I do that, am I not an arrogant,

---

9. The Sedition Act of May 1918, an amendment to the Espionage Act of the previous year, made it a crime to criticize "the form of government of the United States or the Constitution of the United States." Under its provisions, hundreds of critics of American involvement in World War I were tried and convicted. Pacifists were a major target of the legislation, and if the Sermon on the Mount was never officially proscribed, for some enforcers of the law the expression of its sentiments was seditious. In the United Kingdom, there was a similar scrutiny of pacifist sentiments. In October 1914, David Lloyd-George, chancellor of the exchequer, wrote the prominent pacifist Bertrand Russell that he would prosecute a reprint of the Sermon on the Mount if it interfered with war production (Brock Millman, *Managing Domestic Dissent in First World War Britain* [London: Frank Cass, 2000], 180).

10. Thurman references this experience of agreement in a Quaker meeting elsewhere. See Thurman, "The Inward Journey: The Inner Light IV," Marsh Chapel, October 22, 1961.

conceited human being, overbearing, intolerant? Where do I draw the line?

Now there is no simple answer to this. Bernard Shaw has no answer to it. I don't have an answer to it. No one has a simple answer to it, or a complex answer to it, except this, and I have two suggestions to make and that will be all.

The first suggestion is: every person is under obligation, as it would seem to me, to establish for himself private tests for his truth. You know that you have a lot of little private tests for things, don't you? They don't make sense to anyone else, but they are valid for you—little private tests for truth. That is the first thing. You are under obligation to work them out, not my tests or somebody else's tests, but your private tests for truth, so that when this checks and this checks and this checks and this checks, then, as far as is possible for you so to understand, this is it! Now once you get that, then if you are a religious person, you see, that is what you would call the will of God. And what is the will of God? The will of God is that which seems to me at the moment of my greatest honesty to be the truth for me.

Now the second suggestion is: I cannot escape my responsibility as a member of society. I share in the judgments of society, and society as it expresses itself in formal agreements does make demands upon me which demands I must recognize up to the point that in the recognizing of those demands upon me I must not stretch myself out of shape. Then my choice is to either stretch myself out of shape and debase my truth, or on behalf of that to which I am wedded internally I let society do what it wishes to me in fulfillment of its obligation to make everybody fall into line. It is like the frog and the yeastcake seated on the park bench. Someone dropped water on the yeastcake and it began fermenting. The more it fermented, the more it spread, the more it crowded the frog. Finally in desperation the frog said:

—Yeastcake, why don't you stop pushing me off the bench? The yeastcake said:

—I'm not pushing you, I'm just growing.[11]

---

11. One of Thurman's favorite stories and sayings; see *Disciplines of the Spirit* (New York: Harper & Row, 1963), 50.

You see, in following my truth, when I find that I am brought into conflict with society as expressed in any of its institutional manifestations, then the thing that happens to me as I insist upon my truth must never be regarded by me as being personal. For it is the logic of society to guarantee itself by getting rid of heretics, by getting rid of rebels; for if they did not get rid of rebels then they could not hold to the integrity of their position, and it is not that they dislike me or you but that they cannot abide your truth and be true to their own commitments. Either they must relax their insistence upon their own commitments or get rid of you, and they don't mean to hurt you, they just mean to be free of the kind of disturbance that you insist upon generating; and if you take it personally, then you become a martyr, and that is not very good for when you become a martyr in your mind then that is the first time you undermine your truth.

That is the lesson of *Joan*. May God help us in this fateful moment in the world to look steadily at what we see in her and hope that we can recognize in her strength our own strength and our own commitment.

THE POWER OF DARKNESS
[LEO TOLSTOY]

November 12, 1949
Fellowship Church, San Francisco

Thurman wrote little about Tolstoy.[1] This sermon, on a relatively unfamiliar play, The Power of Darkness,[2] *is his most extended consideration of the great Russian writer. But if he wrote little directly on Tolstoy, as Thurman makes clear in this sermon, Tolstoy was an important precursor to his own views of the Christian spiritual life. Tolstoy's message, Thurman writes, was that "no man can come to grips with the meaning of his own life, until he has been stripped of every defense, stripped to the literal substance of himself and must make the decision either to live or die. If he makes the decision to live, then, acting on that decision, he will understand the meaning of life."*

Neither for Tolstoy nor for Thurman was this merely a matter of personal self-examination. Tolstoy, in The Kingdom of God Is Within You[3] *and elsewhere, drawing on the work and life of American abolitionists such as William Lloyd Garrison and Henry David Thoreau, developed his "doctrine of nonresistance." This book, in turn, was a major influence on young Gandhi's ideas about nonviolence and resistance to evil. In his meeting with Thurman in 1936, Gandhi perhaps made a reference to Tolstoy's teaching on nonviolence.[4] Tolstoy, Thurman adds, had a novelist's gift for describing situations in which evil is not a result of weakness of character but strength, a willed separation of means and ends. Evil, he argues, is like "a malignant*

---

1. Leo Tolstoy (1828–1910), one of the greatest novelists and Russian writers, is best remembered for *War and Peace* (1869) and *Anna Karenina* (1877).

2. For an early English translation, see Leo Tolstoy, *Plays*, trans. Aylmer Maude and Louise Maude (London: G. Richards, 1903).

3. This first appeared in English (it had been banned in Russia) as Leo Tolstoy, *The Kingdom of God Is Within You: Christianity Not as a Mystic Religion but as a New Theory of Life,* trans. Constance Garnett (London: William Heinemann, 1894).

4. See PHWT 1:335, 338 n. 18.

growth, like a cell that has outgrown its pattern and is running wild, but it is alive; it is vital; it is quivering!" Thurman argues that only those who recognize the "power of darkness," like Tolstoy, can bring together the light and darkness within themselves and others.

WE COME THIS MORNING, in our series on Man and the Moral Struggle, to a consideration of Tolstoy's *The Power of Darkness*.

Tolstoy was born in Russia in the early part of the nineteenth century, about 1827, I believe. He gathers up within his compass and spirit the vast, elemental reaches of the Slav soul. There is something about the Russian people that has been for a long time a source of bewilderment and awe in my own mind. You will recall that they are, relatively speaking, latecomers to the family of industrial civilization and the pattern of culture as we know it. They lived, for how long we do not quite know, a great, an apparently limitless, people who were in a kind of twilight, whose souls and spirits and minds had a hardness about them due to the kind of endurance to which they were subjected, not only by the impersonal operations of the world of nature expressed in climate but by the peculiar power of their leaders over their lives. It seems as if the czars and all who worked before them were great weights that sat down on the people; they sat and they drew from the people strength and sustenance and vitality, but they could not destroy the people. They are elemental and refined. You listen to a Russian chorus sing, and you are fascinated by the exquisite beauty of the things they are able to do with the human instrument; but yet at the same time there is the stirring of something beyond the grasp of all of the delicate, refined expressions of life and meaning, something with a sweep in it that leaves you breathless. All of that you see in Tolstoy. I'll get him out of our mind pretty soon, but you will have to bear with me a little longer, because he is still hung up in there.

His life, and I suggest to you that if you want some really great reading that has a spiritual impact that is so tremendous it is embarrassing and humiliating as well as inspiring, read his *Confessions*;[5] compare them

---

5. Tolstoy's *Confession* was written in 1879. Because of problems with the Russian censors, it was not published until 1884, and then in Geneva, Switzerland. It was soon translated into English as *My Confession and the Spirit of Christ's Teaching*

with the *Confessions* of Saint Augustine, for instance, or some of the other people who wrote their confessions and whose lives were not altogether beautiful and lovely.

Tolstoy was a living paradox, and he was the kind of paradox that the Russian people represented. He could not relax his hold upon the ideals of perfection that kept calling him, and yet he wasn't ever able quite to fulfill the requirements of those ideals upon him. He was unable to settle for the mediocre and the garden variety, the conventional, and yet again and again he was not quite able to bring within the reach of his power the great dream that hungered him and deviled him and worked on him. He could always see the gross and the refined for he regarded himself (as indeed he was, and as indeed we all are) as gross and refined. A very wonderful illustration of it—I'll just read a paragraph, about five lines, about a struggle he had with a bear. This illustrates what I mean.

> I remember once when a bear attacked me and pressed me down under him, driving the claws of his enormous paw into my shoulder, and I felt no pain. I lay under him and looked into his large, warm mouth with his wet, white teeth. He breathed above me, and I saw how he turned his head to get into position to bite into my temples at once, and in his hurry and from excited appetite he made a trial snap in the air just above my head, and again opened his mouth, that red, wet, hungry mouth dripping with saliva. I felt I was about to die and looked into the depths of that mouth as one condemned to execution looks into the grave dug for him. I looked, and I remember that I felt no fear or dread. I saw with one eye beyond the outline of that mouth a patch of blue sky gleaming between purple clouds roughly piled on one another, and I thought how lovely it was up there.[6]

That is it.

(New York: Thomas Y. Crowell, 1887). Tolstoy's *Confession* relates a mid-life spiritual crisis and marks the transition between the brilliant novelist of *War and Peace* and *Anna Karenina* and the quester for spiritual simplicity among the Russian peasantry, a search that dominated the remaining decades of his life.

6. This passage, translated by Alymer Maude, can be found in his *The Life of Tolstoy: Later Years* (New York: Dodd, Mead, 1910), 74.

When he was ready to get married he sent his intentions to this very wonderful lady[7] using the first letter of the ideas that were in his mind, just the first letters, a whole row of them, then asked her if she would finish the words, and if she did she would know what was on his mind. She did; she wrote out exactly what he was trying to say, and he said, "Yes, that is it." Then he said, "I want you to read my diary." In his diary he had written faithfully, with a kind of relentless attention to details, a kind of thing that makes him the forerunner of the more shoddy school of realism in modern literature.[8] He said, "I want you to read it all, every line of it." And she did, and for three days and nights she wept. Then she said, "All right." They were married, had wonderful children, had wealth, family, recognition, but there was this deep hunger that could find no fulfillment.

He stripped himself bare of all of the things upon which he had depended, trying to see if it was possible for him to get a stranglehold on the meaning of life. He found that if he could be stripped down to life, without all the things upon which men depended, then perhaps he could understand the meaning of life; he could understand life; and if he understood life, then perhaps he could live it with dignity and meaning, and the thing for which he was yearning would be in reach. Almost overnight he became an old man, hair white, face deeply lined. He writes about his experience, and sums it up in terms of an Eastern legend that he had read of a man who was running from a bear, again. He came to an empty well, and he got down in the well to protect himself from this animal. As he was hanging by holding his hands to the limb of a tiny bush, he looked down, and there was a dragon in the bottom of the well. If he falls he will be destroyed by the dragon; if he tries to come up on top he will be destroyed by the bear. Then, as he watched, there were two mice, a black one and a white one, and they were eating away at this little bush that was holding him. Then he looked up. One of the leaves had fresh honey on it, and he said:

---

7. Sophia Tolstoya (1844–1919). She married Tolstoy in 1862, when she was eighteen and Tolstoy was thirty-four.

8. In his diaries, Tolstoy recorded his various sexual encounters with prostitutes, servants, married women, and the details of several bouts of venereal disease; see Tolstoy, *Diaries,* trans. R. F. Christian, 2 vols. (New York: Scribner, 1985).

—Well, at least I can enjoy the honey until my strength gives out or until the mice succeed.

No man can come to grips with the meaning of his own life, not to speak of the life of the world, until he has been stripped of every defense, stripped to the literal substance of himself and must make the decision either to live or die. If he makes the decision to live, then, acting on that decision, he will understand the meaning of life.

We see this reflected somewhat in *The Power of Darkness*.[9] It is a somber, gruesome play. Peter (his name is the only one that I can pronounce easily) is an old man of wealth, and he is sick. He has married a younger woman and has two stepchildren. The younger woman is tired of him. She is in love with the man-servant who is the hero of the story. The servant's mother comes to visit to see how the son is doing, for the son has been rented to this family and the mother comes to collect and see about it. She says:

—Now there is another family that wants to marry my son, but this is a very good thing here. He has good food, and Peter isn't going to live too long, so my son may become the owner of all this. I have some powders here that I brought. I really didn't mean to do anything terrible about this, but I have some powders, two kinds: one kind you feed the person a little every day and they get weaker—they don't die, they just get weaker and weaker; and then here is another kind of powder that you put in the strong tea and that is the finishing blow. Now I paid one ruble for it.

The young woman says:

—Oh, no, that is awful, that is awful! But how did you say you used them?

You see how it goes. There is exchange in these powders. You see the smell of death as it begins to work up, first in the minds of the woman and man, and then it begins to become one with the climate and the atmosphere. As you read the pages, the heaviness in the heart begins to deepen and the shadows lengthen one by one for the kind of death and murder and betrayal that frightens you—why does it frighten you? It frightens you because it is the expression of ideas and impulses the root of which

---

9. Tolstoy wrote *The Power of Darkness* in 1886, based on a true story. In part because of its difficult subject matter, it was not staged in Russia until 1902, when it was staged by the famous director Constantin Stanislavski at his Moscow Art Theater.

each reader recognizes as being within himself. So, Peter dies. Then the marriage takes place, but there comes out of the past of this man-servant some other things that he has done.

Then the story moves very rapidly (it is a gory story) for he becomes interested in one of the stepdaughters. When the stepdaughter is betrayed by him, the stepmother and the mother of the hired servant (who is now the husband) conspire together to marry this girl, whose life has been wrecked by this man, to some young and unsuspecting person with enough money to cover the dower arrangements. The hired servant, who is now the father, goes down into the cellar under the persistent urgency of his mother, down into the cellar with the newborn babe, but he can't bring himself to brutalize his nature completely and finally and unredemptively by destroying the life of this little innocent baby. But she, who represents the wisdom and the guiding genius, even though it is, keeps reminding him of how, as his mother, she has guided him at this point and that point, with the fact always in mind that he, her son, will be rewarded by all the things that she has done. It is one of the most amazing expressions of the complete emptying of one's self of all human decencies and impulses on behalf of the object of one's love, as this mother does with her son. Finally, she makes him kill the child. He says:

—I buried her, and she wasn't quite dead.[10]

Then the nine-year-old stepchild is upstairs, and in her innocence she keeps hearing the cry of this baby. Her uncle tells her she isn't hearing the cry, but this clear bell of innocence, of wholeness, of beauty, of sanctity, of holiness keeps ringing into that darkness; and every time you think the whole sordid thing is over this little girl speaks up again, "But I hear it, I hear it."

Finally when the whole thing is done and the wedding ceremony is set and all the people have come, the hero is sitting out in the barn trying to get enough courage to go in the house and give to his stepdaughter and her husband the formal blessing without which the wedding cannot be consummated. But he can't get out of his mind the long succession of evil that his days have set up. As he sits there he remembers his father, who

---

10. Or, more vividly as in one translation, "It's still alive. I can't do it. It's alive!"; see David Margarshack, *The Storm and Other Russian Plays* (New York: Hill & Wang, 1960), 215.

always reminded him that life was religious in its essence and quality, and that no man can deal with his days without being called finally to account for them. He doesn't commit suicide, but he begins to—you can see it, you can see him begin to knit himself together down in the bottom of his agony and depression and this slough of despondence, until finally there is an accretion of something of integrity and he begins to come up out of that darkness and filth. He moves into the household where all the wedding guests are gathered and he says:

—I cannot give this, but I have something else to say.

Then, step by step, he makes his confession, tells all the things that he has done, and he says,

—I don't know why, why altogether I did this, but I do know that I am responsible for it.[11]

The curtain falls.

Now there are two ideas, two central things I want to suggest to you. The first is that the power of darkness is a power with which the human spirit must always grapple. We do not know what human nature is, quite, but this we do know, that human nature is involved in the kind of predicament that makes of every man one who is both light and darkness. The Pollyanna,[12] sunny attitude, interpretation that we have given to man's nature, that man is good—well, yes, maybe he is good. But man is also involved in the agonizing grapple with impulses and forces that are destructive in character. Any person who acts as if he, for some peculiar reason, is immunized against the relentless boring of that which is diabolical and evil in human life is simply deluding himself. That is the first thing; that the power of darkness is a power that is an essential part of the total experience of man and, particularly, the experience of the individual as well as the experience of the race.

When we say this about the power of darkness in human life, that it shares in all the choices, that it sits there always as a kind of invisible referee, that it reminds us whether we admit it or not when we are voting on [t]his side or on the other side (I don't want to personalize this too much),

---

11. "I did it all myself. I planned it all and carried it out. Take me where you like. I won't say another word" (ibid., 230).

12. Pollyanna, the title character of a 1913 novel of the same name, by Eleanor H. Porter, has become a byword for excessive, unrealistic optimism.

but it means, you see, in the second place, that always in darkness one may find light. In darkness one may find light, for light is also a fundamental part of the totality of man's experience. It is for this reason that the moral struggle becomes finally a religious struggle, for the temptation always is to make the kind of complete separation between darkness and light that will give to us a final dualism, just as in the moral struggle there would be no struggle if we did not rather cleverly and sometimes I think rather stupidly make a distinction between the ends, the goals that we seek, and the means and methods by which we fulfill those ends. Once the means are separated from the ends, then we embrace the dualism, and the solution of the moral problem always is found when it is seen that the means and the end, the goal and the road that goes to the goal, are one and the same thing—so that I cannot be true to my goal, I cannot be true to the ends that I seek and hold those ends steadily before me, if the way that I take to go there is a way that leads some other where. I can't say that I walk over here in this way which is admittedly a complete and radical digression from the ends that I seek while I hold the end clearly in mind as the center of my focus. I'm feeling myself; I can't do it that way, for if I hold the end at dead center, then the reality of the end is constantly contingent upon the reality of the way that leads to that end.

Now that expresses itself in terms of the power of darkness in the function of forgiveness. The thing that impresses me most about Tolstoy, as compared with some of the other men like Augustine, is the fact that the wrong that Tolstoy does, the wrong that he has this man do in *The Power of Darkness*, is wrong done by someone who is strong. Let me say it another way. Please bear with me for I want to get this stated because it is critical. Let me start over again. With some people like Augustine and others who did as many things as Tolstoy has his characters do, terrible things, you always have a feeling that these people did what they did, or are doing what they are doing, because they are weak! They have yielded to an overmastering temptation that brought them under its will and control and power, but in Tolstoy you have a feeling that here is strength that is at the moment unmanageable. It is like a malignant growth, like a cell that has outgrown its pattern and is running wild, but it is alive; it is vital; it is quivering! There is strength, there is power in it as over against the person who does what he does because he is weak. Now, in this action of strength that we see expressed in Tolstoy we find dramatized the authentic significance of forgiveness, for every one of his figures who sins terribly, whose strength runs wild and destroys everything that it touches, has at the very core of his strength a deep, strong sense of inadequacy out of which repentance comes. The forgiveness expresses itself in putting at the disposal of the individual the power to reduce his strength to a manageable unit of control rather than pleading for some additional increment to build him up to a point of forgiveness.

Maybe, as we look at Tolstoy and the type of life he suggests, we feel that we are in fact Westerners;[13] but, on the other hand, if we search our own hearts we will find that there is in each one of us a bit of the Cascade eagle, the eagle that lives in the Cascade Mountains. When that eagle drops down into a gorge, he is higher than the tallest, highest soarer above the plains—because that gorge is in the mountains.[14] There is that element in all of us, and the degree to which it grows, to that degree do we become capable of redemption both in ourselves and in our generation.

---

13. That is, living in California on the West Coast.

14. "And there is a Catskill eagle in some souls that can alike dive down into the blackest gorges and soar out of them again and become invisible in the sunny space. And even if he forever flies within the gorge, that gorge is in the mountains; so that even in his lowest swoop the mountain eagle is still higher than the other birds upon the plains, even though they soar" (Herman Melville, *Moby-Dick*, chap. 96, "The Try-Works"). Thurman confused "Cascade eagle" with the original "Catskill eagle." There is no recognized species or subspecies known as the Catskill eagle, and Melville was probably referring to golden eagles. The Catskills are a mountain range in New York State on the west side of the Hudson River. See also Thurman, "The Narrow Ridge," in *The Inward Journey* (New York: Harper & Row, 1961), 86, and "The Message of Isaiah II," reprinted in this volume.

The Great Hunger
[Johann Bojer]

December 18, 1949
Fellowship Church

In the final sermon in the 1949 Man and the Moral Struggle series, Thurman discusses The Great Hunger, *by the Norwegian novelist Johann Bojer.[1] Long a favorite novel,[2] Bojer's work, for Thurman, is about "the inescapable hunger of the human spirit." This hunger can never be fully sated or fulfilled; and this for Thurman is part of the "tragic sense of life," for life as "it reaches one level of fulfillment, and it absorbs all that there is at that level and then moves on to another dimension and another demand." As in all of the subjects in the Man and the Moral Struggle series, the frustrated search for moral wholeness, at once unappeasable and unfulfillable, drives the characters in the novel onward. Thurman relates the achievements and devastating losses that befall the novel's central character, Pere. This leads to a final reckoning of the hero in a moment of ultimate despair, when he declares that "even if the universe has no meaning in it . . . I must see to it that in me the god-like doesn't die." Thurman was sympathetic to Bojer's notion that all need to share "in the creating of God."[3]*

---

1. Johann Bojer (1872–1959), a Norwegian novelist whose 1916 novel *Den Store Hunger* appeared in English as *The Great Hunger*, trans. W. J. Alexander Worster and C. Archer (New York: Century Company, 1919). Bojer's novels, like *The Great Hunger*, often focused on the lives of poor Norwegian farmers and fisher folk.

2. As early as 1929 Thurman quoted Bojer: "In the midst of his thralldom he has created the beautiful on earth, in the midst of his torment he has so much surplus energy of soul that he has sent it radiating forth into the cold depths of space and warmed them with God" (Bojer, *The Great Hunger*, 327). Thurman compared the novel's characters to the "experience of some unlettered Negroes in the South" (PHWT 1:150). For another reference to the novel by Thurman, see "The Great Moment" (March 3, 1957), reprinted in David B. Gowler and Kipton E. Jensen, eds., *Howard Thurman: Sermons on the Parables* (Maryknoll, NY: Orbis Books, 2018), 108–15.

3. Bojer, *The Great Hunger*, 327.

WE ARE PURSUING another facet of our theme, Man and the Moral Struggle, by calling your attention to a contemporary, relatively, who is from the North Country, and who gathers up into a treatment of the problem that we have been considering tremendous wisdom and a kind of stark power and vitality that are almost overwhelming. The title of the story is *The Great Hunger*, and the writer is Bojer. [It] is a good book to read sometime.

The hunger of the human spirit—what is it? Tennyson puts on the lips of Ulysses:[4]

> I cannot rest from travel
> I will drink life to its less
> For always roaming with a hungry heart
> Much have I seen and known.
> Myself, not least, but honored of them all
> Far on the plains of windy Troy.
> I am become a name; I am a part of all that I have met;
> Yet all experience is an arch where through gleams that untraveled world
> Whose margin, whose margin fades forever and forever when I move.

That is one way. In various aspects of literature and religion we come upon this thing: the inescapable hunger of the human spirit for something. It is a part of the tragic sense of life,[5] you see, for ends and possibilities and glories and wonders, which ends—possibilities, glories, and wonders—stand always just beyond the reach of his strenuous and concerted effort. It is the unresolved dimension of fulfillment that underscores, as it would seem to me, the integrity of the human enterprise. The hunger remains; it shifts its position, its demands; it reaches one level of fulfillment, and it absorbs all that there is at that level and then moves on to another dimension and another demand. I'm never satisfied, really; I'm

---

4. Alfred Lord Tennyson, "Ulysses" (1842). Thurman's quotation is a composite of lines 5–6, 12, 16, 17, 11.

5. See "The Tragic Sense of Life" (January 1949), in PHWT 3:293–97.

never quite it. Now that was true even when I had exhausted all possibilities, you see; and how much more dramatically true in our lives—in my own life, because at no point do I exhaust any possibilities—I'm clear out on the edges all the time.

So that is the idea with which *The Great Hunger* wrestles. It opens with this story which I can sketch very simply, the story of the hero, whose name is Pere, and his wife, whose name is Merle. This young Pere is a boy when the book opens; he is a boy who discovers that he is living with a simple peasant family, and he was under the impression all the time that the man and woman were his mother and father, but they were not his mother and father, as the little children with whom he played advised him. One day a lady swept down into the village. She wore a big flowered hat, and she was beautiful to look at. It was his mother. But the people in the little village were sure that she wasn't quite as good as she should be. Little by little the word began to get around that he was illegitimate, and it did something to him. It would be a very interesting thing for somebody who had the time and the incentive and the emotional and the intellectual resources to make a study of the thing that has happened in terms of the projecting of the will of the individual upon the unresolved aspects of his world growing out of the deeply lying consciousness that he is not within the folds of legitimacy.[6]

People have done a lot of things because—not that they felt they were unwanted but that they felt born out of season. We would not have had the Smithsonian Institute had it not been for that sort of thing because the Scotch boy, whose father did not claim him early—when he made his money he decided he would leave it to the United States of America and asked our Congress to set up this sort of thing.[7] Congress debated for

---

6. This is one of the few places in Thurman's works, if not the only place, where Thurman discusses the subject of illegitimacy. This was deeply personal to Thurman. His birth father was not married to his mother; see PHWT 5:xlii–xliii. Perhaps there is a measure of autobiography when he writes of the "illegitimate boy who was trying to affirm the integrity of his existence despite the withering disillusionments by which his early days had been surrounded." Johann Bojer was also born illegitimate, and his account in *The Great Hunger* likely reflects his own childhood and adolescent feelings.

7. James Smithson (c. 1765–1829), an English chemist and geologist, the illegitimate son of Hugh Percy, the 1st Duke of Northumberland, had no living heirs, and, resentful of his treatment in England, donated his fortune to the United States,

weeks and months and, as I remember reading about it, for years trying to decide whether to accept this grant from this illegitimate boy who was trying to affirm the integrity of his existence despite the withering disillusionments by which his early days had been surrounded.

So we get the same thing here: his father turns up, makes provision for him, gives money to the old people who are taking care of him; and so, overnight now, because his economic position shifted, Pere becomes all right. He isn't quite as illegitimate now as he was because he has crowns in his pocket while the other youngsters hadn't many crowns in their pockets. Then one day the announcement comes that his father is dead, and Pere has a dream that he must be a priest—a priest: that represented the topmost aspiration of his spirit. He goes to the city to see about furthering his education, and the man who is the trustee of the fund is outraged when this country boy talks about learning to be a priest. He says:

—You ought to be an apprentice at some trade and be grateful for that. You don't have any brains, much, and those that you have are not of the first quality.

He then decides that he will go back home, back to this little nest; but when he gets there and realizes that there is no more money to come and the old people realize there is no more money, he begins to feel that he should not eat very much at the table anymore now. More and more the world begins to close in on him. He breaks out again and goes back to the city and becomes an apprentice and works hard, living in a garret; his sister finally moves in and lives with him. Then one day his sister, who has a dream of playing a violin, comes home sick; her throat is hurting, and he looks at the throat and says:

—You had better go to a doctor. She said:

—Oh, nobody has time to go to a doctor. I'm not sick enough for that. I'm no weakling.

He goes to his job and has to sleep on the boat for a week. When he comes back his sister is not there and the lady of the place says, —Your sister was carried to the hospital five days ago.

---

which he had never visited, to establish a scientific institution. After receiving his bequest, and, as Thurman suggests, much debate about it, Congress established the Smithsonian Institution in 1847.

He goes to the hospital, and he discovers at the hospital that his sister is dead. She had died from diphtheria while he was gone. Then he happens to get to the churchyard just as she is being buried, and as they bury her he sits there in the gloom and shadow and decides that from that moment on he will be the master of his world, that God, if there be a God, is only on the side of the powerful and the rich and the dominant and controlling; but God is not on the side of the weak and the helpless and the broken. Therefore he says: —I will be on my own side. He studies now, for the hunger that was in him, for the kind of great creative fulfillment that he dreamed of in terms of the priesthood, now spreads itself out through the corridors of his spirit, and it becomes now something that consumes him with the will to prove—what, he doesn't know.

So he goes to school, becomes an engineer. He meets two friends—they are friends all through the book. Finally, when he is graduated from school, he goes out to Africa and becomes chief engineer at some great engineering project harnessing some aspect of the Nile. He makes a lot of money, and always this hunger. He feels now that this hunger is for knowledge, and he reads all the time, day and night; all the time that he isn't actually working on his problems of engineering, he is searching every little cranny trying to find more truth, more meaning, so that the whole world will be revealed him. He is a little like Faust at that point. Then he discovers that he cannot satisfy that hunger—that it isn't knowledge that he wants but that it is power. If somehow the power that he is able to exercise as his spirit broods over the impersonal and sometimes stubborn and recalcitrant aspects of the world of nature until they become expressive of his private and personal will, if he can take that same power and bring it to bear upon human beings, perhaps that will satisfy his hunger. But it doesn't.

Then he goes back home. He said,

—Maybe the hunger is for my roots. If I can get back, back to the place that fed the little stream originally. If I can bathe myself in those early moments, then perhaps there will be restored to me the lost radiance of a former questing.

So he goes back, and when he gets there things begin to happen. He says: —This is wonderful to be back and be claimed by roots. He goes on a holiday, he hikes, he has all the money he needs, and he hikes around and then he meets the girl. When he meets her he recognizes that she is it; no one has to tell him; no one has to tell her too much. It is a sort of free masonry that springs up. They marry, and they have children, and he has an estate. He finds that he has everything; he is happy; the hunger has been fulfilled!

—So this is what I have been dreaming of; this is hunger; a fireside of my own, a wife and children.

Then there begins to creep up out of that fulfillment the hunger! The hunger expresses itself in terms of the thing to which he has given his life: working in steel as an engineer. He calls it the world-will expressing itself in steel that won't let him alone. He sets up a little laboratory and works on a milling machine. He tries to perfect it, and as he begins to work at it, a bit of the fire begins to come back for he is now putting incense on his altar, you see, and the light is beginning to break more and more. The more it breaks, the more it illumines his face, his countenance; he comes to life now. But that isn't really what he wants.

His friends come to see him. He is going to have his boy christened, and these two friends with whom he was in school, with whom he was in business, come. One of the friends says,

—What are you doing back in this place? You are wasting your time, your energy. With your mind and your genius and your power you ought to be creating things for other human beings; you ought to be making communication more simplified. You ought to be doing these things.

—And for what purpose? Pere says.

—Don't you know that we are not on some kind of rat race on this planet, his friend says, but there is a world will, and that world will is insisting that man must master nature. The more quickly we master nature, the more quickly will we become gods ourselves. You remember the dreams that we had back in engineering school.

—Get away, don't disturb me, Pere says. I'm in love; I'm happy. Of course I have a little experiment I'm working on down there, but that is just to feed something in me.

They leave, but they plant a seed that he should compete for some big dam or something that is to be built, and then the fever starts up again. Figures get into his mind, and he works day and night. Finally he tells his wife: —I'm going into the city, to Christiana,[8] because I want to have a conference. He bids for the thing, soaks up a lot of peoples' money, his money and his father-in-law's money and everybody's money he can get his hands on. He is sure that his figures are absolutely final and that he can do it within the estimate that he has set. But he is not omnipotent; he did not know that the dam would break when they were halfway through the tunnel; he did not know that there would be a landslide and twenty-five of his workmen would be killed and pulled away in green-painted boxes; he didn't know about the exceptionally long rainy spell that would make it impossible for him to fulfill the contract on time. All of that he did not contemplate. One by one, things begin to close in on him, and he discovers that he is going to lose his shirt, everything. The firm in which he had all of his investments went into bankruptcy, so the stock he had put up as security wasn't worth the paper it was written on. Then the day came when everything was auctioned. He and his wife and two children went up into the northern part of the country. He felt he could have licked it, you see, if he hadn't lost his health at the same time. He got sick and had to stay in a hospital, and the bank couldn't wait any longer. All the days involved in the "act of God" were taken up, so everything had to be liquidated.

He and his wife went up into the country to live; he is weak now, but he is recuperating. They have a rich aunt who wouldn't put her money in this thing so she still had hers. She said,

—Let me have your children. I'll take your children.

All over in his mind again went this thing he had been through as a youngster being farmed out, you see, and having no love that he could claim as his own because he found that what he claimed as his own was borrowed. But he had to do it; they had no money. So two of the girls and the boy went to live with this aunt, leaving the mother, the father, and Asta, the five-year-old daughter.

There was a man next door, a brazier who mended pots; he was mean and grouchy. When Pere went to visit him one day soon after he had moved there, he slammed the door in his face and told him to get out.

---

8. The name of Oslo until 1925.

One day when an apple tree branch hung over Pere's yard and he reached up to admire the beauty of the blossoms, this man put his big Russian wolfhound on him. He was a mean man. Then one day Pere heard his wife scream and he ran out into the backyard, and there stood this Russian wolfhound over the dead body of Asta. Pere then, without knowing what he was doing, took the dog and threw him over the fence, in spite of his weakened condition, then picked up the body of his child. The doctor came, but the doctor could do no good. Merle begged the doctor:

—Please do something. She groveled on the floor trying to make the doctor's mind sink into a deeper understanding of the mystery and the magic of the human body and come up with some transcendent cure that would restore her daughter to her. But no, it couldn't be done. So the night came. Pere and Merle sat together in the twilight, and Pere said,[9]

—I seem now to be standing on the promontory of existence. I can't move any farther out. Is this the meaning of my hunger? I've seen men in my time, when they could stand it no longer, rush out into the darkness. I saw, said he, a pale ascetic on a cross who, when he could not stand it longer, said, "Father forgive them for they know not what they do." And he went out into the darkness. But I am not going out into the darkness. I am going to stand my ground and fight! Man must be wiser than the blind impersonal forces that surround him. If the universe has no meaning in it, if the universe is but the steady march of unconscious power, then I have meaning; and I must see to it that in me the god-like doesn't die.

The neighbors of the man who owned the dog decided that they would not let him have any grain with which to plant his field so that he and his wife would starve to death. He went all around the village

---

9. "I sat alone on the promontory of existence, with the sun and the stars gone out, and ice-cold emptiness above me, about me, and in me, on every side. But then, my friend, it dawned in me that there was still something left. There was one little indomitable spark in me, that began to glow all by itself—it was as if I were lifted back to the first day of existence, and an eternal will rose up in me, and said: Let there be Light! ... I understood how blind fate can strip and plunder all of us, and yet something will remain in us at the last, that nothing in heaven or earth can vanquish. Our bodies are doomed to die, and our spirit be extinguished, and yet we still bear within us the spark, the germ of an eternity and harmony both for the world and for God" (Bojer, *The Great Hunger*, 322).

trying to get people to let him have some grain, but they said: —No. No. No. No! So he and his wife were shut up in their own house now with no friends, caught in the agonizing grapple of isolation, a thing that no human spirit can stand.

So Pere gets up from his chair, dresses, takes a basket full of barley, climbs the fence, and under the cover of darkness sows his enemy's field with grain. He said,[10]

—I sowed my enemy's field with grain not because I was responding to the insistence of Jesus Christ; not because I was responding to the thundering voice on some Sinai. I planted my enemy's field with grain that God might exist! Even though the whole universe be indecent, I shall not be, for there is at work in me that which I or nothing can kill; and with that I shall roam the cold depths of space, bound as they be, I shall warm them with God, and in so doing the hunger of my spirit shall be satisfied.

---

10. "I did not do this for Christ's sake, or because I loved my enemy; but because, standing on the ruins of my life, I felt a vast responsibility. Mankind must arise, and be better than the blind powers that order its way... more and more it came home to me that man must create the divine in heaven and on earth—that that is his triumph over the dead omnipotence of the universe. Therefore I went out and sowed the corn in my enemy's field, that God may exist" (ibid., 325).

FAUST
[Johann Wolfgang von Goethe]

February 13, 1955
Marsh Chapel, Boston University

Faust, like Prometheus, is one of the great legends and myths of the quest for dangerous and forbidden knowledge.[1] *The Faust legend originated in sixteenth-century Germany, based on stories of a practitioner of the occult, a Doctor Faustus. From German chapbooks, the legend quickly spread elsewhere in Europe, including England, where Christopher Marlowe's well-known play* Doctor Faustus *was written in the late 1580s or early 1590s. By far the most famous subsequent treatment was by the German man of letters Johann Wolfgang von Goethe (1749–1832), whose verse drama,* Faust: Part One *was published in 1808. In his sermon, Thurman summarizes the play and Faust's pact with Mephistopheles and its consequences for him and the woman he seduced and impregnated, Marguerite. Thurman suggests that the Faust legend raises the question of the "tension that is going on within man himself, the struggle between the impulses of his nature and the insides of his spirit." He gives the example of a lion he met in India that seemed willing to lie down with a lamb; he wonders "is there a clue by which man may see how to honor his feelings without betraying his spirit?"*

In an earlier sermon on Faust, from 1949, Thurman spoke of Faust's desire to experience the full range of possibilities and activities, sacred and profane, and wonders, Is it "necessary to go through all kinds of sin, to have all kinds of experiences, in order to understand the meaning of life"? For Thurman, innocence is "something that is essentially untried; it is fresh, spontaneous, a kind of can't-help-it quality . . . you don't congratulate it; you can't salute it; you don't say anything that is either meritorious or full of

---

1. For Prometheus and Faust, see Theodore Ziolkowski, *The Sin of Knowledge: Ancient Themes and Modern Variations* (Princeton, NJ: Princeton University Press, 2000).

judgment about it. It is; that's innocence." Goodness, on the other hand, is tested and scarred; knowing and having resisted temptation. But the question remains, Can one understand something one has never experienced? The answer for Thurman is unclear. Every person must determine how to limit (or not) the boundaries of their experience. "Life pays me the tremendous compliment of saying to me: You can run the risk. You can run the risk. Sometimes I wish that life wasn't so generous."[2]

In the current sermon, Thurman places the dilemma between experience and wisdom in a broader social and political context. Thinking of recent developments such as nuclear weapons, Thurman wonders if "we have grasped more than we can comprehend," and that if we continue along our current path, without "some kind of creative synthesis," we shall against our will, against our judgment, against our feelings, against our insights . . . as diseased minds, we will destroy ourselves." Thurman suggests, only partially facetiously, given the spectacular failure of humans to understand and creatively use the planet, God might choose other species to be its stewards.

WE PICK UP THE THREAD of our thinking together about man and the moral struggle by considering another of the great myths by which the human spirit, the soul of man, has been able to express that which cannot quite be put into the language of discursive thought.[3] You are familiar with the myth of Faust. You may recall that in one classic presentation of this myth the scene is familiar to the opening scene in the

---

2. "Man and the Moral Struggle VII: Goethe's Faust" (November 9, 1949).

3. In his 1949 sermon on Faust, Thurman had the following to say about myth: "The myth-making tendency of the human mind is a very important one. I sometimes think we tend to say, 'Oh, it is a myth. That is, it isn't true; it is false. Therefore it has meaning, but no veracity.' But when we reflect upon it more deeply we discover that the myth-making tendency of the human spirit is always involved in trying to clarify some dark area, some unillumined area of human experience, and to present that clarification in a form which can be easily apprehended if not quickly understood. It is the way by which the mind seeks to collect the overtones of experience and reduce these overtones to pictures which are understood, which pictures become the vehicle to carry the overtone which cannot quite be grasped by the mind in its pure form. So in this series we have been dealing with myths again and again." Thurman's most extended discussion of myth is in *The Search for Common Ground* (New York: Harpers, 1971), 8–28.

Book of Job. The Prince of Darkness is in the heavenly conclave. It always puzzles me. In time perhaps, I shall find the answer, but at any rate, he is there. And the general discussion goes on about the state of the universe, and the question is raised again about a certain servant, a certain man, Faust. And what a man—brilliant, skilled, creative, seeker after truth. But the Prince of Darkness says, "There really isn't much to him, and I can prove it." He is given permission to do anything so long as it takes place within a certain time interval that marks the measure of a man's life. Then the scene changes, and the doctor himself has come to the end of the road. He has been trying with all of his passion and intellect to understand the secret of nature, the secret of personality, and therefore the secret of himself, but the mind cannot quite grasp what it seeks. He finally gives up in despair and is ready to commit suicide. He is ready to exercise his last option, and as he lifts the deadly cup, there floats on the evening breeze the quiet music from the chapel, and he remembers then his childhood, all the simple beauty and wonder and mystery of life that came to him as part of the early religious experience long before he had become wise and sophisticated, intelligent and smart; and it is this [that leads him] back to an earlier period in his life, when he was surrounded by the fruits of religion, perhaps to the time that he was wise and smart enough to analyze them, and the sediment that was deposited there saved his life.

Now I may take just a minute and three-quarters to say something about this. Apart from the movement of the idea itself, the significance of giving to children the exposure to whatever the race has found meaningful and its high moments of religious interpretation must be faced. It is no answer to the problem to say that as an adult we have outgrown all of these things and we have no particular interest in organized religion, or in institutionalized religion; and why should we therefore expose our children to that which in time they will renounce if they are to be free spirits in a free world? At least we should give them something to give up. That is all I will say about that. That is enough.[4]

---

4. In the 1949 sermon on Faust, Thurman makes the same point at greater length (and arguably, with more reason, since Fellowship Church, unlike Marsh Chapel, had a Sunday School). If it was unusual for Thurman to defend religious education as such, regardless of its quality or nature, it perhaps reflects his conviction that religious belief

The Prince of Darkness encounters Faust and makes a proposition. "I will give you everything you want. I will be your companion, your anchor man, if when you are through with life, you give yourself to me." Well, that is simple to a man who does not believe there is anything left to life. He signed on the dotted line very quickly. Then things begin to happen. The first thing that happens is that he recaptures his youth so that all of the feeling tones by which he wished to involve life and individuals are once again active and dynamic and added to this great feeling quality is the clear focusing of the trained mind. And then he meets Marguerite, the symbol of something else, and she is literally stampeded by his sophistication, by the ease with which he uses words, his manner, just everything that the heart of the country girl wanted but didn't think she would ever get, and here he is. He gives her gifts, the kind the boys and her little community hadn't even seen. She shares them with her mother. "Look what this man has done." Simple mother, who wonders about this. And then there must have been the kind of argument which you can imagine. Well, I can imagine it. So the mother says, "Let's give it to the priest; the church will take it. Then you will be free."

The next time she didn't tell her mother. You know how that is. The thing moves on and on; and yet there is this inner sense of purity that is in this girl, while the thing that harasses and bedevils the mind of the sophisticated man keeps rising up in her and once took the form, "Do you believe in God? Now if you believe in God, then all these things about which I have certain misgivings will be satisfied." And what a speech he gives. I wish I had committed it to memory. All sorts of things about God, wonderful words. She didn't know what in the world he was talking

---

is often at its strongest among children, who can believe without sophisticated doubts, and that, whatever one's later beliefs, a strong childhood faith can anchor a lifetime of religious exploration: "I think that it is just as important for a child to grow up with the experience of religion, with some understanding of what the spirit of man has been trying to winnow out of life in terms of religious experience, as it is for the child to know something about history or about any other thing, for we want the child to be at home in the world. Whether we like it or not, religion is a fundamental part of the experience of the race of man on this planet, and not to be exposed to what that experience has to say to the individual who is trying to learn how to live in the midst of the problems of life is just stupid. It isn't smart; it is stupid. I do not think you have a right to force that kind of ignorance on your child."

about. When he was finished, she said, "But do you?" He communicated to her, however, the feeling that from his point of view, God was feeling, and if you have authentic feeling, that is the spiritual thing, and with that net that had in it just enough of the authentic to be destructive, he seduces her. And then she discovers she is to become a mother. The child is born. She kills her child, is denounced, and languishes in prison. Meanwhile the doctor wanders to another place. He meets her brother, Valentine. The brother invites him to a duel, and he is killed. Added to all these other things, there is murder. On the first of May at the great conclave of the Prince of Darkness, in the midst of the celebration, he sees Marguerite's face, and he then begs Mephistopheles to take him to the prison. He sees her, and in the midst of her agony, there is the vestigial remains of the great moments that she has known with him. As he turns to go, she sees over his shoulder the face of Mephistopheles; and as she cringes away, she dies, but as she dies, she purifies herself before God. All the angels say that as she swings through the gates, she is saved, but Faust has not worked out his salvation. Twenty-five or thirty years later he worked it out. Now that is the story.[5]

There are two or three things I want to point up that have bearing on the moral struggle. Here we see the crucial thing. The focus of the moral struggle shifts for man in his environment to the tension that is going on within man himself, the struggle between the impulses of his nature and the insides of his spirit.

I remember in India walking along the banks of the River Ganges.[6] I saw a holy man coming along leading a lion by the mane. My friend and I approached and stopped at a respectful distance. The holy man delivered a sermon to those who could hear. I asked my friend, "What did he say?" "Behold this lion. I have found him. I have taught him how to restrain his animal impulses. He is so gentle that a little child may handle him without difficulty or threat of danger. Go and do likewise with the unrestrained impulses of your own nature." Is there a clue by which man may see how to honor his feelings without betraying his spirit? That is the first thing. I raise a question. I can't develop it now.

---

5. In Goethe's posthumously published *Faust: Part Two* (1832).

6. In the city of Benares (now Varanasi), which Thurman visited in January 1936, during his time in India.

The second aspect of the struggle here is, What are the limitations of man as the mind of man—who is a part of nature on the one hand and is in a sense always regarding himself as being over against nature on the other—tries to understand nature as if he were other than nature at the same time he is involved in nature? We see it dramatized in our own times. We have brooded over nature until some of its most radical secrets are at our disposal. We can see an inner quality of order, of purpose, of direction in the secrets without making of the secrets the instruments of our own feelings, of our hatred, of our violence. We haven't caught up with ourselves.

On the train last summer coming east, I rode with a traveling salesman. "I have been grounded by my physician," he said. "For the past three years, I've spent five out of seven days flying at least four hundred miles as a salesman covering such and such and such states. Then a fearful thing began happening. I would get to one town and think that I had left something behind, so I spent a lot of time phoning back to hotels. The company finally sent me to a psychiatrist, and after hearing my story, he said, "You have lost your psyche. It is trying to catch up with you. Do not fly anymore now until you get it together." That is a very crude thing, but very far reaching [in] its significance. We are at this moment precisely where in the myth Dr. Faust was. We have grasped more than we can comprehend, and in that knowledge, we try to act as if we ourselves are not earthbound creatures; but we try to assume what our minds have grasped, the totality of our lives, of our experiencing, construction, and we cannot do it. And unless there is some great movement deep within the spirit of man that will relate him to the fundamental purposes of life and their meaning, which purposes include the conscious life of man in the movement of the world of nature around him; unless some kind of creative synthesis, spiritual in character resolves the conflict, we shall against our will, against our judgment, against our feelings, against our insights, but as diseased minds, we will destroy ourselves. God, God may be forced to make a decent world by bringing into his service a whole classification of animals that are regarded by us now as being subhuman. To teach the spirit, to structure the great leapings of the mind, that and that alone will save us.

O God, we make an offering of the best of our thoughts and feelings. What we lack, do thou supply, that all who worship together in this place may walk with more certainty into tomorrow. Dismiss us with thy spirit and give us thy peace, O God, our Father.

> Our little systems have their day.
> They have their day and cease to be.
> They are but broken lights of thee,
> But thou, O Lord, art more than they.[7]

There is so much within us, about us, that we do not understand. We are involved and so great a mass of events, of circumstances, of experiencing, that again and again, we lose our way; and because of this experience which is come to us all, it is well to step aside from the pressures in the carking cares that beset us, to rest in waiting, and behold within us the great settling in the midst of which we may come upon our peace; in the midst of which we may hear thy quiet voice. It is good to turn aside, to wait, to reassess, to reestablish our purposes, to seek forgiveness for our sins, purging for our arrogance, courage for our cowardice, hope for our despair. And we thank thee, O God, our Father, for the resting moment, for the strange settling of the quietness in our spirits, for the whisper in our hearts that purifies. O God, keeper of our spirits, redeemer of our lives, we yield ourselves to thee in quiet confidence.

---

7. From the prologue of Tennyson, *In Memoriam*, lines 17–20.

Brand
[Henrik Ibsen]

March 13, 1955
Marsh Chapel, Boston University

In this sermon from the 1954–55 Man and the Moral Struggle series Thurman discusses Brand *(1866), a play by the Norwegian playwright Henrik Ibsen.*[1] *Unfortunately, the beginning of the sermon is lost, and there are a few gaps in the transcription.* Brand *is the story of a minister—full of passionate beliefs but headstrong and cantankerous—who insists that God demands everything and who in the end is left with nothing. For Thurman, who so often preached on the importance of finding one's true self by placing oneself under the constant scrutiny of God, this sermon was an exploration of the drawbacks of passionate religious dedication. Thurman writes, "Where there is fundamental commitment, there is apt to be a loss of sensitiveness at all the levels of one's awareness." Brand's unbending ideals led him to treat all the people he met with an intolerant harshness that in the end was self-defeating.*

[IN IBSEN'S *BRAND* the title character has an extreme idea][2] of a conception of the will of God. All or nothing. "I want the perfect music or no song," someone has put it.[3] I want the perfect love or not at all. Right is not right when coupled with the wrong. Sweet is not sweet when

---

1. Henrik Ibsen (1828–1906), the Norwegian playwright, was probably the most influential dramatist of the nineteenth century. *Brand* was one of Ibsen's last dramas in verse, before switching to the prose used in his subsequent plays. Another play of Ibsen that Thurman sometimes referred to was *The Wild Duck* (1884); see "The Significance of Jesus V: The Cross of Jesus" (September 1937), in PHWT 2:78.
2. Hypothetical reconstruction of opening.
3. "I want the perfect music, or no song/I want the perfect love, or none at all/ Right is not right when it is coupled with a wrong/Sweet is not sweet when touched

etched with taint of gall.[*] The story is doubtless familiar to you. One feels the ruggedness and the grim struggle as the spirit of man seeks to accommodate itself to the cold reaches of the northland.

Brand is a minister. He has given his life and his mind and his will in one vast and deeply ingrained commitment. The word comes to him that over on an island there is a man who has committed murder; but he is dying, and he doesn't want to die with the blood of his victim on his hands. He wants a minister to help him clear his spirit and prepare to meet his God. It is a stormy night. Brand cannot find anybody to steer the boat across this perilous water. He challenges the men one by one, but they will not run the risk of losing their lives. He tells them that they are weak, that they are full of fear, anxiety, that they are not Christians according to his standards. There is a lady in the group who says as a result of the contagion of his glow, "I will go. I will guide the boat." She was engaged to be married. She renounces her engagement because she feels that the man to whom she is engaged is a coward because he will not do this, and she cannot marry a coward. She and Brand go across this water. They get there. They do the thing that he sets out to do. As a result of this relationship, they decide to get married and devote their lives together to this great commitment which is his and becomes through him her commitment. Mark you, through him, her commitment. They have success, growing out of their devotion. Then Brand's mother, who is a rich lady, who has gotten her money from ways which according to her son were questionable ways, she is dying. She wants her son to do the thing that will help her in her journey out of life. He says, "Of course, I will do it, providing you give over everything you have to the cause." And from her point of view that is irrelevant. She says, "I will give one half. I will give two-thirds. I will give four-fifths." And he says, "You give everything or nothing," and he lets her die without giving to her the tenderness of the love of God, feeling that he is doing the will of God.

Then they have a child, and the child adds wonder and glory to their life. Then the child begins to lose her color, and the doctor says, "Now this is a bad climate. If you want the child to live, you must leave and go to

---

with taint of gall." From William H. Anderson, "Half-Friendship," *Overland Monthly* 3 (March 1908): 287.

some other place." He is tempted to do it because he loves his child. Then he is reminded of his commitment in this place. After that as he works, slowly he sees the life of his only child quietly slip away. She dies. He is thinking all the time, "God requires all or nothing." And his wife keeps some of the little things, you know, a little bootie or dress, just . . . , you know how you do. A gypsy lady comes to the door. She needs clothing for her little child. Brand says, "Give to the gypsy lady all that you have. It is not right for anything to come between you and your commitment." She gives everything but one little woolen cap. She just wants to keep something to finger in the darkness, to comfort her in her desolation. He insists that she give up even the woolen cap. Then little by little her health begins to fail, and the same thing happens as before. If he moves from here, his wife will live. He sees his wife quietly die. Always, God requires all or nothing.

Now he is left with his commitment. He takes the money that his mother left him and puts it into the church, and a new spirit comes into everybody. They have a goal. They are working. Finally, this beautiful church is finished. Then Brand, as he listens to the people talking, as he hears the mayor say nice things to him on behalf of what he has done, on behalf of his mother's money, he says, "You have the wrong idea." He locks the church so they can't get into it to worship. He stands out in front and says to all the people, "Those who are willing to give up everything and come with me to the barren stretches of the wilderness and there in the lonely places work out your salvation, come there." A few people go with him out into the wilderness. Life begins to get more rugged. One by one they get discouraged. They turn on him and desert him. Then in his loneliness, he begins to think a little about his wife and his child, and his whole outlook on life and his experience. Then he has a dream, and his wife comes to him and she begs him to soften up a little, and he interprets the dream as a manifestation of the devil urging him to compromise. Then, as he is in one of the fields, a half-deranged girl whose father at one time was a friend of Brand's mother sees Brand, and she thinks in her mind that he is Jesus Christ. She sees a hawk. Taking a bead she misses him. The bullet goes into a pile of snow and dislodges some rocks, and an avalanche is precipitated and down the mountains there is the snow and the rocks that bury Brand and the girl as these rocks and the snow,[4] as they move on their fulfillment of the logic of their own action, "God, God, God, is love."[5]

That is the story. Now the struggle of the human spirit, of the human will, with its ideal, with its commitment, with its God—and the hard choice that must be made again and again between the loyalty to the ideal and what the individual in the context of his life is able to achieve in terms of the implementation of the ideal—is the heart of the problem. This points up the tragic character of life, for we are always involved in the contrast between the good that we see at any particular moment and the good that we are able to achieve at any particular moment; and the gulf between that of which I am aware when I am most myself in terms of the ideal, in terms of the abstract, in terms of the highest, and that which I am able to do at any particular moment is the measure of the tragedy of human life. Now we wrestle with that, and there are two or three simple observations I want to make.

One is that no man lives in a human situation over which he does not have absolute control without some measure of compromise. The fundamental problem is, "May I live my life under the aegis of my commitment with the kind of sensitiveness that will inform my life when the compromise with which I have to do is one that undercuts the integrity of my ideal and my commitment?" For instance, where does the individual here draw the line?

You remember we touched upon this when we began our series. I believe, for instance, in reverence for life, if I may be personal for just a moment, and yet I have not developed yet to a point that I refrain from eating meat. I am opposed to war and all of the highly organized concentration of the creative fruits of the mind of man towards the destruction of his fellows; and I recognize that a large percentage of all of the income that the government takes unto itself by way of taxes goes to sustain the kind of military enterprise against which my whole spirit stands in revolt.

---

4. As in text.
5. At the end of the play, as the avalanche buries Brand and the woman, Gerd, an offstage voice "calling through the noise of thunder," according to the stage direction, cries out, "He is the God of Love," to end the play; Henrik Ibsen, *Brand: A Version for the Stage*, trans. Geoffrey Hill (Minneapolis: University of Minnesota Press, 1981), 182.

But this year I paid my income tax. So I have arrived at what seems to me to be a working principle which will be [word missing] all the time as I relate to it, and that is this, that in terms of my ideal, in terms of what to me is my commitment to God, I must bring to bear upon it as much integrity as my spirit can generate in terms of what I am able to wrestle from the stubborn, unyielding, recalcitrant aspects of the society of which I am a part, of my own nature.

I make a gain here and a little gain there, always recognizing that what I am able to gain at any one particular moment is far removed in any absolute terms from the thing that I see, so that all of life becomes a process by which the ideal, the dream, the will of God constantly tutors and works over the stuff of human nature, the stuff of human experience, the stuff of social order until more and more there is the yielding, the informing, but at no point am I ready to give myself up because of the gulf between the good I am able to achieve and the good I see. If in my prayers there can come into my mind and spirit more clarity and more insight, not with reference merely to my awareness of the vision but with reference to how I might attack the stuff of life and make it more and more expressive of the will and the purpose of God, then prayer, meditation become necessities for throwing light, insight, wisdom in the hard job of relating the materials of my living to the vision of my heart.

Now just one word; well, not quite one word. There is always the problem inherent in any commitment to God, to the will of God, to an ideal, because in the very nature of the case, no commitment that involves the total of a man's life is ever made on the basis of evidence that is complete. We wait as long as we can, and then we act; and in action there is a margin of the irrational and a margin of that which belongs in a [word missing] to the fanatic. It is for this reason that where there is fundamental commitment, there is apt to be a loss of sensitiveness at all the levels of one's awareness. There is apt to be blindness to all the other values that are involved. A man may be so committed to the ends that he seeks that he is absolutely unconscious of the destruction that he brings into the lives of other people as his commitment deadens his sensitiveness, hardens his heart; and unless he can keep exposing his commitment to the will of God, not his deeds merely, but his commitment to the will of God so that more and more the commitment takes on the conscious character of the mind and will and purpose of God, he becomes [word missing] in his isolation, not only in the life around him, but finally from the God on whose altar he makes the supreme offering of his life. All or nothing? I wonder.

Forgive our wavering footsteps and our wavering mind, and the slackness of our devotion. Breathe into us, O God, as we separate one from the other, all of the fruits of thy Spirit.

Prayer

Deeply conscious are we in varying degrees of the limitations of our lives, the blind spots that cause us to stumble in our pathway, the insensitiveness with which we do the delicate and sensitive thing, the detachment from the struggles by which our lives are surrounded, the condemnation in others of things which we encourage in ourselves, the closing of the doors of our compassion upon the hungry and destitute and naked, the lonely, the troubled, the broken in heart; deliberate actions of violence of the decent impulse and the kindly stern judgment of the spirit of God in our minds and lives. Deeply conscious are we in the quietness of the limitations of our lives and all that they mean in terms of frustration, and the hindering of the kingdom of God in the midst of the people, and we seek in the quietness, the renewal of our minds, the forgiveness for our sins, and the directing of our purposes, and we thank thee, Our Father, for this awareness which we sense as we sit together in the congregation listening to thy voice, feeling the light within us. We thank thee, Our Father, that there is yet available to us time in which to have the [word missing] places of our hearts and lives securely established within us. We thank thee, without pretension, without arrogance, but with great earnestness and integrity. Accept, Our Father, the offering of our hearts and our minds, here now, in this place.

MOBY-DICK
[HERMAN MELVILLE]

April 17, 1955
Boston, Massachusetts

*First published in 1851, Herman Melville's classic work was rediscovered in the early twentieth century and proclaimed one of the greatest of American novels.¹ Moby-*Dick *was Thurman's favorite novel, one that he often discussed in his sermons and writings.² This is his longest discussion of the novel. Interpretations of* Moby-Dick *and its central character, Captain Ahab, are legion. For Thurman, Ahab represents the tendency to reduce "all of the evil in life, all of the problems in life, to one single enemy." He sees Ahab as ultimately a positive figure, "because the thing in him that would make him run away, he conquered. His mistake was to undertake to conquer the whale with the tools of the whale."*

---

1. Herman Melville (1819–1891) was an American novelist and poet.
2. Olive Thurman Wong, telephone conversation with Peter Eisenstadt, January 2012. For Thurman's citation of Melville and *Moby-Dick,* see *Jesus and the Disinherited,* 80–81; *Meditations of the Heart* (New York: Harper & Brothers, 1953), 89–90. Thurman spoke of *Moby-Dick* in his first sermon at Fellowship Church in July 1944; see PHWT 3:87. The lay Episcopal theologian Verna Dozier, who regularly attended services at Rankin Chapel when she was a student at Howard University in the 1930s, writes that "Howard Thurman noted that *Moby-Dick* is the only instance in American literature where white is a sign of evil" (Cynthia Shattuck and Frederica Harris Thompsett, eds., *Confronted by God: The Essential Verna Dozier* [New York: Seabury Press, 2006], 24). If Thurman said this in print or in his unpublished writings, the editors are unfamiliar with it, but it is in line with his critique of the stigmatization of blackness as evil in the mainstream media; see *Jesus and the Disinherited,* 43–44; for similar comments by Thurman in the 1930s, see Quinton Dixie and Peter Eisenstadt, *Visions of a Better World: Howard Thurman's Pilgrimage to India and the Origins of African American Nonviolence* (Boston: Beacon Press, 2011), 185–86. Verna Dozier (1918–2006) graduated from Howard in 1937.

READING: "Because I have loved life, I have no sorrow to die...."[3] We come now this morning to what I think will be the last of the moral struggle. The last in the series on the moral struggle. The moral struggle seems to be most acutely etched in human experience when man is faced with the onslaught that comes from the work, the blind pressure of an impersonal nature or an impersonal social order. When the forces by which he is surrounded cannot be reduced to manageable units and they seem to undermine, and if not to undermine, at least to threaten and jeopardize the essential personal dignity of the human spirit—the struggle of mankind is spent in trying to personalize the impersonal operations of the world of nature on the one hand and the social order on the other.

That is why, for instance, it is so wrong in society to reduce individuals to stereotypes because what happens when we do that is to undermine and reduce to zero the sense of personal dignity by which the individual affirms his life and his significance. We establish a low ceiling and the individual cannot move above it. We see it in families sometimes, and even though you are thirty-six years old, you are still little Johnny or little Mary. You are reduced to a nonentity because you can't get out of the terrible boundary by which you are fixed and which says that your life is not dynamic, vital, growing, but frozen, fixed, stereotyped. The same thing is true of the world of nature. It is amazing how individuals emerge in the process of the impersonal attack of so-called blind natural forces—a flood, a hurricane, and some person who lives three doors from you, you don't know his name, you assumed that he had a name—but when this calamity moves in, reducing all human life to zero, then something begins to stir and man flings the concreteness of his personality into the teeth of this impersonal blind force and makes his character felt on the

---

3. Amelia Josephine Burr, "Because I Have Loved Life, I Shall Have No Sorrow to Die," in Amelia Josephine Burr, *Life and Living: A Book of Verse* (New York: George H. Doran, 1916), 15–16. Burr (1878–1968) wrote numerous books of popular poetry in the early decades of the twentieth century. The poem's opening stanza reads:
  Because I have loved life, I shall have no sorrow to die.
  I have sent up my gladness on wings, to be lost in the blue of the sky.
  I have run and leaped with the rain, I have taken the wind to my breast.
  My cheek like a drowsy child to the face of the earth I have pressed.
  Because I have loved life, I shall have no sorrow to die.

event that would destroy. And we see this in Melville's story. The bare outline I will give.

The hero is Ahab. The hero is the white whale. The story is very simple and yet very complicated. Ahab is a man of the sea, a man who suffered from a calamity. He encountered a white whale once and the white whale chewed his leg off. Ahab had another leg built, but a fever was put in his blood that could never be cured. He organizes a crew, a motley crew, and here the influence of the sense of equality, of social concern, with which Melville was always wrestling, we see it in the cross-section of the crew. Some from the ends of the earth, some are wise, some are simple; there is even one idiot in the group. They are different human beings caught up in the magic of the intensity of Ahab's purpose. And what is that purpose? To find the white whale and to kill him.

The storm comes up and Ahab says to the storm, "You can do anything you want to. You may dry up the bowels of the sea, you may destroy this vessel, you may consume me, but out of my intensity, I can still be ashes." So every time he sees a ship, there is only one question he asks. "Have you seen the white whale?" And if the answer is no, he is through, whatever the person has to say; if it does not have any bearing on the white whale, Ahab has no time for them. He is bitter, difficult, tense, concentrated.

They find the white whale, to skip over miles of *Moby-Dick*, they find the white whale; and when they find him, Ahab is now ready to relate effectively; and they attack and the white whale gets his body full of these barbs and goes down and comes up, and suddenly the white whale that all along has been impersonal seems now to be demonic, personally demonic.

I felt that way last January. I went up to Vermont.[4] Early in the morning, 6:30, I had to get off the train. It was cold, snow, and ice, and the weather suddenly seemed personal. Of course, it wasn't, but I had to do something to survive, so that was the technique I used.

The white whale begins to move on the attack with the result that men are killed, the ship is destroyed, and finally Ahab himself is swallowed up by the deep. In a word, that is the story. And what does it say?

---

4. Thurman spoke at the University of Vermont, in Burlington, January 7–8, 1955.

What light does it throw on the spiritual struggle of the human spirit? There are two suggestions only that I would make this morning.

The one is that Ahab reduces all of the evil in life, all of the problems in life, to one single enemy. (I want you to follow this.) That enemy is the white whale, and that evil thing is external to Ahab, outside of Ahab; and therefore he says if he can but kill the white whale, find him, track him down, and destroy him, then all of the problems of life will be solved. Have you ever felt that way? This thing that I wrestle with is so terrible that it becomes a symbol of all the ill that there is in life. Sometimes we do it with reference to human beings. Here is a person who is close to me and symbolizes all the problems that I have, and if I could just get away from this person, life would be so simple.

We do it as we look out upon society. We said at an earlier period that drink, alcohol, is not only a terrible thing, but it is a most terrible thing in our society; and if somehow we could make it illegal, then all the social problems would be solved. The tendency to reduce all the problems of life to a single simple formula, and to come to grips with that formula and to say that if at last this formula becomes operative, then all the problems are solved. If we could get rid of Hitler, if the Nazi regime could be destroyed, and if all the people who are followers of a policy with reference to that kind of diabolical expression of life were tried, sentenced, and eliminated, then we would get peace in the world.

What Ahab discovered is what you and I must discover, and that is that always there is a straight line moving from the evil in my own heart to the evil that I would eliminate in you and you and you, so that even after you have been eliminated, the central, fundamental, basic problem of wrestling with that which is in my own nature that is against the good, I will have to wrestle with, pluck out, in order that I might get rebirth, renewal; and then I discover that what is true in me is true in others so if I eliminate the man who is the representative of the evil enterprise, all I do on that basis is to eliminate the man. As the Quaker in his letter to John Calvin after he had burned Servetus at the stake in the public square said, "to burn Servetus at the stake is merely to burn a man at the stake. It is not to destroy a doctrine."[5] Now that is the first.

---

5. Michael Servetus (Miguel Serveto) (1511–1553) was a Spanish physician and antitrinitarian Christian theologian and was burned at the stake in Geneva at the

Now the second suggestion I will just touch upon. The great victory in the moral struggle which Ahab had was this: He conquered the thing in him that would make him shrink from the evil thing with which he had to wrestle. When we see the evil, the destructive thing, in our experience, the temptation is to run away, to hide, to seek refuge behind someone else's experiences, concepts, symbolisms, or to say that this thing is not real, it isn't true, to do anything but turn and face that which threatens to deny the essential dignity and meaning and significance and purpose of my life and to look it squarely in the eye and know that I triumphed. If I can relax the thing in me that makes me want to hide and run away. When St. Francis turned the corner on his horse when he was on the way to the great light that has been burning for us all these centuries, he saw a leper, and instinctively he brought the horse around because leprosy was the one thing that he simply could not abide. He had no emotional or religious or philosophical or metaphysical equipment for dealing with leprosy emotionally.[6] He could handle anything else—but don't, I can't stand it. The aesthetics of it is terrifying, and when he pulled the horse around, he realized he could never be able to give his heart to God, he could never be a free man as long as he could not look the leper in the eye. He lay himself bare to it and let it do to him whatever it was capable of doing and survive. That is what we get here. Ahab triumphs because the thing in him that would make him run away, he conquered. His mistake was to undertake to conquer the whale with the tools of the whale. And any moral struggle that would be precipitated for you at one level, for me at another, under God I hope you will be able to conquer in you the thing that is making you run away and to face the adversary until at last he will have no further power over you. This is my prayer both for you and for myself.

---

behest of John Calvin. Thurman was probably thinking of the famous comment about Servetus's murder by the Swiss Reformed divine Sebastian Castellano (1515–1563): "To kill a man is not to defend a doctrine, but to kill a man." The Quakers were first organized in the 1650s, during the English Civil War.

    6. The meeting of St. Francis of Assisi (1181–1226) with the leper is related in the hagiographies of Thomas of Celano (c. 1200–c. 1265).

Dismiss us, O God, with thy spirit riding high in our lives, tutoring us in all the ways by which we may live into tomorrow with courage, with commitment, and with great dedication. And for us, O God, this is enough.

Prayer
It is good to sit together in this time of quiet and meditation, to sense the direction which our lives are taking, to get some sense of perspective with reference to all our purposes and our dreams and hopes and desires, to feel ourselves a part of a company of those who share in this moment the same quiet atmosphere and climate and to sense surrounding us another Presence wooing our spirits into focus, and at such moments it is good to lay bare the heart, to finger gently the private and personal needs, to whisper in silent confession to God the sin, the error, the blindness, the stupidity, the arrogance, the pride, the envy, the weakness, and to hold it there in his Presence until at last there comes stilling over our hearts and minds the great healing of his love washing us clean, renewing our minds, sharpening our purposes, lifting the ceiling of our hopes, directing our thoughts to needs of others, all as we sit together sharing the silence, worshiping God in his holiness.

We rejoice, Our Father, for so great a respite from the pressures of our days, for so much that lifts and strengthens us even as we wait, and we thank thee for the encouragement to our spirits and for the insight into the meaning of our days that thou dost vouchsafe to us now as we wait.

Search us, O God, and know our hearts. Try us, and know our thoughts, and see if there be any wicked way in us, and lead us, lead us, O God, in the way everlasting, Our Father.

The Skin of Our Teeth
[Thornton Wilder]

February 27, 1949
Fellowship Church

This was one of Thurman's first sermons based on a work of literature, a forerunner of the literary themes he would treat later in the year in the Man and the Moral Struggle series. The subject is Thornton Wilder's absurdist, Pulitzer Prize–winning play, The Skin of Our Teeth *(1942), which relates the struggles of the Antrobus family (they are five thousand years old, and live a middle-class existence in northern New Jersey), dealing with climate change (a new ice age, a flood of biblical proportions), and war and its fitful aftermath. The opening of the sermon discusses what he calls the "social revolution" in the black South, a new militancy, and the beginnings of a successful legal challenge to segregation that would culminate, five years later, in the US Supreme Court's decision in* Brown v. Board of Education. *The two parts of the sermon, whether intended by Thurman, share a common theme of looking to what he liked to call the "growing edge," the essential need for new beginnings of life righting and healing itself after setbacks, whatever the impact of previous catastrophes, whether those endured by the Antrobuses, or the first cracks in the regime of Jim Crow imposed on southern blacks.*

The only source for this sermon has various lacunae and inconsistencies, which the editors have silently corrected when possible and noted in the annotation when not.

FOR SOME TIME NOW I have had a growing anxiety to visit one or two important and strategic centers of education in the Deep South. There are great stirrings going on all over the world but particularly in that area because of the rather profound churnings of the customs and habit patterns. Many of us do not realize it but America is going through a very wide[1] period of social revolution.[2] All that we hear and see about civil liberties is but an aspect of the social revolution. The parts of our country that are most—that have suffered most from certain disadvantages—are the parts of the country in which one is able to see, as if under a terrible magnifying glass, the mechanism of this revolution.

In education in the South some very important things are happening. As you know, the US Supreme Court some time ago declared that the policy of the states which did not grant to all citizens the same kind of education was unconstitutional; and since that time, various adjustments have been made to the problem.[3] In certain states, state universities have opened up under certain circumstances. In Arkansas, for example, last year there was a Negro who entered the university and took the same course that other students were taking, but took it in another room. The professor taught this course twice. This year in that same university there is a medical student who is apparently a part of the class.[4]

We should not look down our noses at the state of Arkansas. But nevertheless something is happening. Now they are trying great regional universities that would take in students from several states.[5] The federal

---

1. Struck over for "excited."
2. Struck over for "change."
3. In 1938 the US Supreme Court in *Missouri ex rel. Gaines v. Canada* 305 US 629 (1938) ruled that Missouri had to provide legal education to every person qualified for admittance to law school, in the first significant modification of the *Plessy v. Ferguson* 163 US 537 (1896) "separate but equal" decision. However, the *Gaines* decision did not lead to changes in the segregation policies of southern universities. *Sipuel v. Board of Regents of University of Oklahoma* 332 US 631 (1948) reaffirmed *Gaines* in January 1948 and ordered the admission of Ada Sipuel to the University of Oklahoma Law School, initiating the period of half-hearted compliance with the desegregation of graduate educational facilities in southern states in the late 1940s outlined by Thurman.

4. Stories of this sort were in the news in the weeks before Thurman delivered this sermon: "First Colored Student Enters University of Arkansas," *Norfolk Journal and Guide*, February 14, 1948 (about the University of Arkansas Law School); "Colored Medical Student Files Application at University of Arkansas," *Norfolk Journal and Guide*, February 14, 1948.

5. There were attempts by segregated governments in southern states in 1947 and 1948 to set up regional graduate schools for African Americans. By early 1949 these plans seem to have been abandoned; see "On Regional Universities," *New York Amsterdam News*, February 28, 1948; Mary Spargo, "38–37 Vote Kills Regional University Bill," *Washington Post*, May 14, 1948.

government and several states participating in it give to all the Negroes in that section the same general opportunity for education that are equal to that for the white children. Remember that education at its best in the South, because of its sustained poverty that has its roots in the unique social blindness following the Civil War, does not have any really top schools for anybody. Administrators of the Negro schools are in a very difficult spot; the choice between having regional universities that are being segregated and a watered-down school on the local level is a difficult one to make. And the young students think there is no sound rational basis for accepting either one of the two compromises, and there is a kind of despair in their minds.

I want to go down there as far as Louisiana and Mississippi and feel it at close hand. I hope you will consider that my going is something that you yourselves are participating in. The first few days of my journey I will be doing things on somebody else's terms, for which I will be paid. While I am away Dr. Buell Gallagher[6] will be preacher in our pulpit for a series of sermons on the subject Religion for the Social Order, a field on which he is an authority. I am sure you will find the kind of stimulation that you do not think at the moment you need.

I am put to it about the use to which[7] I want to make of *Skin of Our Teeth*[8] because after reading it very carefully I noticed that it is not permitted to read from the book or quote from it in public without written

---

6. Buell Gordon Gallagher (1904–1978) was a prolific author and educator, and an expert on black education. He was president of the historically black Talladega College (1933–43), and subsequently president of City College of New York (1952–1969.) At the time of this sermon he was serving as minister of the intentionally interracial South Berkeley Congregational Church. See PHWT 3:99 n. 5.

7. As in original.

8. Thornton Wilder (1897–1975) was a novelist and playwright, best known for the drama *Our Town* (1938) and *The Bridge of San Luis Rey* (New York: Albert and Charles Boni, 1927) and the play Thurman is discussing, *The Skin of Our Teeth,* which premiered in 1942 and was published by Harper & Brothers the same year, winning the Pulitzer Prize for drama. Wilder later wrote that the play was in part inspired by James Joyce's *Finnegans Wake* ("Preface to Three Plays" [1957], in Thornton Wilder, *Collected Plays and Writings on the Theater* [New York: Library of America, 2007], 687). Thurman also refers to *The Skin of our Teeth* in "The Quest for Stability," a lecture series he delivered in April 1949; see PHWT 3:312, 317 n. 2.

permission of the author. I do not have that. You are my witness that I am not reading from the book.

The play deals with a perennial problem of human life. I will sketch the story in simple outline. Mr. and Mrs. Antrobus are the central figures. These two people are the human race really. In the first act, the world is slowly destroyed by ice. The Ice Age has come down to the twentieth century, and you get the mixture of the Ice Age concepts and experiences and twentieth-century New Jersey. Long stretch. But as the ice moves across the United States, it becomes increasingly difficult for people to keep warm. It seems that all is lost.

It is then that Mr. A. tells his wife to teach Gladys, their daughter, something of the Bible, how the world began, so that she will have something in her head.[9] He invented the wheel and the multiplication table and the alphabet. He began to teach his son Henry about numbers, about the alphabet, about the multiplication table. And he says that he is doing this and his wife is doing the other, even though all is lost. Perhaps the children will somehow be saved; and if the children are saved, then they will be able to start over again. But to start over means nothing if somehow they have not been able to remember the beginnings that were made by the elders who died in the Ice Age.

The second act is at Atlantic City; there is a convention going on. It is a convention of mammals and vertebrates that represent the human wing of the United Order of Animals. At the same time, others of the orders of the animal kingdom send representatives to this conclave. Male and female. Mr. A. has his family with him at Atlantic City, and many complications arise. His son Henry is off somewhere and has an encounter and hits a man with a stone and kills him. Henry represents up to this point of the story that urge in human life that cannot quite be controlled. He is always getting out of hand.[10]

As it rains, Mrs. A. becomes excited because she did not bring a rain coat. There is an arrangement by which discs are put at certain points to denote certain things. Two discs mean an earthquake; three discs mean

---

9. In the original, there is a semicolon after "head," followed by "who," implying that Mrs. A. or Gladys invented the wheel and the multiplication table. But in the play, Mr. A. is the inventor.

10. A sentence fragment has been omitted here.

tidal wave, and four mean the end of the world. You watch the discs appear. There are three discs finally. Waters are arising. A radio operator finds Mr. A., who is to make the most important broadcast of the year. He becomes involved in all sorts of difficulties. Finally it seems clear that the flood has started and the earth is now being destroyed by the flood. Mrs. A. reminds Mr. A. that there is a boat down at the end of the pier. They can't find Henry; finally Henry comes and says he didn't think anybody wanted him. The animals two by two get into the boat. The kangaroo is asked if he will put the turtles in his pouch.

The heroine of the second act is a fortune teller who constantly predicts that this is going to happen. She urges them to sail. The men taking part in the convention do not pay any attention to the flood. The fortune teller begins laughing when they say they will protect themselves. She says, "You may put stuff in to stop up the cracks and keep the water out but you can't save the world."[11] And as A. goes on his journey with all the primary biological units that will make the new life possible, as they move out from the shore, this fortune teller tells them, "Probably he will be able to start again."[12] This is the second act.

Now, the third act is about a world war. Some war is on and men are coming back; Mr. A. is coming back. They have been living miserably down in a dugout. Down there their daughter's baby was born. They were wretched, hungry, having lived in the dugout without air in wretched circumstances. Now Mr. A. starts to reestablish the family unit. He talks about dreams, of unfulfilled hopes and desires and the dream of peace and the dream about his [...[13]] are suddenly he realizes that his son Henry, who now does no longer represent merely the animal impulses of animal nature but now represents the deliberate clear principle of life, that which is essentially and basically evil, whose basic aim is destruction. And as if by a flash of blinding light, Mr. A. recognizes that all his life the symbol of mankind has been struggling to overcome this evil principle

---

11. "Go back and climb on your roofs. Put rags in the cracks under your doors.—Nothing will keep out the flood. You've had your chance. You've had your day. You've failed. You've lost" (Wilder, *Collected Plays*, 264).

12. "They're safe, George Antrobus! Think it over! A new world to make.—Think it over!" (ibid., 264).

13. Gap in text.

that seems to be a part of the normal, natural [course?] of existence. And it was Henry who was the enemy in war. It was Henry who thought he was always smarting under the prohibitions, the disciplines of life which were determined to destroy him. He has been life in protest. This is why he killed his brother, killed a man in [a] wheelchair. He realizes that between him and his father there must always be this struggle. Now the curiously terrifying thing happens. Mr. A. for the first time realizes that what ice was unable to do, what the flood was unable to do, what all the unrestrained expressions of blind natural force were unable to do, war has done. For he says to his wife, "I have lost it. I have lost it. I have lost it." Lost what? The desire to keep on trying![14]

There it is. Life ceases to be tragic and merely becomes melodramatic. It is like the difference between seeing the man who has been killed by lightning or earthquake or drowning and the man who has been killed by another man. You will discover that in the presence of the man who died from lightning or drowning, there is something in you that even as it recoils from death, there is something clean about it, something that washes you, perhaps because that [way] it seems that the impotence of life is underscored. It drenches you of much corruption, cleans the mind of fear of death. But when you look at a man who has been murdered, there is something nasty about it. You feel unclean, depressed, ashamed of the human race; and in that moment of intensity you wish that [you] could resign, but you can't. That is what war does.

War killed the ground of self-respect, which is the raw material out of which the will to keep on is made.

And then Gladys comes home from school, and senses that all this has taken place in the house. She tries her normal pattern, and then she says, "Papa, I recited today and I had a perfect recitation." He said, "What?" "I had a perfect recitation." Because this girl of his has at her level experienced, in one transcending moment of glory, the vista of perfection. He

---

14. "Antrobus: I'm tired but I'm restless.
Maggie: I've lost it. I've lost it.
Mrs. Antrobus: What, George? What have you lost?
Antrobus: The most important thing of all. The desire to begin again, to start building" (Wilder, *Collected Plays*, 280).

knows now what once again is the destiny of man, and he starts all over again.[15]

Can you do that? Your ice age—you know what it is. Your flood—you know what it is. Your intimate brush with naked brutality, with your fellows or at the hands of someone you trust and love—you know what it is. Can you dig around the rubble until you find the thing upon which you can start building all over again?

If you can do that, there is no power in heaven or hell or in the earth that is capable of destroying you. If you can't do that, anything can get your number. It is not that we escape by the skin of our teeth, but it is that we escape. Do not forget that. To forget it is your peril and mine.

---

15. "Antrobus: You recited in assembly, did you? You didn't forget it?
Gladys: No!!! I was perfect.
Antrobus: Build up the fire. It's cold. We'll do what we can. Sabina, get some more wood. Come around the fire, everybody. At least the young ones may pull through" (Wilder, *Collected Plays*, 238).
Thurman was mistaken about the place of this scene in the play. It occurs in the first act, not at the conclusion of the third.

PART TWO

The Message of the Prophets

The Message of Amos

May 25, 1952
Fellowship Church

This is the first sermon Thurman delivered in the series The Message of the Prophets in the summer of 1952. Thurman arranged the sermons in a rough chronological order, following the dates assigned to them by biblical scholars. Amos is considered the earliest prophet to leave behind a body of writings. Amos, who flourished in the mid-eighth century BCE, was born in Tekoa, a town near Jerusalem, in Judah, the southern kingdom, but he spent his prophetic career in the northern kingdom of Israel. Amos was from humble origins, a shepherd and cultivator of sycamore figs, and was neither a professional prophet nor a farmer. For Thurman this meant that Amos had an unusual degree of independence. "As a shepherd he was psychologically much more independent of the group-folk mind than was characteristic of those persons who were farmers and who were bound or tied to the soil."

Amos's message was consistently one of warning of the power of God's judgment for greed and corruption, and the dire consequences of disobedience. He told his listeners of the likely fate of neighboring countries—Damascus, Aram, Edom, and Moab—for their transgressions, and that a similar destiny could well befall the kingdom of Israel and that their chosenness by God would not protect them. For Thurman, the idea of being chosen leads to the "inevitable conclusion . . . perhaps that we have been favored because we are better." But "the prophet Amos says, that God holds you responsible and you can't escape that responsibility either in fear or in nationalism or any kind of arrogance or pride or might, majesty, strength or wisdom, you can't escape that responsibility. So, if you try to get away from the lion you meet the bear."

Thurman had long been a student of the prophets, drawing both on his roots in the black church and the focus on the prophets in the social gospel.[1] *During the 1950s Thurman was particularly active in writing about the prophets. He delivered two sermon series on the prophets, and published two expositions for* The Interpreter's Bible *of the prophets Habakkuk and Zephaniah.*[2] *For Thurman, what was remarkable about the prophets, despite much that he found narrow and parochial in their thinking, was their call to individual and collective holiness. For Thurman, prophets like Amos preached "how God, how Jehovah, seems to be involved in the life of everybody, all the nations." This was a call that, as Thurman said in his Habakkuk commentary, "has moved through the centuries like the Gulf Stream in the Atlantic, like the deepest and mightiest of rivers.*[3] *Thurman insists that his comfortable congregation in San Francisco "think about South Africa, as we think about Indo-China, as we think about Russia. If we have all that we have—clean beds, all the food we can eat and more, power, money, if we have all these things, it must be because we have been, we have been favored." Do not think that "hiding in your little house, protected by your little acre, under the warmth and aegis and security of your little flag" will protect you from the implacable nature of the divine judgment. "Thus says the prophet," Thurman concludes, "and I don't think either God or human life has changed much since that time."*

[I don't know, as I suggested][4] last Sunday, whether you did read Amos during the week. But in order that you may have a chance to redeem yourself, we will be discussing Hosea next Sunday. Now you have another chance. I'd like to read just a little of Amos for atmosphere:

---

1. Since his time at Rochester Theological Seminary, Thurman was well acquainted with the works of figures in the social gospel movement such as Washington Gladden and Walter Rauschenbusch. Thurman also is an outstanding exemplar of this tradition, particularly among black social gospelers, including Mordecai Wyatt Johnson, Benjamin Mays, William Stewart Nelson, and Martin Luther King Jr. See Gary Dorrien, *Breaking White Supremacy: Martin Luther King Jr. and the Black Social Gospel* (New Haven: Yale University Press, 2018).

2. For the Habakkuk exegesis and the background to Thurman's involvement with the *Interpreter's Bible*, see PHWT 4:136–50. For Zephaniah, see *The Interpreter's Bible* (New York: Abingdon, 1956), 6:1013–34, republished in the current volume.

3. See PHWT 4:148.

4. The opening words of Thurman's sermon are missing. This is a speculative reconstruction.

So now I will deal with you O Israel: since thus I deal with you, prepare to meet your God. For it is He who forms the mountains, and creates the wind, and reveals His inner mind to no man. He who makes the dawn and darkness; who marches o'er the heights of the earth: His name is the eternal God of Hosts.[5] He it is who made the Pleiades and Orion, who turns black darkness into dawn and darkens day again into night, who summons floods and pours them on the earth. His name: The Eternal. He flashes ruin on the mighty till their force fall to the ground.[6]

Your sacred festivals, I hate them; your sacrifices, I will not smell their smoke. You offer me your gifts, I will not take them; you offer fatted cattle, I will not look at them.

No more of your hymns for me; I will not listen to your lutes.

No! Let justice well up like fresh water; let honesty roll in full tide.[7]

Then another little place:

Then the Lord eternal showed me this, a basket of ripe fruit.

Then said He, "Amos, what do you see?" "A basket of ripe fruit," said I. And the Eternal said to me, "so is the doom ripe for my people Israel."

Listen to this, you men who crush the humble and oppress the poor

Muttering, when will the new moon be over that we may sell our grain? When will the sabbath be over that our corn may go on sale? Small you make your measures, large your weight. You cheat by tampering with the scales. And all to buy up innocent folk, to buy the needy for a pair of shoes, to sell the very refuse of your grains.

The Eternal has sworn by the pride of Jacob, "Never will I forget what you have done."[8]

---

5. Amos 4:12–13.
6. Amos 5:8–9.
7. Amos 5:21–24.
8. Amos 8:2–7.

Amos is the first of the writing prophets, and his period is a little beyond the middle of the eighth century. He was a shepherd and a cultivator of rather specialized mulberry fruit trees. And as a shepherd he was psychologically much more independent of the group-folk mind than was characteristic of those persons who were farmers and who were bound or tied to the soil. It would be a very interesting thing if we had time to trace it this morning, the influence of . . . on the history, on the fate of civilizations growing out of the particular kind of social background and orientation to which pivotal personalities in human history have been exposed. For instance, it is a very extraordinary thing that one of the centrally, decisive factors separating Jesus of Nazareth from Paul of Tarsus was the fact that Paul was a city man and Jesus was a rural man.[9] It is very interesting. We can work that to death, but just work it a little bit and you can get some very interesting insight from it. So that a man who lives on a farm, whose fathers before him were there, and for generations this plot has been the place where the family has lived and where the children were born and where they were buried and where they were married and all the other things; the whole life was tied there. It is very difficult for such persons to think of themselves as being individuals. They define the significance of their lives in terms of the group, the rather narrow limitations of the family group and its rootage.

And of course, it is not an accident that no great sense of burning justice has arisen from the prophets whose backgrounds were defined primarily in terms of their being wedded to the soil; for you see you have to become self-conscious, you have to be conscious of yourself before you become aware of injustice to yourself. Oh, you didn't see that. That if I have no sense of self-consciousness, if I have no self-awareness, if to me I am not an individual, then I cannot be aware of what is happening to me

---

9. Thurman again returns to a persistent theme throughout his writings and sermons, that is, a certain class consciousness and cultural location predisposes one to interpret the religious experience through a different lens and therefore informs one's moral perceptions and predilections. Of equal importance, for Thurman, in his review of Amos's prophecy is the notion of the "individual" as being a product of self-awareness and thus able to separate oneself from the herd. At stake in this observation again, for Thurman, is not only the primacy of the individual but the underlying notion of personal worth and value that he ascribes to the message of the prophets and the larger contribution of Israel to religion and society.

as an individual. But the degree to which I become self-conscious, in that sense, to that degree are there exposures in my mind and personality to the things that happen to me. Before that they happen to the clan. It is with reference to the clan that this or that takes place.

We see it in Israel—I am spending too much time on this, but I—we see it in the development of Israel: here is a man who, who goes out to battle and he is ordered not to steal any of the things that he finds on the people who have been killed, and he comes across something, let us say a pretty pair of earrings or something and he says, "Well, that won't make any difference." So he hides that in his saddlebag and goes on; nobody will miss that.[10] But because he does it the whole clan suffers. He doesn't suffer, as such, except that he is part of the clan. And we will watch as we study these prophets, we watch the emergence of a sense of personal responsibility that cannot be present where there is no sense of personal—no personal worth. Well, there is much more to say about that, but let's go on with Amos.

Amos has some visions. He is taking care of his sheep, long watches of the night, thinking about a lot of things. And one of the things he begins thinking about is how God, how Jehovah, seems to be involved in the life of everybody, all the nations. It's not unreasonable that a shepherd who has a primary and sustained exposure to the stars would begin to feel that he is directly related, that all of life, all living things, all the vastness of the universe is under one comprehensive judgment of a universal God. It isn't so difficult for him to arrive at that judgment in the solitariness of his long watches.

At any rate Amos thinks about Tyre[11] and all the other countries around, and they are under the judgment of Jehovah. And if they are under the judgment of Jehovah because Jehovah is the Eternal and is the Ground of all life and activity and is the Creator of all of life, Israel is in some unique way under the judgment of Jehovah because Israel knows

---

10. Although generally the Israelites took spoils after a military victory (including enslaving female survivors) there are some occasions when God expressly forbade this. Violators were punished, such as the tribe of Judah for the actions of Achan in Joshua 7 or Saul in 1 Samuel 15.

11. The ancient city of Tyre (now, es-Sur, a Mediterranean city on the southern border of Lebanon) was a major Phoenician seaport from 2000 BCE through the Roman period.

that it is under the judgment of Jehovah. The others are under the judgment but don't know it. And that knowledge gives to Israel a sense of responsibility; it should give to Israel a sense of responsibility that may not be present in the other nations. So that we see emerging in Amos the thing that will follow us down to latest times: that the measure of a man's moral responsibility is somehow connected, we do not know in detail how, but is somehow connected with the knowledge, with the opportunity, with the exposure that he has to the truth.

Now he comes into town to sell his goods, maybe some wool or something, and he—he's from Judah, you see, but he comes up to Israel because Israel is very flourishing and that's where the money is. I mean, that's where they've been, they've been doing all these things to get the money: robbing people and squeezing the life out of the poor, shortchanging people and putting extra weights and cutting down on the amount; and where the women, he calls these, it is very interesting, he calls these rich, leisurely ladies, he calls them "cows of Bashan."[12] You know they are high-bred cows, you know, well-bred, blooded cows, and they express the intensity of their position by keeping fires built under their husbands so that their husbands would be driven more and more to squeeze more and more to satisfy—more and more. And he watches this. And he is disturbed. And then he goes back. He doesn't prophesize this first time; he just goes back with all these things burning in his mind: I wonder if they don't understand what they are doing? Perhaps they don't understand. I don't know. And then his visions come. He doesn't prophesize until he gets his visions. We may speak of the visions in any way we wish, but I would like to point up one or two of them and then go on to the basic idea and tie it up and I'll be through.

He has a vision of a basket of summer fruit.[13] It's the last go around of the fruit. Israel is the basket of summer fruit that is dead now. This is the last chance. And he has another vision, a vision of Israel, of God stand-

---

12. Bashan cows were a breed of cows, although Amos's vitriolic attack at Amos 4:1 is directed not at the women of Bashan but the wealthy women of Samaria, who, because of their penchant for luxury, oppress the poor. Contemporary biblical scholars find this label insulting and sexist.

13. This is the fourth of five visions that are recorded in Amos: a swarm of locusts (7:1–3); a consuming fire (7:4–6); the plumb line (7:7–17); the basket of ripe fruit (chap. 8); and the Lord by the altar (9:1–10).

ing at the altar, carrying out judgment against the nations of the earth, and his judgment against Israel is far more devastating than his judgment against the others because Israel has had a larger opportunity.[14]

He comes back to that again and again, and because Israel has had a larger opportunity judgment is more severe. Israel cannot say, "But we didn't know." Israel cannot plead ignorance; it cannot plead limited opportunity. It can only say, "We said 'no' to life." So God in this vision hounds Israel and, of course, Israel tries to hide. And Israel can't hide. They run up on the mountain, he pulls them down there; and they go down in hell, and he picks them up. There's an echo of the 139th Psalm there.[15] And then they get down in the sea, and there he lets a serpent chew them. And then he defines it more in detail a little later on: Israel is like a man who flees from a lion and runs into a bear.[16]

Now Amos takes that figure, that thing that belongs to the very heartbeat of the people, and this is the genius of the prophet, you see, he doesn't bring something way out from—but he takes this thing that is a part of the indigenous ground of the life of the people, the very warp and woof of their thinking and feeling, things they'd worked over and worried over and believed in—he takes that and throws the shaft of the divine light upon it, and it becomes something transcendent that they'd never seen before. So he takes this day of Yahweh[17] and says, "Yes! there is a day of Yahweh. It is coming—of course, it's coming. But when the day of Yahweh comes, you will discover that Yahweh has kept books, not on, only on the people who have been doing things to you, but Yahweh has

---

14. As a consequence of Israel's disobedience, God would soon bring about the Assyrian captivity of the northern kingdom (722–721 BCE).

15. "If I ascend into heaven, You are there; If I make my bed in hell, behold, You are there" (Psalm 139:8, KJV). This was Thurman's favorite psalm.

16. "A man runs from a lion, and a bear springs at him: he hides indoors, and, resting, his hand on the wall, a serpent bites him" (Amos 5:19, Moffatt).

17. "The Day of the Lord" has two characterizations in the Hebrew Scriptures. It refers to the divine wrath on God's enemies (Joel 2:1–2; Amos 5:18–20; Zech 1:14–15); or it can signal divine blessings upon God's people (Isa 4:2–6; 30:26; Hos 2:18–23; Joel 3:9–21; Amos 9:11–15; Mic 4:6–8; Zeph 2:7; Zech 14:6–9). In Amos, the former is true. "You long for the day of the Eternal? Ah, what will that avail you ... Is not that the day of the Eternal, danger, not safety, pitch dark, and not a ray of light?" (Amos 5:18, 20, Moffatt).

kept books on you. And what you thought would be a day of light will be a day of darkness, for there is no escape."

Now what does all this mean? It means simply this: that it is so easy for people who are religious, or for people who are secure in the pattern of their culture or their nation or their society, to feel that because of the favorable position in which they are located at a particular time interval in history, that the things, the judgments that apply to people who are not as favorably located do not apply to them. That I am favorably located because the universe is biased in my favor. That's what they felt then—that's what we feel this morning as we think about the hungry people in India, as we think about the Navajos in Arizona, as we think about South Africa, as we think about Indo-China, as we think about Russia. If we have all that we have—clean beds, all the food we can eat and more, power, money, if we have all these things, it must be because we have been favored. That's the most gracious thing we can think, that we have been favored. And then, of course, that raises immediately the question: Why have we been favored and other people haven't been favored? And then we arrive at an inevitable conclusion perhaps that we have been favored because we are better, and the universe has discrimination, and it knows what it's doing and who am I to say that I am not worthy of this if the universe says I am. I mean, I just have one little opinion. Gee, I can't do anything about that. So—I'll enjoy.

And what the prophet Amos says, that God holds you responsible and you can't escape that responsibility either in fear or in nationalism or any kind of arrogance or pride or might, majesty, strength, or wisdom, you can't escape that responsibility. So, if you try to get away from the lion you meet the bear. And when you are sure you have escaped the bear and you are hiding in your little house, protected by your little acre, under the warmth and aegis and security of your little flag, the snake bites—and you have to do finally, with ebbing strength and disintegrating powers, what God required you to do initially while your strength was fresh and your vitality was pulsing. Thus says the prophet, and I don't think either God or human life has changed much since that time.

The Message of Hosea

June 1, 1952
Fellowship Church

In Thurman's second sermon of the series The Message of the Prophets, he discusses the message of Hosea. Hosea, whose name means "salvation" or "deliverance," announced the impending judgment of YHWH upon the northern kingdom of Israel because of its idolatrous participation in Canaanite religion associated with the worship of Baal.[1] A near contemporary of Amos, Hosea's prophetic activity took place during the later reign of Jeroboam II (around 786–746 BCE) and continued until near the fall of Israel (721 BCE). But, as Thurman notes, Hosea's prophesying had less to do with questions of social justice than his call to Israel to return to the covenant with YHWH—"Won't you come back to first principles?" It's an old story, it's as old as life. "Won't you try to recover the lost radiance of a former commitment to God?"

The message of Hosea is difficult and complex, as can be seen in Thurman's interpretation, mainly because the prophet's passionate and mixed declarations of doom and compassion are cloaked in the metaphor of the "harlotry" of his wife, Gomer, which refers to Israel's infidelity to YHWH. Thurman offers a rather creative and sympathetic reading of Gomer (whom he calls "Gomah"), who bore the pejorative labels of "whore," "harlot," and "temple prostitute."[2] He invites the reader to empathize with her desire to

---

1. Baal was an ancient fertility god who was worshiped by the Canaanites and other peoples in the region. Among his many titles, Baal was also called the Lord of Rain and Dew, the two forms of moisture that were indispensable for fertile soil in Canaan.

2. Scholars debate whether Gomah (or Gomer) was Hosea's actual wife or an allegory of the relation between YHWH and the kingdom of Israel. Thurman seems to favor the former interpretation. Described in the King James Version as "a wife of whoredoms and children of whoredoms (Hos 1:2), there are various translations of the pejorative term as "harlot," "prostitute," or "whore." Contemporary feminist/

conceive and her despair as a disempowered woman living within a culture that placed the highest value on procreation. He remembers an experience in India where he saw a Hindu woman place her offering at a temple "hoping that the God that controls all of the processes of life, including the opening of the womb, would be merciful to her and let her have a child, that she might keep her husband."

Today we are dealing with the message of Hosea, and I have written certain excerpts from the book. I'd like to read them to you. The translation is Moffatt.[3] And I am sure that with the promise that was implied last Sunday, you, during this past week, read the Book of Hosea. Now when we start with Isaiah you will have a lot of reading to do. Then, if you haven't been reading all along, Isaiah will be a little more difficult in terms of time. So I thank you very much for your reading.

"Now then"—this is what Hosea says about Israel and then about Gomah, his wife—"Now then I will block up her path with a thorn hedge and bar the road against her, till she cannot find her way."

> She will pursue her lovers and miss them, and never find them: then she will say, Let me go back to my first husband; I fared better with him than today.[4]

---

womanist interpretations dispute these characterizations and argue for ways in which the marriage of Hosea and Gomer point to the hierarchal, dualistic, and paradigmatic power dynamics that influence the reading and interpretations of Scripture. See Renita J. Weems, *Battered Love: Overtures to Biblical Theology* (Minneapolis: Fortress Press, 1995), 22. Other related feminist and womanist interpretations include Phyllis Bird, "'To Play the Harlot': An Inquiry into an Old Testament Metaphor," in *Gender and Difference in Ancient Israel*, ed. Peggy L. Day (Minneapolis: Fortress Press, 1989), 75–94; Alice Keefe, "The Female Body, the Body Politic, and the Land: A Sociopolitical Reading of Hosea," in *A Feminist Companion to the Later Prophets*, ed. Athalya Brenner (Sheffield: Sheffield Academic Press, 1995), 70–100; Gale A. Yee, "Hosea," in *Women's Bible Commentary*, ed. Carol A. Newsom and Sharon H. Ringe (Louisville, KY: Westminster John Knox, 1998), 195–202.

3. *A New Translation of the Bible Containing the Old and New Testaments* (New York: Harper & Brothers, 1922), by the Scottish biblical scholar James Moffatt (1870–1944), based on the latest biblical scholarship of that time, was Thurman's preferred translation.

4. Hosea 2:6–7.

Another excerpt:

> I will make the dale of trouble a door of hope.[5]

Isn't that a good line? Dale of trouble a door of hope. Another:

> Ephraim allows himself to be mixed up with foreigners.[6]

And then this choice piece of imagery:

> Ephraim has become a cake unturned.[7]

Can't you get the figure: done on the outside, raw on the inside. Oh, it's wonderful.

> Foreigners eat away his strength unknown to him, yet they will not return to their God.[8]

Another:

> They sow the wind and they reap the whirlwind.[9]

You've heard that one, haven't you? even though we haven't read Hosea.

> No stalk in their shoot. It bears no fruit. If fruit is born a foreigner would devour it.[10]

And then this:

> A prophet is a crazy fool. A man inspired is a man insane. The prophet is God's watchman.[11]

---

5. Hosea 2:15.
6. Hosea 7:8a.
7. Hosea 7:8b.
8. A conflation of verses from Hosea 7:8–10 (Moffatt). The full passage reads:
Ephraim allows himself to be mixed up with foreigners;
Ephraim has become a cake unturned as it was baked.
Foreigners eat away his strength, unknown to him;
Grey hairs are on him here and there, unknown to him.
Robert Alter (*The Hebrew Bible: The Prophets* [New York: Norton, 2010], 1221) has "loaf" instead of "cake," and compares it to the baking of pita bread on coals.
9. Hosea 8:7a.
10. Hosea 8:7b.
11. Hosea 9:7–8, Moffatt. Full text reads:
Israel clamors,
A prophet is a crazy fool,
A man inspired is a man insane!—

Another:

> Because you relied on your chariots, on your hosts of war horses, in your towns shall tumults rise and all your forts be crushed. I drove them with a harness of love.[12]

Isn't that wonderful?

> But my people are now weary of revolting. They cry to me. Ephraim, how can I give you up; Israel, how can I let you go? I will not execute my anger; I will not ruin Ephraim again for I am God, not man.[13] Thus I, who shepherded you in the desert, in that houseless land, you fed and filled yourselves and grew proud and forgot me.[14] Come back to your God, O Israel, for your faults have made you fall.[15] I will be like dew to Israel: he shall blossom like a lily and strike roots down like a poplar.[16]

Isn't that an interesting imagery? He will blossom like a lily but his roots will be strong like a poplar: a combination of goodness and innocence.[17] Very interesting.

> His branches shall spread out, his leaves fresh as an olive's, his scent like the scent of incense. Once more shall they live under my shadow, well-watered as a garden, flourishing like a vine and fragrant as Lebanon's wine.[18]

Hosea is the second of the writing prophets, as we pointed out last Sunday. Unlike Amos, Hosea was a peasant. He was rural. He was, as it

---

Such is the pitch of your iniquity,
The pitch of your hostility.
The prophet is God's watchman placed over Ephraim,
And yet his paths are snared;
Within the temple of God, men are hostile to him!

12. Hosea 10:14.
13. Hosea 11:7–9.
14. Hosea 13:5–6.
15. Hosea 14:1.
16. Hosea 14:5.
17. For Thurman, innocence is given without knowledge; goodness, however, is achieved through knowledge and responsibility. See HT, *The Search for Common Ground*, 26–27.
18. Hosea 14:7.

were, a dirt man. Sensitive, poetic, gripped by one terrifying passion. And that was that Israel belonged to God and God belonged to Israel. His concern is with the apostasy of Israel in the way in which Israel had taken up idolatrous worship. He is not particularly concerned, as Amos was, with righteousness, with the way the impersonal city dweller, the businessman; the traffic of city life tended to cause men to build power and securities for themselves in a secondary and tertiary manner, being cut off from having a face-to-face contact with the misery that their operations had precipitated. We find nothing in him that says, "Let justice roll down like a river."[19] He isn't concerned with social justice, as such, but he is concerned with personal piety and the way in which that piety makes it possible for an individual to live a life worthy of God.

His story is a very tragic one, in some ways. He married; he married a lady whose name was Gomah. She was the daughter of a man who was one of the leaders of the Baal cult. And their first child was born, and he said the name of this child shall be Jezriel, for it is in the valley of Jezriel[20] that Jehovah will wreak his vengeance upon Israel for violating the covenant and failing to be true to him. And then it seems as if his wife became barren. And the pattern of life in which she had lived, the cultists and the religious experience which was a part of her history and development in the time of her crisis, came to her rescue. It's very interesting how the things that loom in their significance in times of crisis usually are the things that have been an intimate part of the process of your living. It is very interesting. And the things that you study, etc., will make a kind of veneer, and you move on that level; but when the pressures begin to close in on you, the thing that you reach for is the thing that is the deepest part of your experience, the thing that has been the longest, sustained part of your experience.

I remember, when I was in divinity school, one of my very close friends was a Japanese classmate, and he spoke English beautifully. And I shall always remember that when he preached his senior sermon and

---

19. Amos 5:24.
20. The name Jezreel means "God sows" (1:4–5). There were two other children: a daughter, Lo-ruhamah, which means "not pitied" (1:6–7), and another son, Lo-ammi, which means "not my people" (1:8–9). Each child symbolically represents the deteriorating state of the nation.

we were all listening, suddenly he began talking about something that plowed way down in him, and without ever realizing it he began preaching in Japanese, just like that. So when Gomah wanted another child and she couldn't have one, the behavior pattern with which she was familiar came to the rescue. So what did she do? She went to the temple of Baal, and there in that ceremonial, the significance of which we do not quite understand at this far distance, but out of our conceit we have called it temple prostitution, she conceived.[21]

It is very interesting isn't it, this—well I don't want to get off on that aside, but it's interesting. I remember standing outside the Kalighat Temple in Bombay—either Bombay or Calcutta, one of them. Calcutta, I guess it was.[22] Anyway, one of them. And at the temple, the only Hindu Temple in which there is animal sacrifice. And hard by this temple there is a thorn tree, and the thorn tree has tied on it all sorts of offerings. And I stood there watching one day, and I saw a little Hindu lady, with trembling devotion, take from out of her sari a little precious package. Then with some words that I did not understand, she tied that package to the thorn tree as her offering, hoping that the God that controls all of the processes of life, including the opening of the womb, would be merciful to her and let her have a child, that she might keep her husband. And that's what Gomah did; that's what she did. We can understand that.

So at first this child that was born after that was given a certain name by the prophet, and then another child was born under the same circumstances. But all that was deepest in Hosea also came to the rescue of Hosea in his crisis. And what was deepest in Hosea? Jehovah was the only true God, and that Israel had had a private, primary covenant with Jehovah, and that any flirtations with other gods, other cults, whatever may be the nature of the extremity that drives a man, any flirtation with any god other than that of Israel is idolatry, is violation of the love of God and the covenant. Therefore what Gomah had done was to put a Baal cult

---

21. A similar episode, looked on with more favor in the Hebrew Bible, is Hannah going to a priest in Shiloh, seeking an end to her infertility. She subsequently gave birth to the prophet Samuel (1 Sam 1:1–20).

22. At the Kalighat Kali Temple in Kolkatta, dedicated to the goddess Kali, twenty black goats are sacrificed and slaughtered every day. However, animal sacrifice is practiced in many other temples in contemporary India.

over against the worship of Yahweh, and to draw on the vitality of that cult to fertilize her body and add shame to Israel. And she became a harlot, an outcaste in the love of her husband. And he could not forgive her, not merely because she had borne other men's children but because she had dared to insist that Baal could do for her what Jehovah couldn't do. And if she's right, if she's right, reasoned the prophet, if she is right, then the nerve center of my consent is paralyzed. If Gomah is right about Baal, then I am wrong about Jehovah. And if I am wrong about Jehovah, then all of the meaning of life, all of the fateful significance of the covenant, all of the magic and mystery and beauty of the brooding Yahweh over the fluctuating Israelites means nothing.

And so it was an issue on which turned the very fate of a religious faith. There it is. Then, whether it was a rationalization, I suppose some modern students of psychology would say a lot of interesting things about why he did this; why he said this or that, but that is beside the point. He tried to reduce his problem to a manageable unit. Now I will get to the heart of it in just a minute.

How can this problem, this great problem I have make sense? That's what we are always trying to do, isn't it? You see, whatever your problem may be, however great your tragedy may be, if you can somehow pull it down to size, you can take care of it. But if you can't pull it down to size and it romps all over you, then it may actually dethrone your reason. But however terrible it is, if you can somehow reduce it to a manageable unit, then you can ride it rather than having it ride you. And that is what he was trying to do. How can I manage this? How can I think about it in a way that will keep me from being destroyed by it?

"Ah!" said he, "I am being taught something about Israel in this. Look at Israel. She has behaved the very way Gomah has behaved and what has God done? What has Jehovah done? Well, Jehovah was hurt, just as I've been hurt." And when he felt, you see, that Jehovah was hurt as he was hurt and for fundamentally the same reason, then that softened his hurt because Jehovah's shoulders were broader than his. And if somehow he could shift a little of it over to Jehovah, then that was one way by which he could reduce it to a manageable unit. And that is, of course, at once the secret of the confessional, isn't it. It's very interesting. So, he says that Jehovah looks upon Israel with the same sort of, first anger, disgust, disdain, and then pity, then compassion because Jehovah loves Israel. And because Jehovah loves Israel he can never let Israel go. Now that's what he is saying: because he loves Israel he will not let Israel get altogether out of his hands. But how can he keep Israel without condoning what Israel has done? That's his problem, you see. So he says, Jehovah says to Hosea, "Go back and get the lady. Take her from her misery and her sin; reestablish her in your household. Reduce all of her exposures to other human beings to zero, and in the long quiet let your love have a chance to work its way. Don't give her up."

"How can I do that?" said the prophet. "I'll be held up to ridicule and embarrassment and humiliation."

"But this is what you must do because this is what Jehovah is doing with Israel. Then out of the depth of his own struggling and the new and abiding insight that had been generated in his mind and spirit, he looks now, for the first time really, out upon Israel. And he goes from the little town into the city, and in the city his little peasant soul was simply blasted. Of course, in the little town, where there wasn't anything else to do and the pressures were intimate and primary pressures, he could understand why the people would be worshipers of Baal; it was a fertility cult. But in the city, the sophisticated place where they were exposed to books and knowledge and all those things, in the city of course he was not expecting to find it, and there in the city he found everything.

Not only did he find Baal worship, but he found that the leaders of the people, the priests, the politicians, the statesmen, all the guides of the social forces that determine the life of the people and define the significance of that life, that these people were, at their very heart, corrupt: full of panic and fear because they had drifted far away from the security, the emotional and the political and the intellectual security that came from the awareness that they were Yahweh's people, and they were worshiping Yahweh and being true to Yahweh. When they separated from Yahweh and a part of the social process itself became this radical departure from the genius of Israel, then they floundered; they were people without a spiritual home; they were people without any sense of security. And what happened to them? They lost their nerve. And when they lost their nerve then they began doing all sorts of things, and one of the things they did was to try to let political alliances become a substitute for depending upon Jehovah. Assyria, Egypt, running, knocking at every door. We can't stand alone in the presence of the menacing forces that surround us—we must have help. And the only way that we can get the help is to make these alliances, and we can establish out of our own security, our money, that sort of thing, we can make it worthwhile to these other peoples to join with us against the common enemy.

What does that sound like to you? What does it sound like? And because so much emphasis, says Hosea now—since way back, you see, BC—because of this emphasis upon the foreign alliances, Hosea says that all sorts of confusion, chaos, and upheaval turned up at home. Interesting! Because he had said to the masses of the people that there was no longer any confidence in the genius of the people themselves and the religious and political doctrine out of which Israel was born. And if the leaders of Israel have no confidence in that, but must project their fears beyond their borders and hope to guarantee their security by these external alliances, then what happens to the little man who can only depend upon his job or his neighbor or his friend. The fundamental confusion of the prime movers of the state and the church cuts the ground from under the simple man who has nothing to depend upon in his environment but the stabilities of that environment, guaranteed by those who hold in their hands the social process. And if they don't have any faith, then we are bankrupt.

Well, Hosea said, "Won't you come back to first principles?" It's an old story; it's as old as life. "Won't you try to recover the lost radiance of a former commitment to God?" And then he gets angry again. His mind just moves up and down like that: one time crying out against all of this apostasy and then another time saying, oh, how God loves Israel. God will not take his hand off Israel. And finally that shuttling back and forth between these two poles of emotion: "At last," he says, "I see now how to reconcile my problem. God will not let Israel go and yet God cannot condone Israel's sin. If he keeps Israel, does it mean that he condones Israel's sin? No. No! No! No! Perhaps the purpose of the suffering, of the punishment is to redeem Israel and make it possible for Israel to win the right to be in the covenant.

And out of Hosea, then, comes the great doctrine that love has a heart that is as warm as fire, but it works often in conjunction with a brain that is as cold as ice. Punishment of sin, the righteous goal can't withhold that. It's a part of the moral order. But God can keep his hands on you and not let you go while the logic, the relentless logic of the operation of antecedent and consequence works its way out in your life. Now that's it. That's it.

Do you see what he is saying? Do you see? And what it means for us? Have you said over and over again as you contemplated the present moment in human history that God must be evil to keep the world full of war? Have you thought that? It's the same problem that Hosea has. If life in Western civilization had unfolded in a manner (please hear what I am going to say and I am almost through now), if life in Western civilization as it has been for the last hundred years, hundred and twenty-five years, if that life had not yielded world wars, there would be no integrity in the moral process itself.

Wars do not spring full grown like Minerva from the head of Zeus: wars are the unfolding logic, the relentless movement of social processes that end in that kind of disaster. And if that were not true, we could have no confidence in the morality of life. But that doesn't mean that God is outside of it. But to me the logic of history is that God is in history, guaranteeing the relentless movement, the pulsebeat, the flinging of antecedent and consequence, of reaping and sowing inherent in the process.

Now that being the fact, and I think it is, it is my hope, my simple hope, that we will discover, even in the midst of the carnage and the results of our own behavior, some margin of wisdom that will be deep within our social process the symbol that God has not taken his hands off, not only off of America, but off the life of man on this planet. For if something happens to us, my friends, that destroys within us the faith that is as deep as life that the ultimate destiny of man is a good destiny, if that is destroyed in us, then all of life, whatever may be our position in it, will be but a grinning skull and crossbones. But with that faith we can work, struggle, and anticipate the redemptive process of the spirit and the will of God.

The Message of Isaiah I

June 15, 1952
Fellowship Church

As a part of the Message of the Prophets sermon series, Thurman delivered two sermons on Isaiah, the presumed author of the first thirty-nine chapters of the Book of Isaiah. Isaiah, a Jerusalemite, lived in turbulent times and was active from approximately 740 to 700 BCE, a period that included the destruction of the kingdom of Israel by the Assyrians.

In the first sermon, Thurman speaks of Isaiah's prophetic calling and mission, and how prophets need to accept that being misunderstood and traduced are simply part of the calling and the mission. Thurman lauds Isaiah's utopian vision as one that does not focus on material "chicken in every pot" improvements but in humanity losing its fear and attendant "egocentric compulsions."[1] In the second sermon, Thurman says that Isaiah argues against a deterministic view of history, history as simple cause and effect; Thurman argues that Isaiah was encouraging his listeners to try to discern the underlying dynamic of history and God's complex relation to the Israelites, who are sometimes severely chastised but never abandoned. Thurman further states that this is applicable to personal lives as well, and means going beyond thinking that "all of the meaning of your life is wrapped up in the narrow time band of your antecedents and consequences."

For this Sunday and next Sunday we will be working on the first thirty-nine chapters of the Book of Isaiah, and on the last we will deal with the prophetic insight of Deutero-Isaiah, which is Second Isa-

---

1. See the development of this argument in HT, *The Search for Common Ground*.

iah beginning with chapter 40.² So if you are interested, will you read between now and next Sunday, then, the first thirty-nine chapters of Isaiah; and after next Sunday read the rest of the book.

I want to read just a few passages:

"Hear O Is . . ."³

Two aspects of this. I suppose that in all fairness to the background material, I should say that the Book of Isaiah is written by several authors, but you need not bother your minds with all of this. It is divided into two major sections, the first thirty-nine verses [chapters] having to do with the man who lived in one part of the eighth century and the last chapters, from forty on, have to do with a man who lived in another period and another age dealing with another problem. And within the first thirty-nine chapters there are several little poetic gems, prophecies that obviously could not have been written by Isaiah but are introduced into the composite from a point of view and from an historical moment that came long after Isaiah had lived and died. But we need not be bothered about that. The important thing is that the book has been preserved for us, and it is one of the great tidal waves in the religious history of the human race.

Isaiah was an aristocrat, city bred, sensitive, poetic, brooder.⁴ In the year that King Uzziah died, one day when he was seated—he, referring to Isaiah—was seated in the temple lost in meditation and in prayer. He does not tell us what was on his mind; the only thing that he records is that he was in the temple when something very tremendous happened. He had a vision, he had a moment, a moment when like a flash of blinding light the total meaning of human existence flashed upon his mind.⁵ It's a

---

2. The editors are publishing a different sermon on Second Isaiah in this volume, "Man and the Moral Struggle: The Prophet of Deutero-Isaiah," delivered September 25, 1949.

3. Although the transcription indicates that "Israel" might be the next word, the familiar expression "Hear, O Israel" is not in Isaiah. Perhaps Thurman quoted from the opening of Isaiah, "Hear, O Heavens and give ear, O earth, for the Lord has spoken" (Isa 1:2). The recording of the sermon omitted Thurman's other selections from Isaiah.

4. Isaiah, son of Amoz, the author of the bulk of Isaiah 1–39, was probably a well-born native of Jerusalem, but the Book of Isaiah says little about his background.

5. "In the year of the death of King Uzziah, I saw the Lord seated on a high and lofty throne, his trailing robes spread over the temple floor, and seraphs hovered round him, each with six wings, two covering the face, two covering the body, and two to fly

very interesting thing, these moments, and there is nothing more tragic, I think, in human life than to be visited by a moment without realizing it.

The little poem, well, it isn't really great poetry but it's all right, by Sara Teasdale, about the lady who was climbing the mountain, and she said, "When I get up to the top it will be very wonderful because I'll get a view as far as my eyes can reach. I will get pure mountaintop air, and I'll have a sense of tremendous relief that I am not valley bound any longer. But the briars were always pulling at my gown. I must have crossed the crest some time ago, but the briars were pulling at my gown and now all of the rest of the way will be only going down. Crossed the threshold, the crest, the moment, but I was so involved in details, in tiddly-winks, that I didn't know it.[6] Didn't know it. Interesting. Isaiah's moment came and he was ready.

And what happened in that moment? I wish I could tell you. It seemed as if as he looked up towards the altar that all of the temple, the walls, the boundaries, pushed out and out and out and out until at last they enveloped the entire ebb and flow of the life of man and existence. And there was God, seated at the central place, and his glory, the wonder, the awe, the magic, the mystery, the shekinah[7], the uncreated light filled everything. And there were angels in this vision, angels that in the presence of this movement of pure holiness covered their faces with their wings as the symbol of their humility; they covered their feet with their wings and then, then they flew away filling all the space. And while all that was going on Isaiah suddenly realized that he was a man who was dirty, unclean. No one said anything to him about it, but the relentless enveloping of this holy life defined for him the limitations of his own life.

"I'm an unclean man. How do I know that I'm unclean? When I look at this and then look at this, I don't need anybody to tell me. And not only am I unclean and I am on the hunt," says Isaiah, "I am on the hunt

---

with. They kept calling to one another, Holy, holy, holy is the Lord of hosts, his majestic splendour fills the earth" (Isa 6:1–3, Moffatt).

6. Thurman is paraphrasing "The Long Hill," from Sara Teasdale, *Flame and Shadow* (New York: Macmillan, 1920), 121; see PHWT 4:204 n. 9. Sara Teasdale (1884–1933) was an American poet.

7. The shekinah is the Hebrew term for the indwelling presence of God, though it is a rabbinic, not a biblical, term.

for holiness, for the mind and the spirit of Jehovah; I want God, I'm a seeker, I'm searching, the sand is hot under my feet. And if it be true that I am unclean, despite the way my soul is exercised for holiness, what must be true of Israel that isn't even interested in the search! I'm unclean— I dwell among people who are unclean." And then, instead of running away, instead of hiding from the ravages of absolute purity and holiness as Newman, you may recall, makes the soul in the Dream of Gerontius. You remember how he flees from the presence of God when he realizes how whole God is and unwhole he is, and he says, "Take me away. Take me away. Let me go to some dark corner of the universe where I may be hidden, that my soul might gather itself together in recovery from the ravages of absolute purity."[8]

No, not Isaiah. Isaiah kept looking, transfixed, and then something else happened. It seemed as if an angel took a live coal from the altar and put the live coal on his lips and purified them.[9] He didn't rate it: it happened. And then while he was still there, he heard a voice. The voice said, "Who will go for us? Somebody must go to the people. Who will go?" And then Isaiah said, "Here am I. Send me."[10]

How wonderful! to have a tremendous religious experience, a tremendous experience of illumination and then, while you are under the massive pressure of this fresh orientation, to get a job analysis. Wonderful! So that you can implement at once, in detail, against the background of your own equipment before the vision, you can implement the vision now in terms that will be increasingly significant and relevant to your own living. He was a prophet already. And the voice said—his voice said to God, "I'll go. I'll take the message."

---

8. "Take me away, and in the lowest deep/There let me be," from *The Dream of Gerontius,* line 347, a poem written in 1865 by St. John Henry Newman (1801–1890), the English theologian who converted from Anglicanism to Roman Catholicism, and was named a cardinal in 1879. He was canonized in 2019. The poem is best known in its 1900 oratorio setting by the English composer Edward Elgar.

9. "But one of the seraphs flew towards me with a live coal in his hand, which he had lifted with tongs from the altar; he touched my mouth with it, saying,
   Now that this has touched your lips,
   your guilt is gone, your sin forgiven" (Isa 6:7, Moffatt).

10. Isaiah 6:8. These are the same words used by Abraham when God spoke to him in the Akedah and when God called Moses from the burning bush.

And then watch what happens. He said, "Tell the people to listen, but they aren't going to listen. You will break your heart; you will turn your mind inside out; you will pour upon their indifference the priceless ingredients of your spirit: the only thing that I can offer you, says Yahweh, is a deep, profound, ever-circling frustration. That's all. Tell them that they are going to be destroyed, every town burned up, all the people taken into captivity . . . ,"[11] and on and on and on he spells out this doom.

What would you have done? Here is your inspiration, here is your great moment and at last you see clearly the vocational significance of your life. And then as you begin to define that vocational significance it suddenly dawns upon you that you have been sent down a blind alley. Would you go anyway? Or would you say to yourself, "I got my signals mixed?" What would you do? All right. We'll leave that section of Isaiah for a moment, and let's look at one other part of it and that will be all for this morning.

He has a vision of a time when the world will be whole, and it is that vision that keeps him working even as a political advisor to Hezekiah.[12] All about political alliances are in there, and we won't have time to deal with them this morning; but we hope to say something about them next Sunday. But his vision is a kind of utopian thing. But the interesting thing about his vision is this, part of which I read to you—most utopias have to do with how wonderful it would be for all human beings: that everybody will have a nice house, or the utopia during the one period of our history, everybody will have a car in his garage, and everybody will have a stove and on that stove will be a pot, and in every pot there will be a chicken. You remember that part of the political campaign—that was a utopia. Utopias tend to deal, you see, with what's going to happen, what's going to happen to me, you see, what's going to happen to you or happen to you if you like me, etc. But not so altogether Isaiah's utopia. Listen! He says that there shall come a time when Yahweh will be in his holy mountain.[13] And where is this holy mountain? Everywhere. And when he is there, what will happen? To the whole created world? What will happen to

---

11. Isaiah 6:9–13. God's injunction to Isaiah to "make the heart of this people obtuse and block its ears and seal their eyes" has long puzzled commentators.

12. Hezekiah was king of Judah, c. 715–686 BCE.

13. Isaiah 2:1–5.

nature, for instance—not to man, what will happen to nature? The lion and the lamb will lie down together. A little child will put his hand on the hole of an asp, and the asp will relax himself regarding impulse and not sting the child.[14] What's he talking about? When that time comes something else will have already happened among mankind, and what is that? Mankind, too, will lose its self-regarding impulse; it will reorientate all of its egocentric compulsions; he will lose his fear. And when he loses his fear he will beat his swords into ploughshares and his spears into pruning hooks, and it will no longer be necessary for men to study war—not fight—but this antedates all struggle.[15] They will study war no more. They will no longer take the creative resources of their minds and spirits, all of the things with which their lives have been blessed, growing out of the way in which they have reduced all of the impersonal aspects of nature to manageable units of control and utility—all of that becomes the instrument of their fears: therefore they study war.

What have we done? What have we done with the atom? And now the top news is that there has emanated from a semigarrulous congressman, that we have the H bomb, and we are moving into the H-era—going beyond the atomic era to the H-era.[16] And what does that mean? Very interesting, very simple, very terrifying. It means this, that the fruits of our minds, the fruits of our creative endeavors are the vehicles of our fears. That's what it means. And therefore, we turn our back upon the right to the fruits of our minds.

---

14. Isaiah 11:8.

15. Isaiah 2:4.

16. The first hydrogen bomb was detonated at Enewetak Atoll in the Marshall Islands on November 1, 1952, several months after Thurman delivered this sermon. Since President Truman had publicly announced the American development of the hydrogen bomb in 1950, plans for its development were not a secret. Perhaps in the sermon Thurman was referring to the call by Connecticut Senator Brian McMahon for the United States to stockpile thousands of hydrogen bombs, in the news the day of Thurman's sermon, "McMahon Asks Pile of Hydrogen Bombs," *New York Times*, June 15, 1952. In 1958 the Atomic Energy Commission, referencing Isaiah, created Operation Plowshare to promote the peaceful use of nuclear weapons, in such areas as oil exploration or widening or deepening canals. Although none of these proposals were enacted, twenty-seven nuclear explosions were conducted under the auspices of Operation Plowshare, which was discontinued in the 1970s.

So the prophet Isaiah and his utopia include all created things. And they will not find peace among themselves until mankind finds peace. And he says that the symbol of it will be this: that the knowledge of God will cover the earth as the waters cover the sea; and I won't be afraid anymore; even the snakes won't be afraid of me and I won't be afraid of them. Little children can grow up with normal childhood experiences when that time comes. Even those whose minds are sick will be floated by the creative health of us all and will not be a menace to themselves or to others. Do you believe a time like that will ever come? Do you really? If you do, then suppose you try to anticipate it right where you are today!

The Message of Isaiah II

June 22, 1952
Fellowship Church

I SHALL DO part two of the First Isaiah and complete our study of Isaiah, our thinking about the message of Isaiah next Sunday with Deutero-Isaiah or the Second Isaiah. I hope you have been doing your reading.

I'd like to [focus on][1] those parts of Isaiah that are identified authentically with his name. The heart of the message is this: that confidence and trust ultimately and immediately, or immediately and ultimately, are the only grounds upon which the human enterprise can be validated and sustained. Simple. That's the first message, the first part of it, and there follows from that that religion is, in the mind of Isaiah, identified with an attitude of the mind, not the ceremonial, not the ritual, not (it's curious, too) not the act, but it is that which structures the act, says Isaiah. And the third aspect of his message is that pride and arrogance, dependent upon human strength and human ability, is sin against God. Now that's what he's insisting upon.

Now I'd like to spell it out and break it down a little, but if the time runs out, I have said it. The prophets of Israel were intimately tied up with the movements of the periods in which they lived. They were involved in the social process, which is very important to remember. They interpreted Israel and its relationship to God, as to Jehovah, as a primary and personal covenantal relationship. And it is very important to hold that in mind that, for reasons that we cannot quite understand even to this day, in some strange and fascinating and yet miraculous manner this group of people regarded themselves as being some in initially unique relationship with the Creator of their own lives and their little world and their little state. And we see the roots of it in the twilight[2] of their history, in the

---
1. Speculative reconstruction of missing text.
2. As in original, though Thurman presumably meant "dawn."

covenant with Abraham. And the sense of covenant moves down across the pages of human history as a kind of Gulf Stream, giving a moderate temperature to all the surrounding landscape and countryside and continents.[3] And we shall see, when we deal with the Deutero-Isaiah, how this idea of covenant with Israel, this peculiar personal relationship that Israel had with Jehovah, finally becomes a relationship that all the world has with Jehovah.

Now fundamental to this concept, you see, of the relationship of a group of people to God is an interesting and significant philosophy of history. It is a philosophy which to read it says that God is inside the historic process: that he is not outside of it manipulating it or unmindful of it. It isn't like the eighteenth- and nineteenth-century British philosophers who felt that God had wound the world up and set it on its way and he couldn't do anything till it ran down, so he could wait.

The classic example of it is in one of the novels you remember, by the *Forsyte Saga* man—what's his name? Yes, Galsworthy. In one of the novels published after the death of Galsworthy, this lady is complaining to her mother because her husband is . . . , everything that she wanted has disappeared from her and now it seems as if all is lost because her husband is losing his mind; life has become a barren waste for her. And she says to her mother, "I wonder where God is in all this business." And then she says, "Oh, I forgot, He can't be bothered with me in my little troubles. Mother, can't you imagine hearing God say to Gabriel, 'Gabriel, do you remember once upon a time, there was a little speck of star dust that went off around a certain section of the universe, and it was such a pretty speck

---

3. Comparing the legacy of the prophets and the Jewish people to the Gulf Stream was a figure of speech Thurman used on multiple occasions. In his commentary on Habakkuk, published in 1956 but written several years earlier, he stated, "We may quarrel with the way in which the prophet seems to establish squatters' rights over the divine prerogative. We may find it difficult to accept the validity of the ancient insistence of Israel that they are a peculiar people. But the fact remains that the influence of Israel on human history, growing out of that presupposition, has moved through the centuries like the Gulf Stream in the Atlantic. Why this is true remains to this day a baffling enigma" (PHWT 4:147–48).

of star dust that we thought we would put something on it? I wonder how is that fungus getting along, that fungus that we called, man?'"[4]

And the amazing thing is that when human events are regarded merely in terms of events, when there is no answer by the relentless logic of human history, except the logic of the event, it is saying, you see, that all of the possible interpretations that any aspect of human history can reveal is an interpretation that is not in the agonizing grapple of the narrow bounds of antecedent and consequence. And that, in our times, is a rather dominating philosophy; it's a kind of an interesting kind of materialism, and it is also (and I hope you will not misunderstand me), but is also the very important aspect of the philosophy of economic determinism which is one of the basic insistencies of Karl Marx's logic.[5] But we don't have to put up straw horses.

Where do you stand on it? How do you interpret the events of your life? How do you measure them? Do you live your life on the basis that all that there is to you and what you do is wrapped up in the movement, the isolated, circumscribed movement, pulse beat of your little life? Now, if you do, then you know, you see, that the very nature of life is of such that it is fixed (I started to say rationed); but it is fixed, it is finished, it is complete, and you know you can't do anything about anything anyway so you don't try. What's coming to you, you are going to get. My name is there; I can't run anyway, it is there. All of the meaning of your life is wrapped up in the narrow time band of your antecedents and consequences.

Now there is another point of view, and this is the point of view of the prophet. And that is that human life, as well as the lives of nations, takes place within a context that is dynamic. That always when I am in the presence of any event, I am caught in an encounter with a series of potentials that spread out in the widest possible directions and with the most amazing variety of variation. So that if I am alert in the presence of the event, I seek to deal with the event in terms not merely of what it says,

---

4. Thurman was an admirer of the English writer John Galsworthy (1867–1933), who won the Nobel Prize in Literature for 1932.

5. Marxism as a theory of history emphasizes the material and economic factors in history. Many, like Thurman, think Marxist historical theory is deterministic. Karl Marx (1818–1883) was an economic and political theorist, and a founder and leader of the communist movement in nineteenth-century Europe.

what it looks like, but in terms of what seems to me to be the dynamics of the event, the potentials of the event.

Do you deal with events of your life in that way? Do you believe that life is really dynamic? That it isn't quite finished yet? That not only are you involved always in a circling series of potentials, but that you are potential. You, potential. And no time band, no time interval is able quite to contain you and the dynamics of your life and your situation. Do you believe that? I wonder. It seems, doesn't it, it takes a little longer, but it seems, doesn't it, that that's the way you deal with your experiencing of events, isn't it? Haven't you realized that with reference to the simplest experiences of your life that no single event is quite able to deal with all of you. Now let's think now, let's just think about it. We need not hurry.

No event is quite able to deal with all of you. Can you think of a single thing you have ever done in all of your life that was a complete and satisfactory representation of you? Can you think of anything? Is there anything that you have done with reference to which you can say, "Well, this is it. I did it! And I am all present and accounted for in it." No. There is always some part of you that spills over, that can't quite get down in there, you know, which means that that part which spills over, you see, becomes the next basis around which more potential of you begins to be generated. And then that spills over and then . . . Isn't that true? I don't think a person who is sick can ever die until somewhere in his organism a decision is made, a conclusion is arrived at which says that all of me, the totality of my organism, is at last contained in the event; in the event, in the cholera or whatever it is.

Now that's what the prophet Isaiah was telling his people, that you are running down to Egypt trying to get them to sign a treaty with you. You are just running everywhere getting all of these little states to organize themselves along with you in a revolt against Assyria.[6] And you are

---

6. See Isaiah 7, 18–20, 30–31. The main context of Isaiah is the growing power of Assyria. Aram and Ephraim tried to convince Judah to join their coalition against Assyria, which King Ahaz of Judah refused to do, and were attacked by the "Syro-Ephraimite coalition" in turn (Isaiah 7). After 722, when the Assyrians destroyed the northern kingdom of Israel and reduced the kingdom of Judah to vassalage and various voices in the royal household wanted to form an alliance with either Ethiopia (Isaiah 18–20) or Egypt (Isaiah 30–31), Isaiah advised against it, arguing that it would lead to the destruction of Judah.

so sure, so confident that all of the meaning of the events with which you are involved is wrapped up in the mere logic of the events themselves that you say to yourself (and I didn't know, until I studied this this last time, that the quotation is there), you say to yourself, "Let us eat, drink, rejoice: tomorrow we die."[7] It is all wrapped up in now; so what matters? We have repaired every one of the fences; we have done all that we can do because there is no meaning in human history that cannot be included in a formal, discursive logic of my mind and the event.

That's what America thinks today, too; that if we can just get enough support in the world, if we can just line up enough people, we do not have to put our minds on the dynamics of this century and the great upward, surging pulse of the stirrings of the human spirit on this planet. We need not deal with the potentials. We need not concern ourselves with those dimensions of the contemporary scene which point inevitably to the unfolding of the spirit of man as it reaches out for clean air to breathe, for room to move. There was a time when that's what we wanted, what we had to have, 150 years ago. But if we can do that in terms of the superficial events of the historic moment, we do not have to deal with the dynamics of the historic moment.

Now, Isaiah didn't get very far with this. He tried to dramatize it. For three whole years and five months he just walked around, scarcely, without any clothes on, just up and down so everybody could see him. And then they would say, "Why is that strange man dressed that way?"[8] And that would be a chance for the explanation to be given, and the explanation would give him a chance to say his say. Now he said, "The penalty for all of this, the penalty for depending upon man's strength merely is that you depend on man's strength." That's the penalty. Very interesting. What is the penalty? The penalty is that's all you have. That's the penalty. Nothing tremendous about it; just that's all you have. It's just as if, in your own private life you say, "I don't need God; I don't need any other dimension. All of my life is just right here, I see." Now, your tragedy is that that's all there is to you. It's just that. The tragedy is that nothing ever happens. Nothing. You just shut it out. And that was the tragedy of Israel.

---

7. Isaiah 22:13.
8. Isaiah 20. The passage states that Isaiah walked naked and without sandals for three years.

Now two other little things I want to say about the prophet. He had the logic of his idea that God is involved in the historic process, you see, and therefore you relate yourself to God, not to the events. You relate yourself to God, not to the events. If you relate yourself to the events you lose your mind; you'll just be ground to pieces. You can't take it. But relate yourself to the Timeless, to the Eternal, and then you ride with the waves or you go down, but it's all right.

It's like the cascade eagle in *Moby-Dick*, you know, the cascade eagle is an eagle that lives in the mountains, and when that eagle descends into the bottom of the gorge, he is higher than the highest soarer above the plains because his gorge is in the mountains.[9] That's it, when you relate to the Eternal. Therefore everybody, every event is relevant. And he takes this idea and turns it on Assyria. And Assyria has been doing all this trouble, just killing people and wiping out. And what does he say about Assyria? "Assyria is the avenging arm of Jehovah; that Assyria is the whip, the whip in the hands of Jehovah." And then a very curious thing happens to him. (Human beings are such tremendous things.) Assyria laid siege to Jerusalem, but then it got out of hand. It's all right to take all the cities of Judah and all of that, but when he lays siege to Jerusalem, then "Because you did that, you stopped being a whip and thought you were the Controller of the whip." And for that reason you have to be punished.

Now the other thing that the prophet had to say in this connection. I will leave, I will give my message, I will seal my oracles and brood over a little group, whom he calls his pupils. And I will transmit the insistencies in my mind and heart to these pupils who sense and understand, and they will be the growing edge in the historic process. It's very interesting. And he couples with that notion and that insistence which he carried out the idea that, inasmuch as all of human history is in God's hands and the creation of human life and all of life serves some purpose, the significance of which I may not quite understand, all of life, therefore, will not be destroyed; there will be a remnant. And here we get this great idea. You see, what he says, what he decides to do with his little group of disciples; he is going to give to them, you see, the very kernel of his

---

9. Thurman confused "Cascade eagle" with Melville's "Catskill eagle." See page 92, footnote 14, in this volume.

idea, the concepts themselves, so that there would move down through the history of Israel this understanding, this insight about which we are reading today. Now he was doing that.

Now on a wider canvas God was doing something else to match it. And what was this that God was doing? That there would be a remnant preserved, everybody wouldn't be destroyed, there'd always be a remnant, and that remnant would be the rallying point for the new age and the new period.

> Yet all experience is an arch,
> Wherethrough gleams that untraveled world,
> Whose margin fades forever and forever,
> When I move.[10]

Now if you believe as Isaiah believes then you know that the ultimate destiny of man is good, that the contradictions of life are not final contradictions. And that you will cast your vote on the side of the growing edge.

---

10. Alfred Lord Tennyson, "Ulysses" (1842), lines 19–20.

The Message of Jeremiah I

July 20, 1952
Fellowship Church

In the series on The Message of the Prophets, Thurman delivered two consecutive sermons on Jeremiah. Of all the prophets, Jeremiah tells us the most about his life, his political involvements, his confrontations with his enemies, his tribulations, and his imprisonments. For Thurman, Jeremiah, despite his turbulent life, was able to keep his soul from becoming "a highway with traffic going in all directions," and this enabled him, despite being essentially an introverted "country prophet," to be undeterred from his mission. This was, for Thurman, a model for how committed activists need to orient themselves for the difficult acts at hand.

Jeremiah's prophecies were unnerving to his hearers. The sovereignty of Judah was, in the short run, doomed. The stark choice was between Nebuchadnezzar making Judah a satrapy in the Babylonian Empire or Nebuchadnezzar destroying Judah. It was a message few in Judah wanted to hear. But when Judah was destroyed, Jeremiah insisted that God "is a part of the warp and woof, the very structure, the very ground of human life," and if an individual can connect "at the level of awareness that sustains the totality of his life, there he will find God: not only God, he will find the will of God," and a God that can be found not only in the Temple, not only in the Holy Land, but everywhere, even in Babylonia.

I'M BEGINNING THIS MORNING a discussion of the prophet Jeremiah[1] as a part of the series that we have been doing all summer on the mes-

---

1. Jeremiah, born into a priestly family, was from Anathoth, a village near Jerusalem. His active years of prophecy were from about 626 to 586 BCE. His prophetic advice to Judah and Jerusalem that there was no alternative to accepting the domination of Nebuchadnezzar and Babylonia was not well received, and he

sage of the prophets, certain of the prophets of Israel. And I shall be working on Jeremiah both today and next Sunday. I'd like to read a little from this prophet.

My anguish....[2]

I wanted to deal with the prophet this morning from within a context that is in a sense a departure from the general plan of our thinking for the series. For indeed Jeremiah is a radical departure, in some ways, from the emphasis which has been characteristic up to this time. The basic criticism that thoughtful and even sensitive and disciplined minds have against the type of religion that is called mystical religion is this: that it is a religion of withdrawal from life. It is a religion that insists upon detachment, that winnows all of the meaning units of vitality out of the world in which one lives and finds the meaning of life in all of its aspects as a private, intimate, personal, solitary experience of the spirit. And therefore, because this emphasis in mysticism seems basically to be life-denying—you will see the bearing of this on Jeremiah presently—the conclusion, the inescapable conclusion, is that mysticism is negative, leaning back this way, whereas ethics morality is life-affirming, is positive. And now the sensitive mind comes in with, well, the cropper that therefore mysticism as a religion or as an aspect of religion is pessimistic about life.[3] And if you want to retreat, take refuge in mystical religion. Now that's the argument, and there is much to be said about it. But I have always felt from, well I don't know from what point, that this idea over-

---

was subject to persecution and imprisonment. After the fall of Jerusalem in 586, he was given the choice of where to live, and chose to live in Mizpah, in the area of the tribe of Benjamin, with Gedaliah, who had been appointed governor of Judah. After Gedaliah's assassination, around 581 BCE, Jeremiah went into exile in Egypt, probably against his will, where he spent the remainder of his life.

2. O my heart, my heart! it writhes!
Oh how it throbs!
My soul is moaning! I cannot hold my peace,
for I hear the blare of trumpet and the battle cry (Jer 4:19, Moffatt).

The word translated as "anguish" is often translated as "bowels" in the KJV. Robert Alter, in his translation, acknowledging its inelegance, uses "My gut, my gut" (*The Hebrew Bible: The Prophets* [New York: Norton, 2019], 869). The trumpet is a shofar, or ram's horn.

3. As in the sense of "to come a cropper," an unfortunate development.

looks a very simple fact, and that is that all action, all activity, all positive expressions of the personality, therefore all morality, all ethics must be sustained and supported by something that is dynamic, by something that continues to be creative.

I don't know whether you remember the period in our social history not too many years ago, the period of the "tired radical."[4] Do you remember that phrase? You've heard it, the tired radical. Now what was the tired radical? A tired radical was one who had been moving out this way—positively, working towards the re-creation of society, the making over of social patterns, the purging of folkways and mores and the reconditioning of the common mind and the common will around concepts that were more creative and significant than those to which they were devoted. And then he gave out of energy. He just gave out of energy. And first his eyes became dull and his mind became brittle, weary, and he said, "Well, what's the use?" And he sat by the wayside to rest. Now hold that in the background, and let's work for a little while on Jeremiah.

Jeremiah was a country prophet. He was born in a little place, and he had the imagination of a country person.[5] He revolted against all the traffic of the city. He belonged to the open spaces, and therefore when you read him, his lamentations are never for Jerusalem, never for the city, his lamentations are for the people, the people.[6] He was shy, retiring and seems to have been an introvert. He wanted to be by himself and enjoy his company. He didn't like conflict. He just wanted to be quiet, self-contained, modest Jeremiah. And then he had an experience. God called him to be a prophet, and when he wrestled with God about it he told God, "You must have gotten your signals just a little mixed. You really

---

4. See Walter Weyl, *Tired Radicals and Other Papers* (New York: B. W. Huebsch, 1921), 7–16. Walter Weyl (1873–1919) was a prominent Progressive Era reformer, and the phrase was applied to the apparent waning of the militancy of reformers in the 1920s.

5. Anathoth was a Levitical city, that is, reserved for priests and Levites, and had a close connection to the Temple cult.

6. The Book of Lamentations, written in the aftermath of the destruction of Jerusalem in 586 BCE, is traditionally ascribed to Jeremiah, though most biblical scholars doubt Jeremiah was the author. It opens, "How she sits alone/The city once great with people/She has become like a widow" (Lam 1:1, Robert Alter, *The Hebrew Bible: The Writings*, 647, Alter translation).

don't mean me because, first of all, I don't like that kind of mixing and all the work that's involved with people. I don't like that. I find it very difficult to get along, emotionally, with people, and besides I'm young. I'm just twenty-one or -two and I can't carry any message. As soon as anybody looks at me they will say, 'Well, he's scared to death, so he can't speak with any positive character.'"

And God didn't pay very much attention to him but paid a great deal. He said, "You are the one I want and I want you to do a job." "Thee the angel calls as he calls no other. Thou hast thy day to live, thou hast thy work to do. And no one can do for thee what God asks of thee to do." "So, Jeremiah, do thy deed and live thy life."[7] So Jeremiah did. He didn't have much choice. But always he argued, and he is the first one of the inner arguing prophets—always he argued. God told him to say certain terrible things to Israel, and Jeremiah insisted that these things go against my grain.[8] I don't feel that way towards the people. And yet he, God, said, "You do it." "But don't you see that if I do and say these things that all the people will take it out on me, they will persecute me, that they will try to kill me?"[9] "Yeah. I know." "What have I done that I had to be selected to do this? O that I had never been born. O that my mother's womb had been my tomb."[10] And then, while he is in the midst of that struggle, he digs away at his own inward parts until at last he discovers that God is not only in the events, but that God is a movement in his, Jeremiah's heart. And that if he, Jeremiah, does violence to the movement of God in his heart, then he will destroy all of the meaning of God in human history. And it is out of the confessions of Jeremiah that a whole new religious literature emerges in Israel. Read the Psalms, many of the Psalms,

---

7. Jeremiah 1:5–8. Like Moses before him, Jeremiah's first response to the call by God to prophecy is to insist on his inadequacy to the task, though God overrules his reservations.

8. Thurman often spoke of the need to "stay true to the grain in your own wood" (George K. Makecknie, *Howard Thurman: His Enduring Dream* [Boston: Boston University Press, 1988], 65).

9. Jeremiah often writes of the efforts of his enemies to kill and imprison him; see Jeremiah 11:18–20; chap. 38.

10. God tells Jeremiah, "before I fashioned you in the womb, I chose you; ere ever you were born, I set you apart; I have appointed you a prophet to the nations" (Jer 1:5, Moffatt).

so many of them are doing, creatively with literature, with words, with sounds, with vicarious experiencing what Jeremiah did literally with his own inner struggles and conflicts.

Now in Jeremiah then you see two things that I want to emphasize, and I'm through. First that the clue to the outer world—this is commonplace—that the clue to the outer world is the inner world. Very simple, that the clue to the outer world is the inner world; that the battle is won or lost not in the traffic of events, but the battle is won or lost deep within the human spirit. "I laugh when you say"—says the Hindu medieval mystic, "I laugh when you say that the fish in the water is thirsty. / Do you seek the real, the true, the beautiful? / Go where you will from Benares to Mathura, / If you have not found your own soul, / The world is unreal to you."[11] That's what he is saying. That's what he discovered. It's the language of mysticism, but it is a language that is related to the traffic of the world. But the clue to the traffic is not in the traffic. The clue is within the human spirit. You know the story of the musk deer, the doe [sic] of which in the spring of the year is haunted by the odor of musk, and he runs over streams and hills seeking always musk, his little nostrils dilating, his flesh pulsing with desire to find musk that haunts his nostrils, until at last he falls exhausted with his little head resting on his still more tiny paw to discover that the odor of musk is in his own skin.[12] What he seeks yonder is here.

---

11. Rabindranath Tagore, *Songs of Kabir* (New York: Macmillan, 1915), Poem 41. Kabir (1440–1528) was an Indian religious poet. Originally a Muslim, he became a Hindu mystic, opposing both the caste system and the worship of images, and taught the essential unity of Islam and Hinduism. Thurman quoted this poem in an article he published as early as 1925; see PHWT 1:52. The two Hindu holy cities of Mathura and Benares (now Varanasi) are about 410 miles apart.

12. Musk deer are a group of several species of small deer, living near the Himalayas, highly prized (and now, as a result, highly endangered) for the musk glands of the male. The legend of the musk deer chasing his own scent is an ancient Indian legend. Howard Thurman was fond of telling the story of the musk deer as a key to the discovery of inward values. "In the springtime, the roe is haunted by the odor of musk. He runs wildly over hill and ravine with his nostrils dilating and his little body throbbing with desire, sure that around the next clump of trees or bush he will find the musk, the object of his quest. Then at last he falls, exhausted, with his little head resting on his tiny hoofs, only to discover that the odor of musk is in his own hide" ("The Kingdom of Values," in *For the Inward Journey: The Writings of Howard Thurman*,

Now that's a simple insight and Jeremiah is the first of the prophets to come to grips with the essential aspects of this central problem of religion: How can I keep going when the going is difficult and exhausting? Is there something in the external experiences that will yield the clue to my needs? "Perhaps," says Jeremiah. But the real clue is not there. The clue is here. And many, many years after, there was another Jewish person struggling in a garden that we call Gethsemane. And do you remember his struggle? It has echoes of Jeremiah. He says, "Father, let the cup pass from me. I don't want to die. I have a mission yet to do. Nevertheless not my will but thy will."[13] And what does he say? That even though as a result of the relentless logic of events I must drink the cup; that my life faces me with an inevitable gesture, stripping me of alternatives. I'll drink the cup because the most important thing is not the change in the event—please hear this—the most important thing is not the change in the event or events, as important as the change in the event or the events may be: the most important thing is what happens inside of you who may be involved in the event.

Now the second word that we get as we look at this aspect of Jeremiah's life is that every person who is involved in the stresses and strains of living, and we are all involved in one way or another. Perhaps not with the great sense of manifest destiny that a Jeremiah had, but each of us is involved at the level of his own awareness in the tensions of living; that hard by your roadside, where your traffic moves, where the lane of your traffic is crowded, you had better have a little room, a little house, a little spot into which you may retreat so as to catch your breath, to get your compass readjusted, to define your terms again—you'd better have that. Whatever may be the nature of your activity, however crowded your life may be, however difficult and involved your life may be, you had better make provision for your temple of silence into which you may go and get dusted off and cleansed a little and then on your way. For if you do not have that there is no way by which you can keep the traffic of life from moving outside of you to inside of you. And when your soul becomes a mad highway it is the end of the meaning of your living. And your life

---

ed. Anne Spencer Thurman with an introduction by Vincent Harding (New York: Harcourt, Brace, Jovanovich, 1984), 54.

13. Luke 22:42.

becomes barren, and you don't know why; your soul becomes crowded with despair and pessimism, and you don't know why; nothing has meaning, and you don't know why: your soul has become a highway with traffic going in all directions, and there is no place, no place for catching a second wind.

Now that's what Jeremiah found, and it need not be my place, it need not be the prophet's place: it must be your place so that in the twinkling of an eye, in a moment you can be there even though your pace never slackens and your cares mount. And I am grateful for Jeremiah, with all of his tears and his anguish and his symbolism. I am grateful that he has left a witness to the fact that nobody, nobody, is ever too full of responsibility, burdens, cares, problems, joys, or sorrows to be relieved of the personal necessity for discovering for himself a way, a way of renewal and rebuilding. And if you don't do it, it's your fault—your fault—your fault.

The Message of Jeremiah II

July 27, 1952
Fellowship Church

JEREMIAH [INSISTED that there was operating in human life law and order, a moral law and a moral order.]¹ Sometimes it seems as if the God of Jeremiah is deeply involved in the operation of the moral law, and sometimes he seems to be standing outside of the moral law, watching it perform its deeds and fulfill itself. For instance, he says that, to Israel as a part of Jeremiah's foreign policy, if I may mention such a word after the convention,² a part of Jeremiah's foreign policy was the insistence that Nebuchadnezzar was the living instrumentality, the utter embodiment of God.³ And that was true, says Jeremiah, whether or not Nebuchadnezzar was aware of the fact. That is, that Nebuchadnezzar's personal knowledge of the destiny-dealing aspect of his behavior was in a sense completely irrelevant, for beyond the will of man, beyond the normal operation of all of the reflective processes of the human mind and the human judgment and the human will and human skill, beyond all of that, surrounding it all, is the mind of God. And when a man acts, thinking that he is acting out of a process which he himself created and for which he is responsible, let him rethink his position, for he is thinking and acting as a result of a process which—the answer of which he cannot comprehend, and indeed the origins of which he did not create. Now that's one of the central problems, and I don't know what the answer is. I pose it, but I can't deal with it because I'm not mature

---

1. The opening sentences of the sermon have not been preserved. This is a speculative reconstruction.
2. The 1952 Democratic National Convention, nominating for president and vice president Adlai Stevenson of Illinois and John Sparkman of Alabama, was held in Chicago, July 21–26. The 1952 conventions were the first to be extensively televised, and the Democratic convention was the most recent to require multiple rounds of balloting to select a presidential nominee.
3. See Jeremiah 27.

enough. Do you see? Nebuchadnezzar, says Jeremiah, is the instrument of God. And, if Jeremiah is the instrument of God, the wise thing for Judah to do, for Israel to do, is to submit to Nebuchadnezzar. So when these prime ministers from Egypt and other places came to Jerusalem and were having a meeting trying to decide whether or not Israel shall become a part of a military alliance, Jeremiah puts on a yoke and walks up and down outside of the place where this—as a friend of mine says, outside of Number 10 Downing Street, what is the equivalent of Number 10 Downing Street[4]—where the prime ministers were meeting, here is Jeremiah walking up and down with a yoke. And then one of the priests—representatives—took the yoke and broke it. And Jeremiah went back to get some more orders from God. And God told him, "Well, all right. Put an iron yoke on your neck this time. See if he can break that."[5]

Now if the events—now this is the problem—if the events of human life are the results of forces in operation that are not involved really in the private choices of individuals, then whatever may be the collective resultant in any given situation in society cannot be thought of even in terms of personal social responsibility. How can I be responsible, you see, if my behavior is merely the inevitable response which I give to forces over which I have no control anyway? With your permission I'll leave it right there. But I will be back sometime, but not yet.

The second aspect of Jeremiah to which I call your attention is what to me is his completely unique contribution. I may say in passing that it is Jeremiah who introduces the phrase "the grim reaper."[6] The first time in literature, as far as our records go, the first time that death is referred to as the grim reaper appears in Jeremiah. It is interesting to find out that you will discover that when you read the book. But his crucial contribution, it seems to me, is in the way in which he spiritualized religion. Now that sounds like a contradiction in terms: he spiritualized religion. And he did it in an extraordinary manner, because once again he was dealing

---

4. The confrontation with Hananiah, son of Azzur, took place in the Temple. Number 10 Downing Street is the residence of the British prime minister.

5. Jeremiah 28.

6. In Jeremiah 9:16–21 there is a personification of death, but the figure of the reaper is not used in the KJV or related translations, but see the "reaper of death" in Revelation 14:14–16. The phrase "grim reaper" is not biblical. The earliest citation in the *Oxford English Dictionary* is from 1847.

with an inevitable set of political and social circumstances. The people were taken out of Jerusalem into captivity by Nebuchadnezzar. And, of course, when Nebuchadnezzar was laying siege to Jerusalem everybody became frightened. You know when times are difficult—very often people get frightened. You . . . well, they do. So all the people who had slaves freed their slaves while the enemy was knocking at the door. "If there is anything I can do to get myself straight so as to move the enemy, I'll do it. So I'll free all these." So they freed all the slaves. And then a change in political events or something else, and the enemy moved on because of a disturbance in another section, and the siege was temporarily lifted, and so what did they do? They went and got all these slaves back, and said, "Come back now, our situation has changed." Certainly a human thing to do. And Jeremiah watched that. And he said, "That's all your values are? That's all religion means to you that you fall on your knees and pray to God when you think that you have come to the end of the line?"[7] And then they were taken into captivity he said to them, "God is where you are; you didn't leave God in Jerusalem because you have been taken into captivity; God is in Babylon."[8] Of course, it sounds very simple to say that now. But that meant that the whole concept of the meaning of religion had turned a corner: that God is not confined to the soil of Israel.

I remember when I was leaving home to go to school, when I was fourteen, my grandmother called me back to the steps when I had started away and she said, "Remember, Howard, God is as close to Jacksonville (I was going to Jacksonville, Florida)—God is as close to Jacksonville as he is to Daytona."[9] (Daytona was the place where I was living, our home.) "He is as close to Daytona as he is to Jacksonville." In other words, because you are going up a hundred ten miles, he can get up there as well. Now that's what Jeremiah was saying to these people. They were taken into captivity, and they were sure that they had left God back in Jerusalem, back in his familiar place. But Jeremiah said, "No, God is not confined

---

7. For the Jerusalemites reneging on the manumission of their Hebrew slaves, see Jeremiah 34:8–22.

8. See Jeremiah 29. This was probably written after Nebuchadnezzar's first siege of Jerusalem in 597 BCE but before the destruction of the Temple in 586 BCE.

9. In the fall of 1915 Thurman left his home in Daytona, Florida, to attend the Florida Baptist Academy in Jacksonville.

to a holy place." And the world is still trying to catch up with Jeremiah on that. We still don't believe that. God is not confined to a holy place! God is not confined to a holy people. God is not confined to a holy ritual. That's what Jeremiah is saying, that God is in the heart, and wherever you go—wherever you go, there he is.

Now the logic of that brings me to the third thing about Jeremiah. The logic of that is that if it be true—as Jeremiah insists and as Hosea before him and as Micah, as you will see when we study him, and Ezekiel, too, for that matter—if it be true that God is to be found and not confined really in the temple or this place or that place, but God is to be found in the human spirit; if that is true then the logic of it is that God is native to the human spirit—native to the human spirit. Now Jeremiah says that the birds know when to come and go; the birds understand the law of their being.[10] And God is the law of the being of man, but man does not understand. He is not as smart as the birds.

When I was visiting these friends in Canada—they have a dog, one of these combinations of a collie and a huskie and his name is . . . well, he has a name. They were telling me that four years ago—the dog is now five and a half years old—when the dog was a year and a half old, the family, the mother and father, went away for three weeks. And the day after they left, their son was to close up the house and go for three weeks on a camping trip. The friends came by to get the boy, the young fellow, and after he had locked up the house he remembered that he had left his flashlight in the house, and he ran in the house to get his flashlight; and while he was looking for his flashlight the dog slipped into the doctor's office, and then the boy closed the door and went on about his business, not realizing that the dog was locked up in the house. And for sixteen days the dog was in the house without water, without food. And all the neighbors, they even put over the air, the little ham radio thing, asking if this dog had been seen anywhere. When the family came back, here was the dog. And they put water down and food, and even though the dog hadn't eaten for sixteen days he didn't touch the food. He took just a little water. Then he'd lie down. Then he'd take a little more water, then he'd lie down. It was the second day before he dared eat any food. Just a

---

10. Jeremiah 8:7.

dog! Just a dog! And when he was a puppy—as it happens that all these are about the same dog; your dog would do the same, I suppose—when he was a puppy he swallowed a needle, like that, one of these big needles; and Dr. Harkings[11] said that after he swallowed this needle he went out in the yard, started eating dried grass, leaves, and the food that they gave him to eat he would only eat the bread. And for three days he existed on a diet of roughage. And six months after that time they found, in his house, the needle, and all caked around it was this grass, and so forth. Just a dog seeking the roots of his consciousness down into the flow of his being and coming into direct primary contact at that level with the limitless resource of the universe.[12]

Now Jeremiah says that God is native, God is a part of the warp and woof, the very structure, the very ground of human life; and therefore if the individual sinks the shaft of his awareness down to the very grounds of his being, at the level of awareness that sustains the totality of his life, there he will find God: not only God, he will find the will of God. For when the human spirit is stripped to whatever there is that is literal in us, when all of the levels of one's specious desiring have been peeled away, naked and undisguised, without pretense, the human spirit stands bare—it is in that moment that God speaks in a voice that is the voice of your own heart. Therefore Jeremiah says, and I stop now, "A curse on him who depends upon man, who relies upon mere human aid, for he is like some desert scrub that never thrives, set in a salt, solitary place in the steppes. But happy is he who relies on God, who has God for his confidence, for he is like a tree planted beside a stream, sending his roots down to the water. He has no fear of scorching heat, his leaves are always green, he goes on bearing fruit when all around him is barren; and he looks out on life with quiet eyes."[13] That is Jeremiah, and I thank God for him.

---

11. Presumably, Thurman's Canadian friend.

12. Thurman develops the idea that animals have a more acute connection to nature than humans and the need to develop a "kinship with all life" in *The Search for Common Ground*, 56–71.

13. Jeremiah 17:5–8 was a favorite scriptural passage for Thurman, which he quoted in a sermon as early as 1928. However, the final line of his usual quotation, "and he looks out on life with quiet eyes," is not from Jeremiah and is not biblical. Thurman probably borrowed it from the Chicago poet Francis Wells Shaw's (1872–1932) poem "Who Loves the Rain." For Thurman's use of this poem, see PHWT 4:130 n. 20.

The Message of Ezekiel

August 11, 1952
Fellowship Church

If the prophet Ezekiel is not, as a scholar quoted by Thurman stated, "the first fanatic in the Bible," he is surely the strangest of the prophets. A Jerusalemite priest, he spent most of his life in exile in Babylonia, where all of his prophecies took place. He was among the first group of elites brought into Babylonian Exile 597 BCE. He received his prophetic call five years later, remaining active until 570, years that included the destruction of the Jerusalem Temple in 586.

Ezekiel's prophecies of doom and restoration[1] tell us about the lives of Jews in exile and the need to sustain their traditions of faith and practice in a new land where YHWH is no longer bound to the Temple in Jerusalem. Thurman notes this as the central problem for Ezekiel, a problem for "human thought" in general: how to reinterpret "holiness and unholiness," "secular and sacred," and "universality and particularity" in an era of tumultuous change.[2] How can, asks Thurman, "the holy God make any contact, discover any meeting point with the unholy?" Without the Temple, Ezekiel's themes of holiness and sin carry over into the ethical responsibility of the individual.[3] Thurman asks, "Where do I draw the line within myself between that which is really sacred and that which is really secular?"

---

1. The prophet's warnings of doom and threats against Judah and Jerusalem and against foreign nations constitute chap. 1–25 and 25–32, respectively. The later prophecies of restoration and hope are recorded in chap. 33–44. Most scholars treat the material as contemporary with Ezekiel, though a few later additions are discernible.

2. This is also a critical issue for Thurman, a life-long intellectual and personal quest for understanding the nature of the Holy. Rudolph Otto called this nonrational aspect of the religious experience "the numinous." See Rudolph Otto, *The Idea of the Holy* (Oxford: Oxford University Press, 1923).

3. "You cannot say that the parents have eaten sour grapes and the children's teeth are on edge" (Ezek 18:1–4; see also 18:25–32).

Moreover, this sense of individual responsibility for one's actions and reactions, says Thurman, creates a major problem for survival ethics, which was a long-standing personal concern for him and his interpretation of religious experience and morality.[4] *Ezekiel's use of the symbols of Tyre and Egypt as hidden codes to refer to Babylon, Thurman thinks, poses a moral problem and is not dissimilar to his own experiences. The pressure to forfeit one's integrity in the face of danger is universal, but it has implications especially for the politically and socially disadvantaged and their understanding of themselves and their relationship to the powerful. "Under what circumstances do you deliberately lay aside the insistence which you feel natively for integrity and right because somebody you love is being threatened, because your life is in jeopardy, because a cause to which you are committed will go down into disintegration and disaster you think, if you do not prove false in the pressure that is placed upon you?"*

I SHALL UNDERTAKE this morning what essentially is impossible, and that is to do in very short compass, the heart of the message of Ezekiel; next Sunday the heart of the message of Micah. So that if you read the book before you come to church it will be well.

> The hand of the Eternal was on me in a trance,
> And as I gazed there was a storm wind blowing from the north, a huge cloud with fire flashing out of it and with a sheen encircling it and issuing from it the color of amber.
> Out of it appeared the forms of four creatures and this was their appearance; they had the same form each with four faces, and four wings,
> With limbs straight and gleaming like burnished bronze; and with the soles of their feet rounded like the feet of calves.
> Under their wings on the four sides of them were human hands.
> As for their four faces and wings,

---

4. See HT, *Jesus and the Disinherited*, "Deception," 58–73; HT, *The Luminous Darkness: A Personal Interpretation of the Anatomy of Segregation and the Ground of Hope* (New York: Harper & Row, 1964); HT, *Deep River and the Negro Spiritual Speaks of Life and Death* (New York: Harper & Brothers, 1955).

> Their wings touched one another; and their faces never turned as they moved. Each moved straight forward.
>
> As for the likeness of their faces, all four had in front the face of a man, on the right the face of a lion, on the left the face of a bull, and the face of an eagle at the back.
>
> Their wings were stretched out; one pair to touch the next creature, the other pair to cover the body.
>
> Each moved straight forward; wherever the spirit impelled them to go they went; never turning as they moved.
>
> Also in the middle of the creatures there was something moving to and fro like glowing coals, like torches; a fire that gleamed and flashed out lightning.
>
> As I gazed there was a wheel on the ground beside each of the four creatures.
>
> The wheels were the color of topaz, and all four had the same shape arranged as if one wheel were inside the other wheel.
>
> When they moved, they moved in any direction that their four sides faced, never turning as they moved.
>
> The spokes of the four I saw were full of eyes all around.
>
> Wherever the creatures moved, the wheels moved with them; and whenever the creatures rose from the earth, the wheels rose with them.
>
> Wherever the Spirit impelled them to go they went, for a living spirit was in the wheels.
>
> When the creatures moved, they moved: when the creatures stood still, they stood still: when the creatures rose from earth, they rose: for a living spirit was in these wheels . . . etc.[5]

It is very interesting, isn't it? It would be quite an experience to spend the time simply reading excerpts from Ezekiel. He was a very amazing man. He has had a tremendous influence on art, religious art in the Christian movement, a tremendous influence on prophecy.[6] Several con-

---

5. Ezekiel 1:3b-21, Moffatt.
6. Ezekiel was also a founding figure of the Jewish mystical tradition; see Rachel Elior, *The Three Temples: On the Emergence of Jewish Mysticism* (Oxford: Littman Library of Jewish Civilization, 2005).

temporary cults have been built around some of these visions of Ezekiel.[7] His imagery was very impressive to the slaves when they came over and were first brought face to face with these dramatic insights of the Israelitish mind. One of the rather famous and celebrated spirituals, "Ezekiel saw the wheel, way up in the middle of the sky, / The big wheel (something else and something else), / and the little wheel was run by the grace of God."[8] The wheels were alive; you encounter Ezekiel all around. He's become a part of the lore of certain aspects of Protestantism with his figure of the valley of dry bones and certain very interesting, highly imaginative, sermons drunk with poetry have been built around what happens when these dry bones begin to rattle and one bone hooks onto another one.[9] And this is exciting.

He has also influenced our sense judgment for it is he who says that the soul that sinneth, it shall die. It's Ezekiel who does that! He influenced in a rather striking manner the imagination of Jesus of Nazareth. He refers to himself, as I shall point out subsequently, as Son of Man,

---

7. Thurman's reference is not further elaborated, but Ezekiel's prophecy of Gog and Magog in chap. 38 is the source of the prophecy in Revelation 19:11–21:8, a text that has inspired numerous Christian millenarian and apocalyptic groups.

8. Thurman is referencing the Negro spiritual, a favorite song of his childhood and of Morehouse College Glee Club, of which he was a member:
> Ezekiel saw a wheel, Way up in the middle of the air
> Ezekiel saw a wheel, Way in the middle of the air
> Little wheel run by faith,
> Big wheel run by the grace of God.

See John W. Work, *American Negro Songs and Spirituals* (1940; repr. Mineola, NY: Dover Books, 1998).

9. Ezekiel 37:1–14. See especially James Weldon Johnson, *God's Trombones: Seven Negro Sermons in Verse* (1927; repr. *Writings* [New York: Library of America, 2004]), 866.
> And I feel Old Earth a-shuddering—
> And I see the graves a-bursting—
> And I hear a sound,
> A blood-chilling sound.
> What sound is that I hear?
> It's the clicking together of the dry bones,
> Bone to bone—the dry bones.
> And I see coming out of the bursting graves,
> And marching up from the valley of death,
> The army of the dead.

and we hear that phrase ringing on the lips of Jesus of Nazareth. And I think—the critics, many of them disagree with that, but that's all right: they read and I read, so it's all right—I think that they both, both Jesus of Nazareth and Ezekiel, use the term the "Son of Man" in the same way, carrying essentially the same basic insight.[10]

Now there are three aspects of Ezekiel's thinking about which I want to talk for a little while and think about with you. If you want the details and the imagery and the beauty of it, read the book. I will not undertake to do that, but I want to lift out what seems to me to be three of the important insights in this tremendous man who wrestled with emotional disturbances that are almost uncanny. I wonder what a good clinical study of Ezekiel would reveal. It's very amazing. Don't undertake it unless you know what you are doing, but he had visions, hallucinations; as some people call them, he had visions. He had fits, spasms, trances; he was so gripped by the sense of relatedness to the fate of his people and to Jehovah that his body became a living instrument in the hands of the violences of the spirit of God. A man like Pfeiffer refers to him as the first fanatic in the Bible.[11] But there is always an element of fanaticism in any kind of human action, isn't there? When you decide to act, in the moment when that decision grips the mind and galvanizes the total personality into action, what happens? We pull down the curtain of all further reflections and we say, "I wait as long as I can but now I can wait no longer: I act."[12] And when I act there is always a margin in the mind and in the personality that is unstructured, that floats along, that carries the intent that was generated before you pulled the curtain down.

Now the thing that gripped Ezekiel was an awareness of the holiness of God. He reminds you, as you read his pages, of a man who is drunk

---

10. Thurman is referring to the Hebrew rendering for "humanity," the singular, appearing ninety-three times in the Book of Ezekiel alone and fourteen times elsewhere. Thurman thinks that "son of man" as used by Jesus has the same meaning, not an esoteric, christological designation.

11. R. H. Pfeiffer, *Introduction to the Old Testament* (New York: Harper & Brother, 1941), 543.

12. In 1938 Thurman suggested that it was fanatics, rather than intellectuals, who can best experience "the freedom of mind that comes with a great commitment. It causes an orderly recklessness of action and it robs a man of the fear of the death" (PHWT 2:110).

with a sense of the holy. He is—in his vision, in his first vision and in many others[13]—Jehovah has deserted the temple, he has deserted the city, he is in the heavens. And why is he in the heavens? Because the earth has been polluted, not by ordinary men, not by the garden variety of human beings, but the earth has been polluted by those with whom Jehovah has the covenant. The people who knew better have polluted it. And because they have polluted it Jehovah deserts it: he moves up. Because holiness, you see, cannot be brought into intimate, primary contact with unholiness. And that's the first problem with which he wrestles. And if I work at it I may not get to the other two, but . . . how can you make of one piece, human experience, if you have in your mind a concept of the sacred and the secular? How can the holy, the holy God, make any contact, discover any meeting point with the unholy? It's a central problem, not only with Ezekiel; it's a central problem of human thought, isn't it, of human experience? How can the absolute make any contact with the limited? How can the universal still remain universal and make any touch with the particular? You experience it all the time, don't you? Or do you? Have you ever tried to put into words the great feeling that you have for somebody? What do you do? You select, if you have time, you select very carefully a group of words, and you make those words say what you are trying to say. And even as the words come out, what are you doing? You are busily trying to conjure up another set of words because you know that that set of words didn't quite say it. It's what you do all the time, isn't it? Now, so that is essentially the same problem: if God is holy and if he deserted the holy place, the Temple, because of the way in which the Temple was profaned, how can he deal with human life and human beings and at the same time maintain his sense of the holy? Now that's his problem.

Now how does he wrestle with it, without getting too involved? We see in Ezekiel the beginning of the first great movement within the Jewish religion towards angels—angelology.[14] Now what are the functions

---

13. Ezekiel's first vision is normally understood to be Ezek 1:1–28, where he saw the four living creatures and received his calling, which is the scriptural text used by Thurman at the beginning of this sermon.

14. Angels over the course of the Hebrew Bible evolve from human-featured messengers from God to distinctively divine creatures, from the messengers that greet Abraham in Genesis 18 to the cherubim in Ezekiel 9–10. As Thurman states, the word for angel in Hebrew, *malach*, is also the word for messenger.

that angels serve in human imagination and in human thinking; angels make the contact with the—with matter, with the stuff. And they make it on behalf of the God who is too holy, too (I can't get my words) too universal, too self-contained to be broken down into a little piece like a thing, for instance. So the angels do that; the angels are the messengers: that's what the word means: messengers of God. They are the expression, the expression of God. When I was a boy in Sunday school, very often we would have the little penny picture cards with the golden text and then a colored drawing or painting of the main point of the Sunday school lesson. And whenever there was anything from Ezekiel or the prophets, so forth and so on, and Jehovah was brought into the picture, there was a picture of Jehovah. You know, he was ancient and rather mature, and he sat on a throne and [had] a nice beard, a look of timelessness in his face, but suspended in mid-air; on the right and on the left were the angels, who were the messengers; they were to make the primary, intimate, face-to-face contact with the stuff, the limitations.[15]

Now there is another problem in connection with the holiness, and then I will leave it because I must do these other two things, one of the other two things anyway. How much responsibility does the individual have for maintaining a sense of the holy in him? How much responsibility is mine? Is it true that there's a part of me that is holy, that lives in the same house, my body and mind, with the parts of me that are not holy? If so, how may I resolve those? Where do I draw the line within myself between that which is really sacred and that which is really secular? Is one of these related to the other, or is there a desert and a gulf between? Now Ezekiel works that out in an interesting system of morality. For, you see, he cuts across the idea that we mentioned in one of the prophets some time ago, that in which he says that the—"You cannot say that the children, that the parents have eaten sour grapes and the children's teeth are on edge."[16] You can't say that any longer; that heredity, that environment is not the decisive factor. The only decisive factor is the individual act, for in the act there is the effort on the part of the human spirit to be

---

15. See a more critical description of this idea in *Jesus and the Disinherited* (1949; rept., Boston: Beacon Press, 1996), 43–44.

16. "In those days they shall no longer say: 'The fathers have eaten sour grapes, and the children's teeth are set on edge'" (Jer 31:29, RSV).

whole; to be one, to galvanize the two parts: the sacred and the secular, to be the synthesis. That's what the act is. Therefore the moral character of the act is ultimate and absolute and final.[17] So, he says, being consistent after a fashion, that if a man is a good man, and by a good man he means doing good acts, and then in the twilight the same man does a bad act; in the whole sweep of the judgment of life, the only thing that counts is the last act. You don't like that. He says that all these other good acts everyday can't outweigh this one. Bunyan has an idea about that. Do you remember in *Pilgrim's Progress*?[18] Here's the great pearly gates, and right in the threshold of the pearly gates, there's a trap door that goes straight to hell. You might have your hands on the gate, and then—now do you see why he does this? That in the act there is the synthesis of the person, and whatever is the quality of the given act is the final judgment of life upon the act.

Now I won't try to deal with what I think about that, but I am trying to have you understand what it is. Now it works in reverse, you see, that I may have a whole series of bad acts, and each one carrying that sort of judgment; but here now in the twilight I get this one act, this good act; and that good act, says Ezekiel, quoting his interpretation of the movement of the spirit of God in his own mind, that good act counts in a way that all the bad acts don't, because the bad acts were yesterday. So on the basis of that, in one whole tradition in our faith, we get the significance of the so-called deathbed conversion. Interesting.

Now the thing that is behind all of this ethical problem is the impact of his idea of the holiness of God upon his mind and spirit and how he tries to resolve it. But now this brings us to the second thing, the secondary aspect of the bearing of the ethical import. And that is that the individual is responsible for what he does. The responsibility for your own

---

17. Thurman at places refers to this as "the integrity of the act." See *The Inward Journey* (New York: Harper & Row, 1961), 40, 65.

18. John Bunyan's classic, *The Pilgrim's Progress from This World, to That Which Is to Come*, published 1678, is an allegory of the Christian life in which the main character, Christian, passes through the Slough of Despond, the Valley of the Shadow of Death, Vanity Fair, and many other geographic destinations and potential pitfalls on the way to the Celestial City; and there was, as Bunyan states at the end of the first part of *The Pilgrim's Progress*, "a way to hell, even from the gates of Heaven, as well as from the City of Destruction."

actions: a whole school of modern psychology has been built around that idea, you remember.[19] How can you teach people to be responsible for what they do? Even though they were created by an environment and had a mother and father. And it is one of the amazing conveniences that modern psychology has given to us, and all people who are parents recognize this, that I wouldn't be as I am if my father, my mother hadn't done so and so, etc. And that may be true. I'm not saying it isn't true, so don't misunderstand me. But I am just saying be very careful how we take advantage of it because the human spirit being what it is, we can't stand the risk of having anybody around on whom we can hang these things. Because it tends to postpone for ourselves the reckoning about which this prophet is insisting.

Now, it is interesting how at last every insight, every vision that he had was finally broken down in terms of the prophet himself and where he was living and what he was doing. So, for instance, when he, in exile, suddenly found that he was in a society that had become, at least temporarily, a classless society—for all of the people who had been taken into captivity were all of the professions and the classes that they represented when they were living in a stabilized society, those things meant nothing in captivity: they were just captive Jews.[20] And the fact that one was rich in Jerusalem and one was powerful or one was a prestige-bearing individual with highly developed skills that gave to him a unique place in the mind and the thinking of his fellows, all of that was irrelevant. You are now in Babylon, just a captive, that's all. And therefore, the movement of the experience of authentic democracy becomes operable in that situation, forced as it was due to the movement of history. So to dramatize that Ezekiel refers to himself not as the prophet, not as the anointed one of God, but he refers to himself as what? As son of man—just a son of man. I am just—we are all one—just son of man. So, many years after Jesus picked up the echo and he refers to himself as son of man, not [him],

---

19. The Viennese psychologist Alfred Adler's (1879–1938) theory of "individual psychology" popularized the notion of the "inferiority complex."

20. The first deportation to exile in Babylon occurred in three waves from 597 to 581 BCE as a result of Judean rebellions against Babylonian rule and mainly affected those of the upper class of society.

but we, in our thinking, have made the little "s" a capital "S." But I feel confident that in his mind it was a little "s"; just son of man.[21]

Now you can see the logic of that in terms of the ethical concept, you see, of personal responsibility.[22] If I am responsible for what I do, then I am responsible. I'm not responsible as a doctor, I'm not responsible as a social worker or as a housewife or as a son or a daughter; I'm responsible as, well, just as me. That's bad English, but you understand me—just as me, I'm responsible. And what I am in terms of the pretensions of my life, however clearly defined and accurate those pretensions may be, is irrelevant: I am responsible. I am an individual and I rate being held responsible for what I do. I do not seek to hide behind this, this, this, this, etc. Well, that's pretty rugged, but that's what he is insisting upon, and these are the reasons for it.

Now there is just one more thing and I'm—well, yes, just one more, and that is a personal problem that Ezekiel had growing out of all of this thinking. He was gifted, you know. A poet. You read this—even as we read it, translation of a translation of a translation, etc., it still sings. So what it must have been just listening to it is overwhelming. And people just flocked to hear him even though he was a prophet of doom and they didn't like what he said. But they ignored that because it was so good listening to it, you know. And he thought at first that everybody who was goggle-eyed in front of him was goggle-eyed because of the impact of the

---

21. Thurman's interpretation of "the religion of Jesus" and "the religion about Jesus" is captured in a number of his books, sermons, and essays, most notably *Jesus and the Disinherited* (1949). The latter designation depicts Jesus as a human being who achieved a supreme God-consciousness that is available to all. The latter, he thought, was the product of the apostle Paul and the early church's construction of Jesus as the Christ of God. See "Man and the Moral Struggle: Paul," published in this volume.

22. Responsibility is a major ethical concept in all of Thurman's sermons and writings. Thurman suggests that responsibility is the corollary of freedom because when the individual assumes responsibility for his or her actions, she or he confirms the integrity of the self and its authenticity. Therefore, one can never unshoulder responsibility for one's actions and reactions without forfeiting one's own being. This emphasis on responsibility has profound implications for the moral imperatives to practice love and integrity in *all* encounters and situations. For the oppressed, claiming responsibility for one's own destiny is the initial act of freedom and selfhood. Thurman writes, "The moment I transfer responsibility for my own actions, I become an instrument in another's hands. This is the iniquity of all forms of human slavery" ("Freedom under God" [February 1955], in PHWT 4:113).

spirit of the living God that he was talking about upon their minds. And it dawned upon him that they were just delighted with the way he talked.

If you will forgive an extremely personal reference to California, but the first time I arrived at Palo Alto, and Sunday morning came, and I preached myself.[23] The chaplain at that time was a wonderful man, Dr. Godwin. He said, at the end of the sermon, "Before the young people come to take you to the place where you are having lunch, I want to take you down to my cottage for," as he called it, "a spot of tea." He was this very nice Englishman. And we were walking down the road at Palo Alto. He had his arm in my arm, and he was telling me about the countryside in England and various other things, and then suddenly he stopped talking to me and stopped walking, released my arm, squared my shoulders with both hands up like that and looked me straight in the eyeballs. And he said, "Too beautiful. Too beautiful. Truth is rugged, deckle-edged; it comes out in hunks, dripping." And then he said, "Young man, God has been very good to you. He has given you gifts. Don't show your ingratitude to him by working over your gifts till you take all of the life out of them with polish." And then he released my shoulders, and picked up the thread of his conversation. And I have thought of it many times since. And when I read about Ezekiel's experience (and please do not misunderstand the reference—I do not put myself in Ezekiel's category), but I know that the temptation is to let the beautiful turning of the phrase, the happy creative rendering of the word, divorce themselves from the movement of the spirit that generates the word, and the listener becomes so involved in the histrionics that the impact of the word dies before it ignites the spirit in you.

Now that was Ezekiel's personal problem. And I realize that I should stop, and I am going to stop in a minute because I am not going to preach on Ezekiel next Sunday. So if you'll just give me another three minutes or four, I will finish what I have to say.

The final thing with reference to Ezekiel was the way he had to deal in a secondary manner with the ethical problem. I don't quite know how

---

23. Thurman's first trip to California was probably in June 1929 when he attended a YMCA student conference in Asilomar Conference Grounds in Monterey, about ninety miles down the coast from Palo Alto. Whether he visited Palo Alto at the same time is unknown.

to put it. But you see, when Jerusalem fell and when the chances for recovery, as he saw it, dimmed, and he began dreaming about the restoration, the new Temple and the way he works it out as an architect and a mathematician, I won't have time to go into that, and carrying out this idea of holiness with which he opens and closes, he had to give comfort to the people.[24] And he had to give them comfort in the language that they could understand but, at the same time, language that would not get him into difficulties with Babylon. Do you see his problem? How can I say what I need to say to the captives and at the same time not make their condition worse than it is? Can I veil my words? Can I make certain false references? He deals with the problem in two or three ways. He uses a cipher, he refers to Tyre and Egypt and using the descriptive language that applied only to Babylon. And every Judahite captive who was listening to him knew about whom he was talking. But his words said Tyre, Egypt. So the Babylonian secret service couldn't do anything with him because he wasn't talking about Babylon. Gog, Magog—his use of those two terms belong in that same category, and it poses a very fundamental problem that I'll just present and have you live with it for a little while.

If I am under a great threat and on behalf of the guaranteeing of my own existence, I resort to duplicity and hypocrisy, does that make the duplicity less duplicit? It is a crucial problem. It isn't a simple problem; it is a crucial problem. If my life is in jeopardy and I lie my way out, is there a different quality in the morality because of the circumstances under which it took place? What about it? It is the persistent moral problem and ethical problem wherever people are trying to live.[25] The whole morality of the underground during the dictatorship ties in right here. Many people deal with this same problem in the way in which they have handled the loyalty oath that they have had to sign to get their paychecks to bring

---

24. Reference here is to Ezekiel's vision of the new Temple and a New Jerusalem, chaps. 40–48. See, for instance, Ezekiel 40:2–3, "In visions of God he brought me to the land of Israel, and set me down on a very high mountain, on which was a structure like a city.... There was a man whose appearance was like bronze, with a linen cord and a measuring reed in his hand. And he was standing in the gateway."

25. Deception or lying is never a viable moral alternative for Thurman because it destroys the value structure of the one who deceives and lies. "The penalty of deception," Thurman writes, "is to become a deception, with all sense of moral discrimination vitiated" (*Jesus and the Disinherited*, 65).

it home. Or as one of the prophets in the Old Testament, as he walks into the temple with his—by his religious standards, his heathen king who is his employer—and as he walks before the throne he has to genuflect his knee as an act of sacredness and holiness before a foreign god. And the prophet cries out in his agony and says, "If when I walk into the house of and bow my knee before that altar, do not hold it against me, O God of my fathers."[26] What about it? Under what circumstances do you deliberately lay aside the insistence which you feel natively for integrity and right because somebody you love is being threatened, because your life is in jeopardy, because a cause to which you are committed will go down into disintegration and disaster you think, if you do not prove false in the pressure that is placed upon you. What about it? What about it? Ezekiel's answer, "I'll just say what I am going to say in language that everybody who'll want to hear it can understand it and hope it will be so veiled and involved that people who shouldn't hear it, won't hear it." What do you do when you are faced with that kind of circumstance? And it is no answer to say that you are never faced with that kind of circumstance. You are, almost every day of your life. How do you deal with it? I wonder.

---

26. For Naaman, see "Man and the Moral Struggle: Introduction," published in the current volume.

The Message of Micah

August 17, 1952
Fellowship Church

In his sermon on Micah, as in other sermons in this series, Thurman emphasizes the historical and social context of the prophet's activity. Micah, a native of Moresheth-Gath, a town in Judea, flourished as a prophet from c. 740 to c. 697 BCE, was a contemporary of Isaiah, Hosea, and Amos, and witnessed the threat to Israel and Judea from the Assyrian Empire. However, many scholars believe some of the later chapters of Micah (4–5; 7:8–20) were written several centuries after the time of Micah, at the time of the final organization of the book.[1]

Thurman again makes the distinction between the city dweller and the country person in respect to Micah, and argues that his roots and message were akin to those of Amos, neither a rustic nor a city dweller. Like Amos, he preached against false piety and corruption among elites and called for social justice for the poor.[2] A considerable portion of the sermon is spent on the relationship of "mercy" and "justice," a persistent theme in Thurman's writings and sermons. Does justice precede mercy or does mercy precede justice or can both exist in a simple act of kindness that is nonretaliatory and treats the other with humility and grace? In closing, he asks with Micah, "What does God require of thee, then, O son of man? To do justly, to love mercy, and to walk humbly with thy God." To this, he adds, "And that perhaps is the meaning of religion. Certainly it is the meaning of the good life."

---

1. Micah 1:1 states that Micah's prophetic activity took place during the reigns of the Judean kings Jotham, Ahaz, and Hezekiah, roughly from 756 to 697 BCE, though in Jeremiah 26:18 Micah's prophetic tenure is limited to the reign of Hezekiah.

2. Thurman asks his congregation to compare Micah's exalted view of Zion (used interchangeably with Jerusalem and Israel) in 4:1–4 with Isaiah's similar ascription (Isa 2:2–5), both of which reflect the ideology of the Zion tradition in Jerusalem before the exile.

[This is the] end of the series that we have been working on having to do with the message of the prophets of Israel.[3] It has been a very significant journey that we have been taking together, and I hope that as a result of it many fresh insights have come to us all and that we subsequently will draw rather heavily upon the written pages of the prophets as we try to think our way through the fitful days that stretch out immediately ahead of us.

I want to read a little from the prophet Micah, the fourth chapter of Micah:

> But in the last days it shall come to pass, that the mountain of the house of the Lord shall be established in the top of the mountains, and it shall be exalted above the hills; and people shall flow unto it. And many nations shall come, and say, Come, and let us go up to the mountain of the Lord, and to the house of the God of Jacob; and he will teach us of his ways, and we will walk in his paths: for the law shall go forth of Zion, and the word of the Lord from Jerusalem.[4]

Locate that in one of the other prophets?[5] I read it to you a few weeks ago. I'll say who he was a little later. "But they shall sit every man under his vine and under his fig tree; and none shall make them afraid for the mouth of the Lord of hosts hath spoken it."[6]

Every man under his vine and under his fig tree—there's a passage you may recall from your history; it was quoted by George Washington when, on the occasion of the inauguration as president of the United States, a synagogue, a Jewish Synagogue, through its leader addressed a letter to the president congratulating him and congratulating the country because they had finally come through a rather difficult time and established what seemed to them at that time to be the foundation of a new

---

3. Several weeks later Thurman did add a concluding sermon, "The Message of the Prophets," published in this volume.
4. Micah 4:1–2.
5. Isaiah 2:2–5.
6. Micah 4:4.

and creative experiment in government.⁷ And when George Washington answered this Jewish synagogue, he expressed his deep appreciation for the fact that they had so recognized the significance of this moment in American history, and then he said that it is my wish that the future of America will be of such that "every man will sit under his vine and under his fig tree and none shall make him afraid."⁸ I wonder what would he say today.⁹ Could he quote that? But that is not on the point.

Now there is one other passage I'd like to read that also has been on the lips of someone very recently:

> Wherewith shall I come before the Lord, and bow myself before the high God? Shall I come before him with burnt offerings, with calves of a year old? Will the Lord be pleased with thousands of rams, or with ten thousands of rivers of oil? Shall I give my first-born for my transgression [that reference is to child sacrifice], shall I give my first-born for my transgression, the fruit of my body for the sin of my soul? He hath showed thee, O man, what is good; and what doth the Lord require of thee, but to do justly, and to love mercy, and to walk humbly, with thy God?¹⁰

---

7. President Washington responded to the Hebrew Congregation in Newport, Rhode Island, on August 18, 1790, thanking them for an earlier letter of support, writing, "may the Children of the Stock of Abraham, who dwell in this land, continue to merit and enjoy the good will of the other Inhabitants; while every one shall sit in safety under his own vine and fig tree, and there shall be none to make him afraid" (George Washington, *Writings* [New York: Library of America, 1997], 767). At the time, the United States was the only country that gave Jews full citizenship rights. The Constitution abolished religious tests for holding federal office. The congregation's home, the Touro synagogue, built in 1763, is the oldest standing synagogue building in the United States.

8. Micah 4:4 was a favorite Scripture of President George Washington and other early leaders of the new republic. See Carl J. Richard, *The Founders and the Bible* (Lanham, MD: Rowman & Littlefield, 2016), 75–76.

9. A possible reference to either McCarthyism or the expanding US–USSR nuclear arms race.

10. Micah 6:6–8, KJV.

Who quoted that not very long ago? Do you remember? Well, I heard you. It's very interesting.[11]

Now I would like to read Moffatt's translation of that same passage just for your own . . . :

> How shall I enter the Eternal's presence and bow before the God of heaven? Shall I come to him with sacrifices? With yearling calves to offer? Would the Eternal care for rams in thousands or for oil flowing in myriad streams? Shall I offer my first-born son for my sin, fruit of my body for guilt of my soul? O man, he has told you what is good. What does the Eternal ask from you but to be just and kind and live in quiet fellowship with your God?[12]

Now the prophet Micah was a contemporary, a younger contemporary of Isaiah. And he was a bit like Amos because he was a country boy, and Isaiah, of course, was city-bred. And if you bear that in mind as you read the prophets much light will be thrown on the insights which they give because the attitude and the point of view of a city dweller is different from the attitude and the point of view of a non–city dweller. A city dweller has to struggle very hard for his individual survival. He is not cushioned by the group awareness that surrounds the person who lives in a more . . . in a simpler, more pastoral environment and therefore, the city dweller is apt to be very much more self-conscious. And if the city dweller is more self-conscious than the rural dweller, this is generally true, then it means that the city dweller is much more conscious of any impositions upon him. If he is more conscious of himself, he is therefore more conscious of everything that happens to him. So that always it is this self-consciousness on the part of the city dweller that again and again is responsible for the emphasis in the prophet on social justice, social

---

11. A possible reference to a speech President Truman had delivered the previous fall to a convention of the Union of American Hebrew Congregations (the main organization of Reform Judaism) in which Truman condemned "atheistic communism" and quoted Micah 6:8 ("Truman Acclaims Judaism's Center," *New York Times*, October 28, 1951).

12. Micah 6:6–8, Moffatt.

inequalities, as contrasted with the emphasis of a more rural-minded prophet at another level of concern.

Now the prophet Micah believed that people under stress and strain, when things are not going well, they are willing to make any kind of dramatic gesture to appease the gods. So, he says, "Wherewith shall I come before God?" He is disturbed—God is disturbed about me. He is not kindly disposed because I have not been just, I have not been … He lists all the things. So can I placate him with offerings? Even ten thousand rivers of oil, or if I sacrifice my own child,[13] would that satisfy him? It suggests something very interesting that I just want to look at for a second, and that is that for the most part human beings even then and now have not grown very much in the quality of their religious experience. It's very hard to get beyond the stage of superstition in religion. Just straight superstition. Do you believe that? When your times are out of joint, when things are not going right with you, when event after event seems to disintegrate instead of holding together where you are concerned, when everything you touch withers and turns to ashes, when all the tidings that float in your direction are bad tidings, your temptation is to try to placate the forces that you think control that. Isn't that true? You find yourself sometimes even reading the Bible, you know, just reading the Bible, and learning how to pray in your way, dropping into a church. Superstition. That's what he is talking about.

Now that's a superficial way to look at that, of course, and I do not mean to be ungracious. It suggests, however, that there is a recognition when we turn in times of distress to something that is more stabilizing than anything that we know; there's a recognition that life is not completely without morality, and if we can … that the thing that we relate what has happened to us in terms of our private character: that's what is back of that. And it has taken the human race hundreds and thousands of years to move beyond that check-and-balance attitude, beyond the atti-

---

13. There is a debate among scholars as to whether human sacrifice took place in ancient Israel, but there are many instances in which the people of Israel followed the practices of neighboring tribes, especially their conquerors. As Thurman notes, child sacrifice seems to have been taken for granted in the text. The concern, according to most scholars, is that it does not appease God. See Stephen G. Dempster, *Micah* (Grand Rapids, MI: Eerdmans, 2017), 159.

tude of reward and punishment. And even Micah isn't quite beyond that, you see, for he insists that "What does God require but to do justly?" And what is justice? It's still in the category, you see, in that initial statement, of reward and punishment, of balance. One of the earliest of American social philosophers, a man who first wrote in the field of sociology in America, gave a definition for justice that has remained a part of the lore of sociology if not its insight for a long time, and that is that justice is the "artificial, equalization of unequals."[14] Now think about it. Just . . . the artificial equalization of unequals. Where there is inequality it is built up so that it balances something over here. Where there is inequality that moves up this way, it is shaved down so as to fill in the gap over here.

Now the concept has had a very interesting development for at one time, in all human relations, as far as Jehovah was concerned, there was the insistence on the part of the prophets that God, Jehovah permitted, yea, blessed and endorsed, an attitude which says that if I am injured by someone then I am at liberty to injure my injurer to the limit of my strength and ability and his endurance. And for hundreds of years that was it. If you injured me, then I could pay you back as long as I have the will and the strength and you survived. And then there was a shift, a growth, a whole new process, and we see it emerging in some of the codes: something that is called the *lex talionis*,[15] they call it. It's the eye for an eye and the tooth for a tooth doctrine. If I put your eye out, then you may put my eye out. You see that is a great advance over this other one, you see, that if you put my eye out then I can do everything to you as long as I have the strength and ability. But the *lex talionis* moves up a step, you see, a great step, a long stride. It represents a whole growth of maturity of the

---

14. Thurman was paraphrasing Lester Frank Ward (1841–1913), an American scientist and a pioneering sociologist, who said that "individualism has created artificial inequalities" but "socialism seeks to create artificial equalities" (Lester Frank Ward, *Outlines of Sociology* [New York: Macmillan, 1897], 292). For other uses of the quotation by Thurman, see Walter Earl Fluker, *Ethical Leadership: The Quest for Character, Civility and Community* (Minneapolis, MN: Fortress Press, 2009), 141–42; "The Grace of God" (August 1948), in PHWT 4:284; "Justice and Mercy," in *The Growing Edge* (New York: Harper & Brothers, 1956), 79; and "Justice and Mercy" (a different sermon), in Gowler and Jensen, eds., *Howard Thurman*, 132–42.

15. The law of retaliation, whereby a punishment in kind and degree resembles the offense committed.

human spirit, a deepening of an awareness of the meaning of life in terms that extend beyond the event in which human beings are involved. So an eternal note begins to appear in human relations under this *lex talionis*, this balance: I will do to you precisely what you have done to me.

Now the third step is the step that appears in the second part of what Micah has to say: to love mercy. And we find this expressed in the Sermon on the Mount. All this review of the evolution of the doctrine of justice in human relations appears in the Sermon on the Mount in the same manner that I am describing it here. And Jesus insists, you see, that mercy is more important than justice. Micah says that you should love—Israel should love mercy, and if it loves mercy, then will it do justice? Or is mercy something that is in another category completely from justice? Under what conditions do you regard yourself as acting mercifully towards someone? Let's just think about it. In your own experience, when you have done a merciful deed, what kind of deed is it? Is it one in which you could have been destructive but you weren't? And you congratulate yourself because of your self-control? Is that being merciful? When you are merciful, what happens to the person who is on the receiving end of your mercy? Maybe that's the way we should look at it. Let's think about it now. What kind of test, as seen through the eyes of the person who experiences your mercy: Does it inspire ill will and contempt in him? Does it make him feel that it would be very much better if you had been unmerciful because then, at least, he would have had his self-respect intact? Is that what it means? Is there a difference between being merciful and being kind? Or are they one and the same thing? What about it? When you are kind, what are you? Is there ever an element of obligation in kindness? Can you be kind to someone because you are under some obligation to be kind to them, or is there in kindness always the element that is stripped of all obligation? What about it? So that when I am kind it is as when I am merciful. Is it? That I confer upon the other person, gratuitously, without obligation, the gracious act. Does kindness, does mercy mean dealing with individuals as if they were yourself?—Or is that too narrow an interpretation? Does kindness mean dealing with people as if they were more than yourself? Or is kindness surrounding your relationships with little or big deeds that are gratuitous and obligation free and responsibility free so that when I do this thing not only is it true that I do not bind the recipient but I release the recipient? Is that what we mean by it?

One very subtle thing about mercy and about kindness is that when someone has been kind to you, one thing is always true, you can't ever pay them back; you can't repay the kind act. Have you ever tried? Because, you see, you can't establish any basis for measurement. When Oscar Wilde was being brought from the court of bankruptcy back to prison, handcuffed to this arm of the sheriff, as they walked down the long corridor in this great place, the crowd milling all around, and they jeered and did all sorts of things because Oscar Wilde was a very unpopular prisoner. Then when they came to the center of this jeering group of people, one man stepped out from the crowd, lifted his hat, held it at attention and bowed his head until the prisoner and the sheriff passed. And that silent act hushed the jeering crowd into silence, and Oscar Wilde writing about it the next day from his prison said, "This simple act of unasked for kindness, this gratuitous expression of a kind and gracious heart has made," to quote him, "the desert of my prison blossom like the rose."[16] When someone has been kind to you, you can't repay it. And that is why there is something that has the element of the eternal about kindness, for invariably, at long last, the kind act of which I have been the recipient multiplies itself in my spirit and expresses itself in this way and that way and the

---

16. Oscar Wilde (1854–1900), the Irish playwright, poet, essayist, and novelist, was convicted of sodomy and "gross indecency" in 1895 and sentenced to two-years hard labor at Reading Gaol. Thurman is quoting and paraphrasing from *De Profundis*, "Where there is sorrow there is holy ground. Someday people will realize what that means. They will know nothing of life until they do. Robbie [a correspondent and friend of Wilde] and natures like his can realize it. When I was brought down from my prison to the court of Bankruptcy, between two policemen, Robbie waited in the long dreary corridor that, whom before the whole crowd, an action so sweet and simple hushed into silence, he might gravely raise his hat to me, as, handcuffed and with bowed head, I passed him by. Men have gone to heaven for smaller things that . . . the memory of that little, lovely, silent act has unsealed for me all the wells of pity; made the desert blossom like a rose. . . ." From Oscar Wilde, *The Complete Works of Oscar Wilde, Volume 2, De Profundis, "Epistola: In Carcere et Vinculis*, ed. Ian Small (Oxford: Clarendon Press, 2005), 85. See also Oscar Wilde, *The Ballad of Reading Gaol* (1898). "Robbie" was Robert Ross (1869–1918), Wilde's close friend, his literary executor, and the editor of the first, expurgated edition of *De Profundis* in 1905.

other way in a wide variety of relations that are not tied up at all with the individual who was kind to me.

And now—so the prophet Micah says, "If you want to be pleasing to God," he said to his people, "don't waste time with burnt offerings. Don't waste time making sacrifices of rivers of oil. Don't bow down before Jehovah and say all these things. There is only one thing that you need to do: deal with your fellow men justly." And to be sure that there was clear understanding as to what he meant by that kind of justice, he said, "And to do it justly as men who love mercy, as men who are kind." So that you go around releasing people from prison in the way you deal with them. And then finally he said, "Walk humbly with God." Humbly with God. Just one word about that.

How do you walk humbly with God? How do you? How do you walk humbly with anybody? By always measuring yourself by the other person? Or by pretending that you are really worse than you are, you know. I remember when I was a boy, a rather elderly lady, in the presence of my grandmother, said something very nice about me, about a little speech that I had made in the Children's Day cantata. Well, you don't make a speech in a cantata. Well anyway it was something like that. And when she said this very nice thing to me, I said, "Oh, Mrs. Murray, don't say anything like that." And my grandmother watched this performance, and then when Mrs. Murray went on her way my grandmother said, "I'd like to tell you something, and that is that before life gets through with you, there will be so many people who will say ungracious things about you that whenever anybody wants to say any kind word about you, be sure to let them do it. And stop pretending that you don't enjoy it." Is that what they mean by humility? Always selling one's self at a discount in the open market? Is that humility? Or is that arrogance, pride, conceit gripped by the deep notion that you can outsmart life? Interesting. But is humility understanding what my equipment is? Coming to grips with who I am, what I am as accurately and as fully as possible: a clear-eyed appraisal of myself. And in the light of the dignity of my own sense of being I walk with God step by step as he walks with me. This is I, with my weaknesses and my strength, with my abilities and my liabilities; this is I, a human being myself! And it is that that God salutes. So that the more I walk with him and he walks with me, the more I come into the full-orbed significance of who I am and what I am. That is to walk humbly with God.

"What does God require of thee, then, O son of man? To do justly, to love mercy, and to walk humbly with thy God." And that perhaps is the meaning of religion. Certainly it is the meaning of the good life.

The Religion of the Prophets

September 7, 1952
Fellowship Church

In this, the concluding sermon in the Message of the Prophets sermon series, Thurman tries to summarize his view of the Hebrew prophets. The prophets rooted their mission in the sovereignty of God and God's covenant with the Israelites. They wrestled with the uniqueness, what Thurman calls the "peculiar" relationship between the Israelites and their complex history and their God, "who is the righteous will expressing himself in these events." They wrestled with the universality of God, and whether "if behind this fence there is any meaning, it must be a meaning that also includes the other side of the fence." Christianity, which now claimed to have replaced Israel in God's covenant, faced the same questions about the universality or particularity of God's message, and arrived at the same inconclusive results.

The deepest message of the prophets for Thurman is that "the ultimate, the ultimate *meaning of human history is never in the events of human history. But the ultimate meaning of human history is in the mind and the spirit of him out of whose stirring movement the whole creative process emerged." This meant that no one could be sure of their role in this history, and anyone and everyone could be crucial in the process of redemption, with the "God of the whole universe who has a covenant with all of humankind and all of human history." But in the chaos of the present, "the prophets placed a social responsibility upon the individual even though the ultimate responsibility for the redemption of the world rested in the mind and on the heart of him who by a series of mighty events, created the world." And this, Thurman concludes, is the legacy of the Hebrew prophets, "so rewarding and so disturbing," for "Jew or gentile, agnostic, atheist, free-wheeler, whatever we may be."*

The Religion of the Prophets   199

I WANT TO DO what it has not been possible to do, pull together in one sermon the heart of the prophetic intent as far as its religious insight and implications are concerned. For, even though the prophets of Israel apparently were concerned with events, their deep concern was with religion and its meaning. And the concern with religion and its meaning was for them rooted in two or three simple things to which I would call your attention, because I think they may be basic to the whole religious quest of the human spirit. Technically the first and important segment about the religion of the prophets is this: a conception of the sovereignty of God. For them God was a present fact in their experience. God represented for them righteous will. God was personal. Creator of the world he was, and as righteous will (bear in mind now the basic idea is the sovereignty of God: that's the hook on which they hung all this), that God, as righteous will, expressed that will in a series of mighty events. The first event was the creation of the world. So that all through the prophetic literature there is a sense of the movement of the first chapter of Genesis: "In the beginning God created the heavens and the earth...." Righteous will. Self-conscious. Therefore, you see, expressing himself in a series of events, one of which was the creation of the world. And in the creating of the world, time, also, was created. And the stage was set, then, for a series of other events connected one with the other.

Now, many times, when we study the Book of Genesis (and this is not a discussion of the Book of Genesis, as such)—but many times when we study the Book of Genesis, we are puzzled because we try to make of the Book of Genesis a treatment of geology or one of these other long "ologies" about how the world was made—a theory of creation, to make a scientific treatise out of it, and, of course, we can't do that. We get into every kind of difficulty. Men have done wonderful things with it: they've said the six days do not refer to six twenty-four-hour periods, but they refer to the six eons of human history—anything to try to satisfy East and West at the same time. But the insistence of the Book of Genesis is merely that the creation of the world was a divine act—a mighty act. And in the creating of the world, the whole time-space process was set in motion. And once the time-space process is set in motion, then there is a climate, an atmosphere, in which antecedent and consequence, reaping and sowing, the whole logical process of events could be fulfilled.

Now another one of these mighty acts was the calling of Abraham and harassing Abraham's mind with a dream, with a vision that caused the sand to burn hot under his feet always until he could get to some resting place, some specially prepared place, and that all of Abraham's seed would be blessed and would multiply, etc.

Another one of these events was the calling of Moses. And here the prophetic movement begins to take place. For the calling of Moses ties up, intimately, with what, from the point of view of the prophets, was one of the central events in human history: and that was the redeeming of the Jewish people from their Egyptian enslavement. Moses, inspired by this God who is the righteous will which expresses itself in a series of mighty acts in human history, causes Moses to lead this little band of people out of their enslavement into a Promised Land. And, as a result of that event and as an expression of its meaning, there emerged a peculiar relationship between the people, who themselves were pulled out of captivity, and the God, who is the righteous will expressing himself in these events.

So the covenant, then, between God and his people becomes the centerpiece around which all of the religious experience and the prophetic fire of this long line of distinguished human spirits got its rights. The covenant was an agreement between this self-conscious righteous will, this God, and a group of people. If you are true to the covenant then you do show forth the fact that you are my people; if you are not true to the covenant, then you are welching on your word and on your agreement. Now that's the thesis. I don't care which prophet you look at, he moves back and forth in that area: the covenant, which is a formal and informal agreement between the God who expresses himself in these mighty acts, and the people, carrying with it mutual responsibility: "I will be your people and you will be my people—I will be your God."[1] Now in order that you might know the meaning of the covenant, I will move in your minds and in your spirits so that there will emerge in you a guide that will protect you. Pillar of fire by night, pillar of cloud by day—the external expression of that. There will turn up in your midst people who will guide you, lead you; a whole succession of people.

---

1. See Exodus 6:7; Jeremiah 30:22.

Now sin then, for the prophets, became any deviation from the private, primary agreement between Israel and Jehovah.

Now, if God is righteous will, expressing himself in human history in this way, then it suggests, and this is the second thing in the religious insight of the prophets, it suggests that there is no event that is outside of the scope and the inclusive concern of this God, who expresses himself in a series of mighty acts: One of those acts is the covenant and the covenant people. Now see what that does. The prophets could not arrive at that position immediately, for at first, you see, the covenant is something that belongs to me and to my people. And it belongs to us because of a peculiar relationship between us and between God. Standing within that context we can look over there at all the other people and say, "Well, I don't know how it happens that we are over here. But we are and you are over there. I'm sorry for you. I would like to—I wish, somehow, you could be included with us, but you can't be." And we all like that, don't we? We like to feel that in some way we are peculiar: that the thing that we enjoy because of this advantage or that advantage or this gift or whatever it may be is ours in some exclusive sense. And the human spirit has never been able to solve that conflict, the conflict that arises between this deep conviction that there be few in all the world who rate being saved, for instance, on the one hand, and on the other hand the deeply lying conviction that is just as insistent, that if, behind this fence there is any meaning, it must be a meaning that also includes the other side of the fence. So between those two points we are squeezed back and forth, and Israel was no exception. Now if God—if we are God's people, you see, and the covenant is in some peculiar sense our covenant, our relationship with God, then our responsibility, only, is within this compound, within this context. And we can't possibly have any responsibility for people outside. So all the Deuteronomic codes or laws: for instance, loving your neighbor as you love yourself—loving your neighbor meant your neighbor over on this side, not over there, but over on this side.[2] Let your land lie fallow for seven years and then you free all the slaves, and if anybody comes, during that period, if anybody comes who is hungry, you feed him.[3] If he needs,

---

2. Leviticus 19:18.

3. Thurman combines several passages from the Torah; letting your land go fallow during the Sabbatical year (Exod 23:11; Lev 25:4); freeing Hebrew slaves after

you give it to him—all on this side, and be true to the covenant. And we've never been able to get rid of that in human history, have we? I don't know. We can't get rid of the feeling that what is binding for my group is binding in a way that does not reach over.

Now there were prophets then, and this is the important thing, there were prophets then who couldn't ever get outside this fence. And they felt, if you read certain words of Amos, for instance, even though he was very revolutionary in some other ways; read certain words of Jeremiah, certain words of Hosea, even though Hosea pushes it, pushes the boundary out in another direction. In any of the prophets, practically, you see that there is a big movement in their minds and spirits that resisted any insistence that what is discovered over on this side, in the covenant relationship of Israel with God, is ultimately significant for Israel, only if it be significant for the rest of the world.

So the movement catches up with us in the development of the Christian church. So the Christian church becomes what in the New Testament? The Christian Church becomes the group of people with whom this God, who expresses himself in self-conscious acts of will, in mighty events in human history—the people with whom this God has a peculiar relationship. So that in the New Testament development, the church takes the place of Israel. In the Old Testament and with the prophets, Israel has this covenant with God. So the apostle Paul talks of what? A new covenant.[4] What's he talking about? What's he mean? That God now has a relationship with a new group of people, namely, the church, which relationship transcends his old relationship that he had with these old people. So that the church then becomes the battleground for the same kind of struggle between exclusiveness and inclusiveness that we experienced in the Old Testament and the prophets in Israel.

So, how does it express itself, then? I remember when I was a boy—maybe you will remember too, when you were something else—how, in my community a man died, and he was not a member of the church and

---

seven years of bondage (Exod 21:2–11; Deut 15:12–18); and feeding the stranger (Lev 19:33).

4. Second Corinthians 3:7–11. Paul's understanding of God's covenant with Israel is more complicated than in Thurman's account; see E. P. Sanders, *Paul: A Very Short Introduction* (Oxford: Oxford University Press, 1991), 137–49.

the minister of the church said, "Well, we can't bury you from the church. We can't bury you from the church because you died out of Christ. Now you should be buried, but not from the church." And then—so he refused to do it. But there was an evangelist in the community who recognized that this was a golden opportunity. So he volunteered to take the sermon for this man. And when all the people gathered together and went to church and he preached the funeral, he preached the man into hell.[5] And he called attention to the fact that this is an object lesson: if you live out of the church you die in your sins and you go to hell. Now, that is just the logic of the various levels of exclusiveness that we practice. It doesn't have to be in religion, but that's the exclusiveness which the prophets felt as true Judahites, and the exclusiveness, the inclusiveness, rather, which they felt at moments when the movement of the spirit of God was triumphantly radical in them, precipitated a conflict that moves straight down the center of Israel. And the same now—dear old Augustine, with that mighty mind of his, holding in its power the mental stability of an empire, while the political expressions of that empire disintegrated. And how did he do it? He did it by insisting that the kingdoms of this world and the kingdom of God—the kingdom of God transcended the kingdoms of this world—and therefore, the kingdoms of this world may disintegrate and collapse, etc., but if you are in this other kingdom you will be salvaged. And out of that came, quite logically and consistently, a doctrine which is fundamental in Catholicism even to this day, that the church, which now is just equivalent to the community of Israel—the church, outside of it there can be no salvation. So if you accept the church, then it means you accept the medicine of salvation and the medicine of salvation is what? The sacraments: baptism, this, this, this, this. And if you accept that medicine, then you are on this side. And what happens to people on the other side who are outside of that? Go back and read the prophets, and at once you will see the struggle that the prophets had with reference to the ethical meaning of all kinds of human relationships in the context of this covenant. And transfer the same thing into the New Testament,

---

5. Thurman was describing his own experience as a young boy at the service for his stepfather. Thurman had not yet publicly described the incident and the hurt it caused him, and would not do so until 1959; see *Footprints of a Dream: The Story of the Church for the Fellowship of All Peoples* (New York: Harper & Brothers, 1959), 15–16.

on to our own period in human history, and you will see the problem has remained essentially the same.

Now, finally, even though the prophets did not consistently solve the problem, they recognized it. And you see what the problem is now. But one or two of the prophets spilled over and felt that the only meaning that the covenant had was at last expressed in spreading the boundaries of the covenant until it included the whole human race. And God, then, becomes not merely the God of the covenant with Israel, but the God of the whole universe, who has a covenant with all of humankind and all of human history. And, therefore, the logic of that is that since the creation of the world, and I'm almost through now, since the creation of the world was one of the mighty acts of God that precipitated this whole process, and since he is involved, then, in the world and all the events of human history . . . human history has a great meaning and a great dignity, for how desolate is the human spirit if it feels that in all of the ebb and flow of events, the individual or groups of individuals are stranded, isolated, and alone in the vastness: that's the desolation where men do not have this other position.

Now the prophets said since God did this, then the redemption of the world is the concern of God. The redemption of the world is the concern of God. And how did the prophets deal with that? They dealt with it in terms of their interpretation of the meaning of the future. And what is the meaning of the future? The meaning of the future expresses itself in terms of the remnant! So all the people may be apostate, but not quite all. There is always a remnant left on the basis of which the one who precipitated these mighty events in human history can fasten his dream upon their mind, and they will build again. And then, even though that civilization disappears, out of it will be another remnant—a remnant: a growing edge, if you please. So the prophets felt that even though they had a conscience about human history and about human sin, the redemption of the world was also to be one of the mighty acts of God. It is a very interesting thing. So in all the pictures that you get—even in the New Testament with the church, because the church picked up the same idea—the redemption of the world finally will be one of the mighty acts. And for Christian theology, again and again, it is regarded as the final act. And in the thinking of Jesus, you remember, the same sort of picture emerges:

at the end of human history, the great judgment scene: all the people are there, sheep on the right, goats on the left.[6] The ultimate, the ultimate meaning of human history is never in the events of human history. But the ultimate meaning of human history is in the mind and the spirit of him out of whose stirring movement the whole creative process emerged.

Now that means what? It means, you see, that you can decide that since the remnant is in God's hands, God is going to do this anyway, there just isn't any point in your doing anything. You can just sit it out. If you can just sit it out, then he will do it. Now there is an abundance of material on that side, because when you examine your own life, you see, many times, that after you have worked hard, exhausted everything you know to exhaust, the thing happens without your effort. And then sometimes when you put forth every effort that you can to hold it back, it moves on: when you put forth every effort you know how to make it come to pass, it doesn't come to pass. The same movement expresses itself in our religious development, where any person who is acquainted with prayer, the meaning of prayer, recognizes at once that sometimes you fulfill all of the requirements of spiritual exercises; you get the spirit quiet, your mind in focus, everything in you is in one moment of suspended waiting for the invasion of the spirit of God, and nothing happens. And then there are some other times when your mind is full of all sorts of things and you are just in one ball of chaos and confusion: and right in the midst of all of that churning disorder a strange new sense of meaning begins to gather inside of you and you feel warm and whole and clean, even though you know you are dirty: the movement of God. So that even in the dimension of the spiritual life there is this process. So, the prophets insisted that everybody, and this is the cleverest insight of them all, I think, clever in the true sense of the word, everybody in any civilization, any community of Israel, everybody stood in candidacy to be the remnant. So I'd better be careful because I might be the remnant. Because, who knows, I might be the one, the fruit of whose womb will be the creative remnant, the Messiah. And with that notion, you see, with that notion, the prophets placed a social responsibility upon the individual, even though the ultimate responsibility for the redemption of the world rested in the

---

6. Matthew 25:33.

mind and on the heart of him who by a series of mighty events created the world.

And so, whether we be Jew or gentile, agnostic, atheist, free-wheeler, whatever we may be, every single fundamental moral and ethical concept that influences the thinking and the overtone of Western culture and civilization finds somewhere, within the restless minds of the prophets, streams that feed them and sustain them. And I am happy to be a part of a tradition so rewarding and so disturbing.

ZEPHANIAH: EXPOSITION

The Interpreter's Bible, 1956

In 1946 George Buttrick engaged Thurman as one of the editors of the massive Interpreter's Bible, *a twelve-volume edition of the Old and New Testaments with extensive commentary.[1] Of the several dozen editors of the* Interpreter's Bible, *Thurman was the only African American. At some time in the early 1950s, Thurman was asked to write the exposition, a commentary, for the Books of Habakkuk and Zephaniah.[2] It is not clear why Thurman was asked to write on these two books or why he agreed to write them, but it speaks to Thurman's close connection to the prophets and their message, and his interest in the prophets in the early 1950s, when he delivered his sermon series on the prophets.[3] Because of space limitations, the Zephaniah commentary was omitted from the* Papers of Howard Washington Thurman.[4]

---

1. Howard Thurman to George A. Buttrick, May 3, 1946, in PHWT 3:190–92. George A. Buttrick (1892–1980), born and raised in England, was one of the most prominent preachers of his time, a prolific author, and the Plummer Professor of Christian Ethics at Harvard University from 1954 to 1960. He was the chief editor of *The Interpreter's Bible*, 12 vols. (New York: Abingdon Press, 1951–1957).

2. We are not certain when Thurman wrote the two expositions for the books of Habakkuk and Zephaniah, but both were published in 1956. The Habakkuk commentary was reprinted in PHWT 4:136–50. See the annotation for more background into Thurman's only efforts at extended biblical commentary. *The Interpreter's Bible* included three kinds of commentary in addition to the biblical text itself: the introduction to each biblical book, an exegesis, and an exposition, which consisted of more general reflections on the text.

3. One possible reason for the assignment of these two books to Thurman is their relative brevity.

4. "Zephaniah: Text, Exegesis, and Exposition," in *The Interpreter's Bible, vol. VI* (New York: Abingdon Press, 1956), 1013–34. Only the exposition is reprinted here. Biblical quotations use the RSV.

The Book of Zephaniah is set during the reign of the Judean king Josiah (640–608 BCE). Like his probable contemporary Jeremiah, Zephaniah castigates the Judeans for their idolatry, calls for their repentance, and concludes with an eschatological vision of God restoring justice in the world. For all that Thurman found narrow and minatory in Zephaniah and the other Hebrew prophets, he applauded the potential breadth of their vision. "The idea of monotheism," states Thurman, "leads irrevocably to the idea of one people—one family inclusive of all peoples—under God." This seeking the unity of all peoples in the unity of God, he adds, "is just the reverse of the modern tendency." Zephaniah's message for Thurman was that "the time shall come when there shall be no alien lands, no strange peoples, and no expression of life outside the divine accord. Every knee shall bow and every living thing and all creation shall join in the grand paean of praise and worship of the God of life who is at once the God of faith."

1:1–18. The Day of the Lord.—Zephaniah[5] is dealing with mighty words of judgment. It is the judgment of God upon Jerusalem and Judah. The mood is that of the sensitive religious spirit so outraged by the collective unrighteousness of an age or a people or a civilization that all of life seems to be stained, to be unholy. It can find rest only in the thought of some kind of complete and final decimation. And such a decimation bears most heavily upon those whose iniquity is deliberate, who have put aside the knowledge of a better way. It is one thing to run afoul of righteousness in a mindless, amoral manner. Under such circumstances the penalty is nevertheless exacting, but somehow it seems to be softened by the fact of innocence.

There is a sense of justice which ultimately takes into account the fact that the offender against God was not quite aware of the awful import of his deeds. It is revealed in one's innate reaction in the presence of death caused by nature as over against death caused by a deliberate act of violence on the part of human beings. When we are faced with death by what may be called "an act of God," there is something clean

---

5. The Book of Zephaniah identifies its author as flourishing during the reign of Josiah, the Judean king who reigned from 639 to 609 BCE, though portions of the book might date from the time of the exile in Babylon.

and unfouled about it, despite the fact itself. We may be filled with awe or overwhelmed by a profound sense of mystery or even helplessness. But when we are faced with death by another human being, there is something nasty and foul about it. It depresses, humiliates, and degrades; it is an attack upon the very grounds of the integrity of the race. The same qualitative difference appears in the reaction to the innocent man or nation who runs afoul of God's law. Jerusalem and Judah know what the law of God is; he has planted it in their hearts. The judgment of God against them has to do therefore not only with the external aspects of their situation; in their inward parts there is a laying waste. This the prophet sees with deep clarity.

The conception of human history as being a climactic movement is most significant. It occurs many times in the thought of Israel. It points up the basic difference between a philosophy of history and a theology of history. Both of these get their meaning from the theory of time upon which they are projected.

There are at least two important theories of time that have influenced the thought and behavior of the race. One is what may be regarded as circular. All creation is involved in an endless series of repetitious events, occurrences, or even existences. All creatures are time bound and cannot escape the time-space necessity of their existence. No margins of reality can be experienced outside this necessity. It is important to make clear that this conception of time is in some sense transcendent, as far as any particular time-space event is concerned. All events are conceived as taking place in time, even though time itself is not an event. Even dramatic events such as birth and death are seen as taking place in time: thus time becomes coterminous with existence itself. Outside time there is no existence, because there can be no frame of reference for awareness. Such a view really means that time itself is a perpetually revolving image of eternity, if eternity is regarded as an awareness without differentiation.

Given the fact of existence as the beginning of the time process, continuity is made possible by it, and the only relief from that continuity must mean release from time. The interpretation of history (time-space events of long or short duration) growing out of such a theory must result in a long-drawn-out or endless futility unless there is some device for breaking the perpetual rotation. The meaning of history must be very narrowly circumscribed in terms of a sheer antecedent and consequence relation, with ample provision made for the swift judgment of the act; or the meaning of history must be determined by the possibility that certain events will break the cycle of repetition and make possible the escape from the time-space predicament. The bearing of all events upon this possibility becomes at once the basis of the philosophy of history.

The other theory is one which regards time as an irreversible process moving in a definite direction. In this theory time has a beginning and an ending. The beginning and ending are not involved in the fateful resultants of events, but rather in the quality of time-space experience. It suggests that within the time band the event may take on the character of the timeless, the finite may become involved in the infinite while it remains finite. It was this manner of apprehending time that claimed the mind and the thought of the prophet.

But to return to the distinction between a philosophy of history and a theology of history. A philosophy of history seeks to make an end of historic process. If there is a goal in history, it is thought of in terms of process itself. Such a goal is the product of historical evolution and can have meaning only in direct relation to the facts of history. In no sense can such a goal be regarded as transcendent or having a meaning beyond and perhaps outside history. A theology of history, however, views history as a process in time moving always toward a definite goal. The total process is relevant to a wider plan that includes but is not derived from human history. Such is the conception of the day of the Lord (vs. 7)[6] of which the prophet speaks. It is the moment when the true meaning of life, of event, of history, of creation itself will be made clear. There is no escape from it. God will search Jerusalem with lamps (vs. 12).[7] From the divine scrutiny there is no hiding place. Of this the prophet is so sure that he calls the roll of those who seem to think that God has been unmindful of their deeds because they are the prestige-bearing members of society (vss. 4–6).

---

6. "Be silent before the Lord God! For the day of the Lord is at hand" (Zeph 1:7). All biblical quotations and citations in Thurman's exegesis and the endnotes are from the Revised Standard Version (RSV), unless otherwise noted.

7. "At that time, I will search Jerusalem with lamps, and I will punish the men who are thickening upon their lees, those who say in their hearts, 'The Lord will not do good, nor will he do ill'" (Zeph 1:12).

The sweeping character of the divine accounting is completely devastating. It falls upon those in authority as well as upon the less responsible. For the day of the Lord is the ultimate guarantor of the equality of man. It is a grand and noble affirmation. Soon or late, one by one, each must account for his deeds.

The same conception appears in the thought of Jesus concerning the Last Judgment. Here is the climax of human history and before God all peoples of the earth appear (Matt. 25:31–46). They are divided into two groups: the sheep on the right, the goats on the left. But unlike most of the picture that Zephaniah draws for us, it is a time of reward as well as of punishment. The thing that determines whether a man goes to the left or to the right is not the arbitrary will of the judge but the deeds of the man himself. In the thought of Jesus the moral judgment does have an empirical basis in history.

Near the end of the chapter the prophet draws a most striking picture of the distress of those upon whom the day of the Lord makes its sudden appearance. They are dazed. They shall walk like the blind (vs. 17).[8] All the grounds of their security have given way; the evil in which they have been engaged has moved from outside them in their deeds and actions, and now has taken over the deep center of their souls. For the first time in their lives they cannot pay their bills. All of the accumulated security which they have built up is completely worthless. At last here is something from which their gold and silver cannot deliver them. They are stripped to the literal substance of themselves, face to face with God; and there is nothing they can say to him.

There is nothing they can say to him because already in their hearts they have said that God is completely without moral character. The prophet states that they say in their hearts, The Lord will not do good, neither will he do evil (vs. 12). This is the final atheism, because it reduces all values to zero and strips life of its moral significance. It is a form of moral nihilism in which the point of reference for value-judgment is locked within the confines of ends that do not extend beyond the individual. The behavior pattern resulting from such amorality finds its

---

8. "I will bring distress on men, so that they shall walk like the blind, because they have sinned against the Lord; their blood shall be poured out like dust, and their flesh like dung" (Zeph 1:17).

dynamic in the temporary success it may achieve in fulfilling itself. If it is true that the God worshiped is the God with whom we must deal at last, then to such as worship a God to whom moral values have no significance there can be no alternative but an end that is like the life, barren and meaningless.

2:1–7. The Way of Escape.—There is but one way to escape the wrath of God—that is to change one's direction. The judgment of God may be averted by Judah if she stops and considers. If she will hold assembly,[9] surely there will be opportunity under God for the distilled wisdom of the race to come to the fore, reminding all of the meaning of the life that is being lived. There is a chance that disaster may be averted if action is taken before the wrath of the Lord is unleashed. In the general assembly there will be a chance for the simple of heart and the humble to be heard. It is they who are not smart enough to go against the divine will.

Here is something that men often overlook. The strong, the powerful, those who carry great authority and upon whose decision turns the destiny of the body politic, are apt ever to ignore the humble and the simple man. The responsibility of the ordinary, garden-variety individual must never be forgotten. In one of Petrarch's *Letters of Old Age* appear these words:[10]

> When a word must be spoken to further a good cause, and those whom it behooves to speak remain silent, anybody ought to raise his voice, and break a silence which may be fraught with evil. . . .[11] Many a time a few simple words have helped further the welfare of the nation, no matter who uttered them; the voice itself displaying the latent powers, sufficed to move the hearts of men.

It is so easy to underestimate the potential power of one word spoken at the critical moment! We say to ourselves sometimes that because we are not famous or learned or rich or powerful or gifted, our word means

---

9. "Come together and hold assembly, O shameless nation" (Zeph 2:1).

10. A favorite quote of Thurman, from J. Lohse, ed., *Thoughts from the Letters of Petrarch* (London: J. M. Dent, 1901), 125, from the Italian humanist Francesco Petrarch (1304–1374), "Senile," or "Letters of Old Age," Book VII, Letter 1.

11. Ellipsis in Thurman's original source.

nothing in the presence of a great injustice or a great iniquity. Who would pay attention to us? Many good causes are hindered, often nameless persons are brought to untimely ends, because "those whom it behooves to speak remain silent"; and because they do not speak, we do not speak. It is important to remember that there is no limit to the power of any single life or any single voice when it is the only outlet, the only channel for righteousness in a fateful situation. The silence of the high and mighty sometimes gives greater power to the simple voice of the solitary individual.

There is still another aspect to be noted here. The perspective from which even the prophet looks at human history can become distorted due to the despair growing out of the hopelessness of the situation. The more closely he is associated with the life of his times the more clearly he may see the starkness of the depravity of his people. The surer he is of the judgment of God the more convinced he may become that in its clear sweep all will be carried away. That any may escape because they have sought righteousness is a rare but highly precarious prospect. What saves him from complete despair is the recollection that God will somehow be mindful of a remnant of the house of Judah (vs. 7).

No situation is ever completely without hope as far as the divine option is concerned. God is never without a redemptive alternative. This is the meaning of the remnant. And that meaning becomes clear the moment we apply the insight in terms of personal behavior. Despite a man's pretensions, as long as he has a fair degree of mental health he does not give up his sense of self. True, he may not be as good as his admirers think he is, or as good as his mother thinks he is, but he does not give himself up. On the contrary, he clings to himself with an abiding enthusiasm. Somewhere deep within him is the assurance that he can and will be a better man. Something seems ever to be arguing on the side of the wisdom of a better alternative. The margin favoring the seed of the remnant concept is resident in the life of every man.

But this is not all. The psychology of the remnant is manifest in every situation where love abounds. Where there is love between human beings the allowance, the exception, is always made. Somehow the blow is softened and the harsh judgment mellowed into something which redeems. We are never quite willing to say that the bad deed done by the beloved is quite what it appears to be. If we can get the true story, the accurate account, there will appear sufficient reason to make forgiveness a mutually shared experience. Always this is implicit in Yahweh's relationship with Israel. The judgment of the prophet bears down mercilessly in the fulfillment of the task appointed him by God, but running through it all is another note, full of the warm overtones of lovingkindness. This total tendency becomes articulate at the place of the remnant in the stormy experiences of God with his people.

8–15. The Enemies of Judah.—The rest of the chapter deals with the judgment of God against the enemies of Judah. The proof offered as justification of the judgment is the fact that they needled and taunted God's people and made boasts against their territory (vs. 8).[12] For this they will be punished by a complete destruction of their cities and their civilization. Even their gods will be destroyed. When this is accomplished,

> . . . to him [the Lord of hosts][13] shall bow down,
>   each in its place,
>   all the lands of the nations.[14]

The tendency on the part of the prophet to regard the enemies of his people as also the enemies of God is a very human one. The destruction which is to be meted out is all-inclusive—those who are responsible for policies and those who are not, the guilty and the innocent. At best, in retrospect, it is a curious kind of ethical behavior. There is to be no discrimination in judgment. The assumption is that even the alien nations are responsible to God. This is equivalent to saying that even though the other nations worship other gods, the fact of their being regarded as morally responsible to God means that they are in candidacy to worship the true God. An attitude of exclusive relationship to the one true God leads inevitably to the conclusion that the borders of such exclusiveness must be widened until all are included.

---

12. "I have heard the taunts of Moab and the revilings of the Ammonites, how they have taunted my people and made boasts against their territory" (Zeph 2:8).
13. Bracketed text is in original.
14. Zephaniah 2:11.

Of course there can be no universal worship of the true God unless all people are one. The idea of monotheism leads irrevocably to the idea of one people—one family inclusive of all peoples—under God. This is just the reverse of the modern tendency. The unity of the peoples of the earth is manifest in a wide variety of interdependencies made possible by the annihilation of space and time. This has been achieved by the application of scientific method to the world of nature. Given the facts making for one world, they lead irrevocably to one faith as the logic of the modern experience. The demand for one faith to match one world means that the concept of monotheism is the only one that provides a religious basis for modern life. The insight of the prophet becomes the necessitous affirmation for modern man.

3:1–20. Beyond Judgment.—Jerusalem has betrayed the Eternal. The proof of her apostasy is the fact that

> her prophets are wanton,
> > faithless men.[15]

Even her priests do violence to God's law. This has happened even though it is clear that it is not the Lord by whom they are guided in this disgraceful behavior. These men are acquainted with the righteousness of the Lord. They know what his record is; it is its own witness. Surrounded by the evidence of his righteousness and his wrath, they have not taken it into account. They have gone on their relentless way, unmindful of what their eyes have seen and their hearts have felt.

It is important to note the crucial problem ever present for the man whose daily work involves him in the use of the holy materials of religious worship and dedication. First, such a man tends to develop a veneer of professionalism. He is a prophet, not a religious man; he is a priest, not a religious man. This professionalism becomes a part of the etiquette of his calling. Second, there is an increasing immunity to the personal moral demands of his work. It is true that no man can handle the holy materials of worship as a part of vocation without either becoming more holy thereby or developing an immunity so that he will not be affected by his

---

15. Zephaniah 3:4.

function. The rationalization is that what God requires of the average layman is not required of the priest: "Become more holy and genuine or less holy and unreal." The handling of the rites of the office turns into a substitute for becoming one with one's function.

The time will come, so the chapter declares, when God will be his own witness.[16] He will gather together all peoples and enter into judgment against them. At such a time he will change the speech and give to all a common tongue, the purpose of which will be to enable all to worship God and serve him with one accord. The dream of seer and prophet finally comes to the same resting place. There is one God, one family, and one habitation. God is the creator of life and all that therein is. The mark of the creator is on every forehead and his signature is in every living thing. What is inherent in life will become manifest in deed. This is the destiny of man, this is the destiny of all of life. The homing instinct is given, and the time shall come when there shall be no alien lands, no strange peoples, and no expression of life outside the divine accord. Every knee shall bow and every living thing and all creation shall join in the grand paean of praise and worship of the God of life who is at once the God of faith.

---

16. "'Therefore, wait for me,' says the Lord, 'for the day when I arise as a witness. For my decision is to gather nations, to assemble kingdoms, to pour out upon them my indignation, all the heat of my anger; for in the fire of my jealous wrath all the earth shall be consumed" (Zeph 3:8).

Index of Names

Abraham, 152n10, 157, 180n14, 190n7, 200
Adler, Alfred, 183n19
Aeschylus, 52, 52n2, 53, 54, 55, 58
Ahaz (king of Judah), 159n6, 188n1
Alter, Robert, 141n8, 164n2
Amel-Marduk (king of Babylonia), 25n11
Amos (biblical prophet), 24n10, 131–38, 188, 202
Atkins, Gaius Glenn, 66n2
Augustine, 86, 91, 203

Bach, Johann Sebastian, 13
Baudricourt, Robert de, 75, 75n4
Bell, Derrick, xi
Bennett, Lerone, Jr., xi
Bojer, Johann, 93, 93n1, 94, 95, 100
Bunyan, John, 182, 182n18
Burr, Amelia Josephine, 116n3
Buttrick, George, 207, 207n1

Calvin, John, 118, 119n5
Castellano, Sebastian, 119
Charles (king of France), 76n5, 79n7
Croesus (king of Lydia), 25n12, 26
Cyrus (king of Persia), 25, 25n12, 26, 36

Deutero-Isaiah (biblical prophet), 19–29, 32, 36, 44, 149, 156, 157

Dixie, Quinton, 115n2
Dozier, Verna, 115n2

Eisenstadt, Peter, xii, 115n2
Elgar, Edward, 152n8
Elijah (biblical prophet), 37
Ezekiel (biblical prophet), 23, 24, 173, 175–87

Farmer, James, x
Fluker, Walter Earl, xii
Francis of Assisi, 119, 119n6
Fullerton, Kemper, 19n2

Gallagher, Buell, 123, 123n6
Galsworthy, John, 157, 158n4
Gamaliel the Elder, 46n11
Gandhi, Mahatma, ix, x, 84
Garrison, William Lloyd, 84
Gedaliah (governor of Judah), 164n1
George, David Lloyd, 81n9
Gladden, Washington, 132n1
Godwin, Dr., 185
Goethe, Johann Wolfgang von, 102
Gomah/Gomer (wife of Hosea), 139, 139n2, 140, 143, 144, 145

Habakkuk (biblical prophet), 132, 132n3, 157n3, 207n2
Hananiah (biblical prophet), 171n4
Hannah (mother of Samuel), 144n21

Harding, Vincent, xi
Harkins, Dr. (friend of Thurman), 174
Hezekiah (king of Judah), 153, 153n12, 188n1
Hitler, Adolf, 118
Hosea (biblical prophet), 24n10, 139–48, 173, 188, 202

Ibsen, Henrik, 109, 109n1, 112
Isaiah (biblical prophet), 19n2, 140, 149–55, 156–62, 188, 191

Jackson, Jesse, xi
Jeconiah (king of Judah), 24n9
Jeremiah (biblical prophet), 163–69, 170–74, 202, 208
Jeroboam II (king of Israel), 139
Jesus, 30–40, 44, 45, 48–50, 134, 168, 183, 184n21, 194, 204, 211
Jezriel/Jezreel (child of Hosea and Gomah), 143n20
Joan of Arc, 74–83
Job, 59–65, 66–73
John the Baptist, 33
Johnson, Mordecai Wyatt, viii, ix, 132n1
Jones, Rufus, ix
Josiah (king of Judah), 208, 208n5
Jotham (king of Judah), 188n1
Joyce, James, 123n8
Judas (apostle), 39

Kant, Immanuel, 12
Kelley, Katie, ix
King, Martin Luther, Jr., x, xi, 132n1
Kropotkin, Pyotr Alexeyevich, 71, 71n11

Lo-ammi (child of Hosea and Gomah), 143n20
Lo-ruhamah (child of Hosea and Gomah), 143n20

Marlowe, Christopher, 102
Marx, Karl, 158, 158n5
Mays, Benjamin, viii, 132n1
McMahon Brian, 154n16
Melville, Herman, 115, 115n1, 117, 161n9
Micah (biblical prophet), 173, 176, 188–97
Moffatt, James, 140, 140n3, 191
Moses, 152n10, 166n7, 200
Murray, Pauli, x

Naaman (Syrian commander), 4, 7, 8, 187n26
Nebuchadnezzar (king of Babylonia), 23, 23n7, 24, 25, 170, 171, 172
Nelson, William Stewart, 132n1
Newman, John Henry, 152, 152n8

Otto, Rudolph, 175n2

Paul (apostle), 41–51, 134, 184n21, 202
Percy, Hugh, 95
Peter (apostle), 49
Petrarch, Francesco, 212, 212n10
Pfeiffer, R. H., 179, 179n11

Randolph, A. Philip, 3, 3n3, 4
Rauschenbusch, Walter, 132n1
Ross, Robert, 195n16
Russell, Bertrand, 81n9

Samuel (biblical prophet), 144n21
Schweitzer, Albert, 9, 11–18
Schweitzer, Helene Bresslau, 13, 13n7
Second Isaiah. See Deutero-Isaiah

Index of Names

Servetus, Michael, 118, 118n5
Shakespeare, William, 4
Shaw, Francis Wells, 174n13
Shaw, George Bernard, 74, 74n1, 75, 76, 77, 79, 80, 82
Shelley, Percy Bysshe, 52, 52n3, 53, 55–58
Sipuel, Ada, 122n3
Smithson, James, 95–96n7
Sparkman, John, 170n2, 171
Stanislavski, Constantin, 88
Stendahl, Krister, 46–47n13
Stephen (martyr), 41, 45, 46, 47
Stevenson, Adlai, 170n2
Story, William Wetmore, 53n4

Tagore, Rabindranath, 167n11
Teasdale, Sara, 151
Tennyson, Alfred Lord, 63n6, 94, 94n4, 162n10
Thomas of Celano, 119n6
Thoreau, Henry David, 84

Thurman, Sue Bailey, ix, x
Tolstoy, Leo, 84–88, 91, 92
Tolstoya, Sophia, 87
Truman, Harry S., 154n16, 191n11

Uzziah (king of Judah), 150, 150n5

Van Dyke, Henry, 8n10

Ward, Lester Frank, 193n14
Washington, George, 189, 190, 190n7, 190n8
Wells, H. G., 66, 67, 67n6, 68
Weyl, Walter, 165n4
Widor, Charles-Marie, 13
Wilde, Oscar, 195, 195n16
Wilder, Thornton, 121, 123n8, 125n11, 126n14, 127n15
Wong, Olive Thurman, ix, 115n2

Zephaniah (biblical prophet), 132, 132n3, 207–16

www.ingramcontent.com/pod-product-compliance
Lightning Source LLC
Chambersburg PA
CBHW062006180426
43198CB00037B/2483